FOREIGN ADVENTURES *of an* ECONOMIST

Raymond F. Mikesell

UNIVERSITY OF OREGON PRESS
EUGENE

University of Oregon Press
Office of Communications
1281 University of Oregon
Eugene, OR 97403

Edited by Tom Hager
Designed by Jeffrey Jane Flowers

Manufactured in the United States of America

10 9 8 7 6 5 4 3 2 1

Library of Congress Cataloging-in-Publication Data

ISBN 0-9702134-0-9

CONTENTS

Chapter 1: Introduction

I grew up in a Midwestern Bible-belt town where the trial of a teacher (Scopes) accused of teaching Darwinian evolution was the most important event of the early 1920s, and foreign economic relations were mainly concerned with keeping out competitive imports. I was an only child and my parents worked together in a petroleum distributing firm that earned sufficient income for almost anything we wanted to do. I was a voracious reader and read widely on the social and physical sciences, but I was particularly interested in reading about other countries and foreign relations. My parents had little formal education but regularly followed the news. After we acquired a radio in the early 1920s, listening to news broadcasts was a family routine. My parents almost never traveled out of Ohio, but I had the opportunity of attending summer YMCA camps in Michigan, an exciting two-week canoe trip in a Canadian wilderness area when I was thirteen, and the following year an Alaskan trip—called "On to Alaska with Buchanan"—sponsored by a Detroit businessman. I loved to travel. During my junior year in high school, I spent one entire summer in Europe, and the next summer I visited several countries in Latin America. My parents had complete confidence in me and provided the money for these and other trips. They seemed to enjoy traveling vicariously through their son, as I wrote long descriptions of my foreign adventures.

As far back as I can remember, my parents emphasized to me the importance of a college education, but they knew very little about college and the fields in which one could major. My father, who used a certain amount of elementary chemistry in his business, was acquainted with a chemical engineer whom he admired. After consultation with his friend, my father strongly advised me to major in chemical engineering at what was then called the Carnegie Institute of Technology in Pittsburgh, where I enrolled in the fall of 1931. I did well in chemistry, mathematics, and economics but hated the

1

engineering shop courses and engineering drawing. Much of my spare time was spent with music students; I joined the Carnegie Tech glee club and sang in a church choir—for which I was rewarded with a suite of rooms in the church office building. I probably would have graduated with a degree in chemical engineering, but during my second year I developed a very serious allergy infection requiring that my sinuses be drained twice a week. Pittsburgh was one of the dirtiest cities in the world, and the smoke from the steel mills and other industries made the air almost impossible to breathe on many occasions. When my physician suggested that I not return to Pittsburgh for my third year, I decided to continue my studies at Ohio State University in Columbus.

The move to Ohio State was a very fortunate one for me. I took elective courses in philosophy and economics, and I became acquainted with liberal arts students and with several members of the faculty. I became president of the Ohio State Philosophy Club and won a medal for the best philosophical essay written in 1934. While I did well in chemistry and chemical engineering, I took as many elective nonscience courses as possible and also attended summer school.

Early in my third year at Ohio State, I discovered I had enough credits to graduate with a major in chemistry but not in chemical engineering. By that time I had decided I did not want a career in chemical engineering, so I took a bachelor's degree in chemistry in March 1935 and entered graduate school with a major in philosophy. I finished the work for a master's degree in philosophy in three quarters. My master's thesis, titled "Natural Rights in the History of Economic Thought," combined my interests in philosophy and economics. I loved being at the university, but my father began talking to me about making a living. His preference was for me to come into the petroleum business with him, but this did not appeal to me. I asked him if I might delay beginning work in his business—which I knew very well from working in all aspects of the business during my vacation periods—and continue for another year at Ohio State. Although I am sure he questioned my wisdom, he agreed and I turned to majoring in economics. When I was offered a teaching fellowship in economics in the fall of 1935, I knew I was on my way to an academic career. The teaching fellowship was followed by a research fellowship with no teaching duties. I devoted all my energies to earning a Ph.D., which was made easier by a close friendship with Henry Bittermann, a faculty member who became my dissertation adviser. I finished my general examination for a Ph.D. in economics in the spring of 1937 and, with Bittermann's aid, received an offer from the University of Washington in Seattle. In 1943 I introduced Bittermann to several officials in the Treasury Department and he was hired as a senior economist—a position he held until his retirement in 1961. My close relationship with Bittermann continued until his death in the 1970s.

Going to the Pacific Northwest, which I had visited earlier, excited me because of my love of mountains and wilderness areas. When I knew I had the job, I felt secure enough to ask my lady friend, Desyl, to marry me, and we drove to Seattle, where we found a small apartment near the university.

The first year at the University of Washington was very hard. I taught large lecture classes, one with 450 students and another with 250. In addition, I taught an upper-division course called Trusts and Estates, a subject I knew, and cared, nothing about. The following quarter, my third course was labor economics, in which I also had no interest; my students knew more about current developments in labor than I did. It was customary for people teaching labor economics to invite the head of the regional Teamsters Union to lecture to the class. It was especially important to do so since he was a member of the university's board of directors. He was later convicted of fraud, and I believe he initiated a pattern for Teamster officials.

Nearly every evening I spent from 7 p.m. to 10 p.m. working on my lectures and from 10 p.m. to 1 a.m. on my dissertation, waking in the morning in time for an 8 a.m. class. My wife was very helpful to me during this period. She did not press me to do household chores, and she typed my dissertation and correspondence. Despite the heavy working schedule, I was able to get in some golf every week at a course near the university. I finished my dissertation in the fall of 1938. Thereafter life was much easier, especially since I was able to teach advanced courses and had only one large elementary economics class. I was anxious to receive tenure, which required at least three articles in leading economic journals. Fortunately, my dissertation, titled "Unemployment and Marginal Productivity Theory," provided the basic analysis for the articles, and I received tenure in 1939. While writing my articles, I was assisted by Paul Douglas, who was a former professor of economics at the University of Chicago and later a U.S. senator. A specialist in the field in which I was working, he spent an afternoon helping me with the articles while on a visit to Seattle.

A number of years later, I appeared before a Senate committee chaired by Douglas to talk about U.S. economic policies. He had invited several economists, including Milton Friedman and Paul Samuelson (both of whom were Nobel Laureates in economics). Douglas requested that no official transcript be made of the meeting and treated it as if it were a private seminar of economists. Friedman argued that governmental activities should be largely limited to security, while more liberal members of the group argued that government should be involved in controlling a wide variety of activities having to do with business practices and social welfare. Samuelson said that Friedman's *laissez faire* position suggested that the best way to have fought World War II would have been to give $50 billion to Dwight Eisenhower in Europe and $50 billion to Douglas MacArthur in Asia and let them accomplish their military goals without further government interference. I wish I had a record of everything that was said at this meeting.

Early Work in the U.S. Government

I was interested in the wartime preparations in Washington, D.C., and in October 1941 an economist whom I believed I had met sent a telegram inviting me to work with him in the Office of Price Administration (OPA). To take advantage of this opportunity, I requested leave from the university until March 1942, fully intending to return to my academic post.

When I arrived in Washington, D.C., in October 1941, I learned that the person who contacted me was not the academic friend I had known but a man with the same name who somehow was misinformed regarding my background; neither of us wanted to work with the other. However, I did get on the OPA payroll and spent several days looking for a suitable job. I had five offers in three days, including a job I almost accepted at the Federal Reserve Board. I ended up as a senior economist in the OPA working under Richard Gilbert, an economist who was special assistant to Leon Henderson, the director of the OPA. Shortly thereafter Pearl Harbor was attacked, and the next day I dutifully went to the Navy Department to find out where I would be assigned as a reserve officer. (In 1940 I had accepted a reserve commission in the Navy to teach at a proposed Navy supply school, which was never established.) However, the Navy had no time to find a job for an economist with no training in naval arts. I was told to stay in my position in the OPA until called. This did not happen until nearly a year later, when an economist with the Navy asked for my services as a liaison between the Navy and the OPA—a job in which I had no interest because of its routine nature and absence of concern with broad national policies.

My initial experience in Washington, D.C., reflected the confusion in the U.S. government, which was trying to create a wartime economy that required an enormous production of munitions, ships, and factory capacity, with considerable resources drawn away from production for the domestic economy. Purchasing power in the hands of the public soared, and actions were required to prevent inflation by controlling wages, rationing goods and services, and redirecting investment from less essential industries to produce goods needed for war. The government had little experience in these functions, and there was a great demand for professionals of all kinds, including economists.

The OPA job was a lucky one from several standpoints. First, I worked mainly with academics on leave from universities and made acquaintances who were useful to me in later years. Second, I was thrust into an environment in which nearly all of the problems were new and required innovation and experimentation. I was asked to prepare price control and rationing programs for a number of commodities about which I knew very little, and there was no literature on the subject. This taught me that an economist did not need a background in a particular area to make a contribution, and from then on I never avoided an assignment because I lacked knowledge or experience in the field. Finally, the OPA job enabled me to apply my skills as an economist—preparing economic models and statistical analysis to deal with urgent problems in the U.S. economy.

One project to which Richard Gilbert, the OPA's chief economist, assigned me was preparation of a model for calculating the effects of a change in the agricultural price support legislation on the U.S. cost-of-living index and on the federal budget. My model ran to 200 pages and was worked out with a 1940–vintage calculator (since computers were not yet available). Gilbert called me at home one evening to say that he had just returned from a Senate committee meeting where he was arguing against proposed legislation to increase farm parities. He said he had promised the committee a numerical estimate of how the proposed change would affect the cost of living and the federal budget, and asked me to have a memorandum on his desk by 9 the next morning. I went immediately to my office to do calculations and asked my secretary to be in the office at 6 a.m. to type the tables and memorandum. The committee was sufficiently impressed by my memorandum that it rejected the proposed change in legislation. My memorandum appeared in the *Federal Register* the following day.

I also prepared models for determining the effects of commodity subsidies, and these models turned out to be useful for the OPA. I sent one of my OPA memoranda on subsidies to the *American Economic Review,* where it was published with very few changes. Subsequently, several other internal government memoranda were published in economic journals, which helped to increase my professional standing. My wartime publications resulted in several academic offers, including one I later accepted at the University of Virginia at four times the salary I was earning at the University of Washington.

In the summer of 1942, I met Edward Bernstein (who was Harry White's deputy in the Treasury Department's Office of Monetary Research) at a cocktail party, where he learned that I had used his book on monetary economics as required reading in one of my classes in Seattle. This impressed him sufficiently to ask me to work with him in the Treasury. Bernstein was on leave from the University of North Carolina but never returned. We became close friends and I worked with him for the next four years.

I wanted to work in the Treasury Department, but had first to deal with my obligation to the Navy, which was complicated by the fact that I did not pass the medical examination for Naval service because I did not have enough of my own teeth! I spent a day at the Navy offices locating the physician who would determine whether my medical disability would be waived. After looking at my record, the physician suggested that perhaps I could better serve my country in a civilian position—the choice was up to me. It was an easy choice, and I was given a medical discharge in August 1942.

When Bernstein introduced me to Harry White on my first visit to the Treasury Department, White hired me immediately without bothering to check on my background. Bernstein wanted me to assist him in developing White's preliminary proposal for an international stabilization fund and world bank into a full-fledged plan. White impressed me as someone who was both well organized and authoritarian, but not oppressive. With the help of well-chosen economists and a good legal staff, White had built a small division in monetary affairs into a highly influential office in government, especially in the field of international economic relations.

Working at the Treasury Department introduced me to the field of international finance, which along with international trade became my areas of specialization. I worked in a number of areas during my first year in the Treasury Department. But working under both Bernstein and White, I tended to specialize on plans for the postwar economy. I benefitted from frequent meetings with economists in the Federal Reserve Board, the State Department, the Department of Commerce, the Export-Import Bank, and other U.S. government agencies.

Harry White had been appointed to his position by Treasury Secretary Hans Morgenthau, who was a close friend of President Roosevelt. I was privileged to attend a number of Cabinet-level meetings in Morgenthau's office and also became acquainted with Lauchlin Currie, who was a special economic assistant to Roosevelt. These contacts proved quite valuable for my work in government after the war, and they provided opportunities for me to serve as a consultant to several presidential commissions and in the White House itself.

Harry White, with the backing of Secretary Morgenthau, sought to expand the influence of the Treasury Department in various branches of government and frequently sent me to meetings on matters not related to the responsibilities of the Office of Monetary Research. One example was my participation in the initial preparation of the international trade proposal under the jurisdiction of the State Department, which eventually became the General Agreement on Tariffs and Trade.

Another was my work with Eleanor Roosevelt. White requested that I respond to a call he had received from Mrs. Roosevelt for assistance on a speech she planned to give. At our first meeting in the White House, the First Lady explained to me the economic and social welfare points she wanted to cover in her speech, and she asked me to prepare a draft. I recall that some of her ideas on public welfare and income distribution were much more liberal than those of the Roosevelt administration, but I kept most of her ideas in the draft. After sending my draft to the White House, I received a note of praise and an invitation to the International Student Assembly Conference where the talk was to be given. There I met Joseph P. Lash and other good friends of Mrs. Roosevelt. Her talk was in support of international student cooperation and toleration of the economic and political philosophies of other countries. Virtually nothing in it reflected the material I had sent her. Nevertheless, she told her friends that I had made a very important contribution to her talk.

Mrs. Roosevelt's activities and some of her friends were under suspicion by the Federal Bureau of Investigation (FBI). An FBI observer at the conference reported that some of those attending, including representatives from Russia and several other countries, were sympathetic to Russian aggression in Lithuania and elsewhere. I heard nothing at the conference to confirm this, and I believe some of the FBI report was fabricated. Following the conference, my wife and I were invited to a White House reception, during which we had the opportunity to talk with Mrs. Roosevelt as well as with some of the leaders of the International Student Assembly. We were impressed with what we heard about the assembly and saw none of the negative aspects reported by the FBI observer. We were even more impressed with the warmth of Mrs. Roosevelt's personality. The first time I met her, she gave me the feeling that I was a close friend in whom she had the greatest personal interest.

Under thirty years of age and still new in government, I was somewhat overwhelmed at meeting with Cabinet-level officials in other government agencies and representing the position of the Treasury Department, especially as that position was not always well received. Several examples of the friction between the State and Treasury Departments are discussed in later chapters of this book. These conflicts surprised me since there is a tendency for outsiders to believe that federal administrators speak with one voice. But I learned that national policies, even those relating to dealings with foreign powers and international agencies, are often complicated by ambiguities arising from U.S. intragovernmental conflicts. As a junior employee representing the position of the Treasury Department, I was always treated with respect by high officials, but I sometimes experienced embarrassment—a reflection of my self-consciousness. On one occasion I was sent to a meeting chaired by Dean Acheson, who at that time was Undersecretary of State. In the course of the meeting, I called him "Dean" as did the others, but I had not intended to call him by his first name. In academia, "dean" is a title, which is appropriate to use when addressing college deans, and I was embarrassed when I realized I was calling the Undersecretary of State by his first name. When I apologized after the meeting and told him why I had used his first name, he laughed heartily and said I should always call him Dean. Several years later, when he was Secretary of State, I reminded him of this during another meeting.

My early experience in the Treasury Department not only acquainted me with the major foreign economic policy issues facing the government but gave me confidence to negotiate with foreign government officials whom I was to meet at conferences and bilateral meetings. No longer feeling restrained by my rank, I met with officials with a sense of parity because of my knowledge and the confidence instilled by the U.S. government officials whom I represented.

Missions to Algiers and the Middle East

My first overseas missions for the U.S. government provided an education in foreign diplomacy, but they afforded me little satisfaction in terms of either accomplishment or interest in the work. In neither Algiers nor Cairo was I assigned a specific function, and my presence made little difference to the success of the U.S. government programs in the areas. Perhaps it was expected that I would find sufficiently useful work to justify sending me; in fact, my lack of specific responsibilities and short tenure confined me largely to attending meetings and keeping the Treasury Department informed. But this is why I was sent.

In Cairo I learned much about Middle Eastern culture and politics that proved useful for my later work in the area. Moreover, by living with a French family, I developed some facility in French. My health was poor from having acquired a series of local diseases; I missed my family, and I was increasingly anxious to return to Washington to pursue my work on plans for postwar international organizations. Some people are mentally suited for long periods abroad, but I am not one of them. One cannot work well in a foreign country if his heart is at home.

Algiers

Following the defeat of the German army in Libya in 1942, American and British forces occupied French North Africa. Prior to the occupation, French North Africa was under the Vichy government of France, which in turn was heavily controlled by Germany. After the Allied occupation, an agreement was negotiated with the North African government: military and political matters would be under the control of the U.S. and British forces, while local governmental affairs would be left to the French Commissioner, Admiral Jean Darlan. In addition to the Allied military presence, the North African Economic Board (NAEB) was created as a joint British-American agency for dealing with a range of economic problems, both directly and in cooperation with the local French African government. The NAEB's functions included supplying essential commodities for the civilian economy, controlling all foreign trade, allocating Lend-Lease shipments, determining foreign exchange and other financial policies, and expediting the local production of commodities needed by both the civilian population and the armed forces. The NAEB staff included several representatives from the State and Treasury Departments. When one of the Treasury Department people was transferred from the NAEB, Harry White asked me to take a temporary assignment in Algiers to work with the board. He was quite vague about my duties, other than keeping the Treasury Department informed of economic activities in French North Africa. Since the assignment was to be temporary, I thought a visit to North Africa in wartime would be both interesting and instructive for postwar reconstruction, which would soon encompass all of Europe.

In September 1943 I flew to North Africa aboard a military transport on a nonstop flight from Newfoundland to Prestwick, Scotland. The plane flew at over 25,000 feet to avoid turbulence; since the plane was not pressurized we needed to breathe oxygen from tubes. I arrived in Prestwick with severe head congestion and was immediately sent to a U.S. military hospital, where they cleared my head. That same night I was visited by a military official who asked if I felt well enough to board a plane leaving about 1 a.m. for North Africa, because transport planes flew at night to avoid being seen by German aircraft. I agreed to do so but later learned that two nights before, the same flight had been intercepted and shot down by the Germans. All of the passengers slept on the floor of the plane in the dark, and I stepped on several Army officers trying to find my way to the head.

Algiers was a city with a modern sector, good hotels, restaurants, office buildings and a large native sector of narrow streets lined with beggars, prostitutes, and peddlers. The native area was fascinating, but I always felt insecure visiting it. The modern sector was heavily occupied by military people—American, British, and French North African. Aside from occasional air raids, there were no signs of war or devastation. I ate at the officers' mess and had a comfortable room in the best hotel.

When I arrived at the NAEB, the Treasury Department people treated me politely although they were not prepared for my arrival and seemed uncertain why I had come or what I was to do. After spending time reading documents, I was assigned to several committees and met from time to time with local French officials. These meetings gave me an opportunity to practice speaking French. A major problem for civilians was inflation caused by the scarcity of goods and heavy military expenditures financed by the exchange of dollars and sterling for the local currency. I recall writing memoranda on price controls and rationing. There was considerable controversy, however, both within the NAEB and with the local government, on how to apply these controls in the North African situation. Nothing I suggested was put into practice. The meetings I attended dealt largely with local and administrative issues regarding which I had little interest.

The more important economic issues—such as the exchange rates between the North African franc and the dollar and between the franc and sterling—were settled in Washington and London, although the NAEB did supply background information. The Americans and the British disagreed over whether certain imports should come from the United States or from Britain. I never thought this commercial rivalry was a significant issue in U.S.

national policy during the war, since all international goods and their transportation were in short supply.

According to State Department regulations, communications between Americans overseas and their Washington offices had to be cleared and sent by the U.S. legation. Since the NAEB was a wholly American institution, the Treasury Department took the position that activities of Americans in North Africa were outside the jurisdiction of the American ambassador, and that Treasury Department officials should be permitted to communicate directly with their department in Washington. Although this dispute was officially settled in favor of the State Department, I found ways to send my personal reports to the Treasury Department with individuals traveling to the United States or by direct mail.

The Treasury Department official from whom I learned most about what was happening in Algeria and elsewhere in French North Africa wore the uniform of an enlisted American soldier. He had been working as a civilian in the NAEB for about a year when he was drafted to military service by his draft board in the United States. This happened occasionally to both reserve officers and draftees, and it was the practice of the Treasury Department to request that they continue to serve with the department overseas. As a rule, no opportunity was given for draftees to return home as long as they were needed abroad.

I became well acquainted with the Treasury Department man and frequently had lunch or dinner with him in the enlisted mens' mess, where the service was cafeteria style but the food just as good as in the officers' mess. He told me that before he was drafted he had been going to meetings with local French government people, but he could no longer do so because he was required to wear an enlisted man's uniform. Subsequently he received permission to wear civilian clothes and thereafter could resume contact with French North African officials. When I met him at the Treasury Department a couple of years later in Washington, he was wearing the Purple Heart medal. He told me that when he had landed in southern France with the American troops who were accompanied by a civilian corps to establish a government in the occupied area, he had been hit in the back by shrapnel.

Cairo

I had only been in Algiers a few weeks when I received a cable from Harry White asking me to spend a few months in Cairo as U.S. Treasury Department representative in the American Embassy. I agreed to do so: first, because I was bored in Algiers, and second, because I had read a great deal about the Middle East and wanted to see the pyramids and other Egyptian archaeology. I accepted the assignment with the understanding that I would return to Washington the following year, before the planned international conference on the establishment of the International Monetary Fund and the World Bank.

White wanted the Treasury Department to have a representative in the Middle East because of the economic importance of the area and the emerging conflict over Palestine. In 1943 President Roosevelt appointed Harvard Law School Dean James Landis as Chief U.S. Representative in the Middle East. Landis served as the principal American representative in the Middle East Supply Center (MESC) with the personal rank of minister. I was supposed to serve under Landis, but my functions were never spelled out and Landis never gave me direct orders. In fact, I never had any orders at all except to keep the Treasury Department informed. This seemed to me primarily a bureaucratic effort to expand the influence of a particular branch of the government in the area.

Although I had no specific function in the MESC, I did attend meetings and serve on several committees whose primary activities were controlling inflation and distributing Lend-Lease imports. The MESC began as a wholly British organization, but in 1942 it became a joint Anglo-American agency. It controlled the allocation of imported supplies of food and other consumer goods, both from commercial sources and from U.S. Lend-Lease shipments to the area. It also sought to promote domestic production of the goods needed by the region and by the Allied military forces. The largely British staff consisted mainly of specialists in particular commodities such as foods and raw materials.

One of Landis's objectives was to reduce or eliminate what he regarded as British discrimination against U.S. trade and investment in the Middle East.

He also espoused greater political independence of Middle Eastern countries from Britain. He developed a secret liaison with the young Egyptian King Farouk and sympathized with the king's efforts to become more independent from Britain. This relationship became known to the British, who quite naturally were disturbed by it. Landis frequently accused the British officials in the MESC of discriminating against American goods. The British government had a special interest in such discrimination because, when imports were paid for in dollars, the dollars would be acquired by converting sterling into the dollars held by the British Treasury. When sterling was used to pay for imports, there was simply a transfer from one sterling bank account to another and no loss of dollars. For Britain, dollars were scarce but an unlimited supply of sterling could be created. Landis did not receive much sympathy from the U.S. Department of State on his criticism of British policies relating to Middle East imports, largely because the State Department was much more interested in overall U.S.-British cooperation in all phases of the war effort. In his messages to Roosevelt, Landis complained that the department did not support him in his efforts to eliminate discrimination against U.S. commercial interests. Although Landis was the co-head of the MESC, he was thwarted in his efforts to increase American influence by the fact that the personnel were largely British.

Landis was much less formal and scholarly than I had imagined a dean of a prestigious law school would be. He seemed consumed by protecting American commercial and political interests and acted more like an American businessman might act in the same position. I got along well with Landis, but he struck me as a disturbed and unhappy man. On one occasion while I was in his office, he was frustrated by not being able to find a memorandum in his desk that he wanted to show me. In my presence he took out every drawer in his desk and hurled it violently against the wall. I learned from his secretary that his personal discontent could be traced in considerable measure to the breakup with his wife, Stella, and to his falling in love with Dorothy Purdy Brown, who had worked with him in Washington, D.C. He had wanted to bring Dorothy to Cairo with him, but she thought it best not to go. According to his biographer, Landis was in a bad mood on days when he did not receive a letter from Dorothy. They married following his divorce from Stella in 1945.

One of the problems I worked on as an economist in the MESC was local inflation, which was largely a result of the scarcity of goods and large local expenditures by the Allied military. Inflation made it difficult for the poor to obtain consumer goods. Since the exchange rates between the local currencies and the dollar and sterling remained fixed, the local currencies became overvalued. That is, their value in terms of commodities declined while their foreign exchange remained fixed. This overvaluation had an adverse effect on trade within the Middle Eastern region, and it reduced the incentive for Middle Eastern producers to participate in the world market.

I participated in a Middle Eastern financial conference in April 1944. It was attended by ministers and technical experts from eleven Middle East governments and by representatives of the governments of India, Britain, the United States, and France. The principal purposes of the conference were to educate officials in the domestic governments on methods of controlling inflation and to provide an opportunity for the delegates to voice their opinions on these and other economic issues. But the conference turned out to be of little value either as an educational exercise or as a means of finding a solution to the inflation problem. Local Middle Eastern governments were not very concerned about inflation, and some denied that it could exist as long as their currencies were fully backed by foreign exchange assets—mainly sterling. Sterling, which was being accumulated by the local governments as well as by private entities, could be used for purchasing goods and capital equipment after the war whenever these goods became available for export. Most of the local government delegates blamed price increases on Allied military expenditures and the limitation of imports; they argued that the only way to solve the inflation problem was to increase imports from abroad. This was correct, but commodities were in short supply, largely because of shipping limitations. The MESC representatives urged the local governments to reduce their fiscal expenditures and tighten credit conditions. This was unacceptable to the Middle Eastern governments because they believed such actions would reduce their output.

Landis wanted to free the local foreign exchange markets from the existing controls that prevented the free purchase of dollars and other currencies with domestic currency. This would have violated sterling area controls designed to limit the acquisition of dollars. While supporting Landis's position, I also suggested that since the local currencies were overvalued, they should be devalued in terms of both sterling and dollars. The local governments were against devaluation, largely for political reasons. Governments that permit their currencies to depreciate are nearly always criticized. My reasoning was that devaluation would make the locally produced goods more competitive in world markets, especially since at the end of the war Lend-Lease supplies would be terminated and the countries would need to depend upon exports for their foreign exchange requirements.

Landis continued to argue for the elimination of restrictions on foreign exchange transactions, but this was opposed by the British Treasury representative, G. H. S. Pinsent, because of the drain on Britain's dollar reserves. I pointed out that the Allied governments were planning a financial conference in 1944 to establish a system of foreign exchange convertibility among all currencies, and that a step in this direction in the Middle East might be desirable. Landis introduced a resolution endorsing the abolition of restrictions on the purchase and sale of foreign exchange for current transactions, but he was unable to obtain a majority vote in the conference. Instead, he had to settle for a rather general statement on the desirability of reducing foreign exchange restrictions.

Visit to the Levant

In December 1943, I visited several other Middle Eastern countries to report on economic and political conditions. I flew on small Egyptian passenger planes, which provided only large spittoons as a toilet! An American vice counsel met me at the Tel Aviv airport and drove me to Jerusalem's best-known hotel, the King David, built in the nineteenth century. Across the street was a modern high-rise American YMCA building whose Christian visitors were a distinct minority. Neither Muslims nor Jews were reluctant to enjoy the services provided by a Christian institution. In Palestine, I visited the major historic shrines and talked with British, Arab, and Jewish leaders about the political future of the areas. There was political turmoil, but the economy appeared to be prosperous. Despite British efforts to control immigration, Jewish refugees were arriving in considerable numbers, financed mainly by American Jewish organizations. I believed then that there would be a Jewish state in Palestine after the war, but I never imagined I would be working in a Jewish state a few years later.

In Lebanon I was impressed by Beirut as a resort haven in the midst of a war, and by my ability to ski in the mountains above the city in the morning and bathe in the Mediterranean in the afternoon. Beirut had long been a pleasure mecca for wealthy Arabs to escape Muslim fundamentalist restrictions. Many wealthy Arabs kept Western-born wives there. I also enjoyed visiting the world's oldest city, Damascus, and its excellent restaurants. I believed that all the Levant had great potential for development after the war, but only Israel has succeeded.

Knowing that final preparations were being made for the Bretton Woods conference and having been promised participation by Eddie Bernstein, White's deputy in the Treasury Department, I became very anxious to return to Washington. Although orders for my departure were not forthcoming, I simply decided to leave, especially as my replacement was expected to arrive shortly. Landis had no objection, so I left on a military air transport on the first of May 1944. The trip home took more than a week instead of the two days I had expected. The plane developed engine trouble before it landed in Khartoum, Sudan, and it was two days before I could get a plane to Accra, Ghana, where I spent another two days resting on the beach. My plane to Brazil was scheduled for a fuel stop on Ascension Island in the mid-Atlantic, but before our arrival two of its engines stopped and it landed with two propellers feathered. The next day I made it to Brazil and arrived in Washington, D.C., two days later. Most of the military planes available for civilian passengers had no regular passenger seats. Crossing the Atlantic in a B-29, I spent most of the time in a seat designated for the rear gunner.

In Retrospect

U.S. and British occupation of Algeria and Egypt did little to prepare them for successful development as independent states, which they became after the war. Neither has made significant economic and social progress in the half-century since World War II. Wartime occupation did not provide a good environment for modernization, and the two occupying countries were more interested in using the areas as military bases than in contributing to their future.

Sources

Some of the information on Eleanor Roosevelt was based on Lash (1982). The source of some of the material on James Landis came from Ritchie (1980). My discussion of the Middle East Supply Center was based on Lloyd (1956).

CHAPTER 2:
BRETTON WOODS: PRECONFERENCE NEGOTIATIONS

The negotiations leading to the establishment of the International Monetary Fund (IMF) and the World Bank were important because they determined what kind of a trading system the world would have after World War II. Before the war the dollar was fully convertible into all currencies and had a stable value in gold. The world payment system of the 1930s disadvantaged both U.S. exporters and domestic producers competing with imports; the trade controls used by other countries discriminated against U.S. exports, and the competitive devaluations of other countries rendered U.S. exports less competitive in foreign markets. One form of trade control was the bilateral trade agreement in which countries agreed on how much each country would buy from the other and forced their traders to comply with these agreements—rather than buying and selling competitively in world markets. These arrangements discriminated against U.S. exports since this country did not use them. Most countries, including the United States, also maintained high tariffs and import quotas on some imports to protect their domestic producers from world competition. These conditions were also disadvantageous to U.S. exports, since U.S. import restrictions tended to be lower than those of most other countries.

For these reasons, an important objective of U.S. postwar planners was the establishment of a world system of convertible currencies, stable exchange rates, a substantial reduction of tariffs, and the elimination of import quotas. The U.S. government took the initiative of calling international conferences for reaching agreements on foreign currency practices and trade restrictions. The IMF Agreement on rules governing international monetary practices was negotiated at the international conference in Bretton Woods, New Hampshire, in 1944. An agreement on trade restrictions was embodied in the General Agreement on Tariffs and Trade (GATT), negotiated by a number of countries at a conference in London in 1947.

Free trade is not possible unless traders are able to exchange their own currencies for foreign currencies without restrictions. In other words, currencies must be convertible into one another for purposes of financing trade. During the 1930s, most international trade (other than that of the United States and Canada) was conducted under bilateral agreements that the national currency paid to exporters by the trading partner could only be used to pay for imports from the country whose currency was paid. This meant that when France received sterling from a trade surplus with Britain, it could use that sterling only to buy goods from Britain or from other countries that were members of the sterling area. France could not use this sterling to make payments to Belgium or to buy goods from the United States. France gave preference to imports from sterling-area countries, thereby discriminating against the United States and other non-sterling countries.

Besides requiring nations to allow their currencies to be convertible into one another for financing trade, the Bretton Woods Agreements established a system of fixed rates of exchange between currencies, subject to adjustment in accordance with rules administered by the IMF. This system differed from both the gold standard in operation before World War I, in which most national currencies were convertible into a fixed amount of gold, and the government-controlled exchange rates of the 1930s. The IMF system also differed from the freely fluctuating exchange rate system used by some countries during the 1920s. Under the government-control system, nations frequently depreciated the foreign exchange value of their currencies as a means of improving their competitive trade position with other countries. When a country depreciates its currency, the prices of its exports decline in terms of currencies of its trading partners, while the prices of its imports rise in terms of its own currency.

The White Plan

According to Treasury Department legend, the ideas embodied in the Bretton Woods Agreements arose in late December 1941 from a dream Treasury Department Secretary Morgenthau had of a world in which all countries used the same currency. The following morning, Morgenthau called Harry White and asked him to prepare a post-World War II plan for a single

Raymond F. Mikesell

world currency. White, however, believed a single world currency was impractical. He favored a plan for interconvertible national currencies stable in value in relation to one another. White wrote Morgenthau a memorandum in which he explained the difficulties in achieving a single world currency and showed that most of the advantages for world trade could be achieved by world currency interconvertibility and stable exchange rates. White provided Morgenthau with a rough outline of what later became the White plan for an International Stabilization Fund (ISF). It was reported that White's initial outline for an ISF was formulated in the summer of 1941. I believe he had been thinking about an international financial agreement well before he prepared the memorandum to Morgenthau.

The first definitive draft for establishing both an ISF and a World Bank was dated April 1942. This mimeographed document was presented to me for study and comments on the day I arrived for duty at the Treasury Department in August 1942. Bernstein asked me to prepare for him any comments I had on the White plan. I recall being astounded at the many functions the plan assigned to the two new institutions, which went well beyond stabilizing exchange rates and providing rules for foreign exchange practices of its members. However, at that time I was too new in the field of foreign exchange and international financial relations to realize that many of the powers given to the institutions were well beyond what would be acceptable to other U.S. government agencies or to foreign governments. It was only after I became well acquainted with the background of the plan that I could make useful suggestions for amendments.

The basic components of the White plan for an ISF were (1) currency convertibility, (2) exchange rate stability, (3) elimination of exchange controls on current transactions, and (4) assistance to countries experiencing balance of payments deficits that threatened their ability to maintain their exchange rates or currency convertibility. The concept of a World Bank was included in the original White plan as a source of loan funds for both post–World War II reconstruction and financing the development of poor and middle-income countries. White looked upon the World Bank as an inducement to countries for accepting membership in the ISF, and he made membership in the Bank conditional on membership in the ISF.

Most other countries were dissatisfied with the motley foreign exchange system of the 1930s, but they did not want to return to the gold standard system of pre–World War I in which the par value of each currency was fixed in terms of gold. This system was regarded as a cause of recession when a country was forced to impose monetary and fiscal restrictions in order to maintain the convertibility of its currency into gold at the fixed parity. Countries needed to adjust their exchange rates in accordance with international monetary rules. However, there was considerable disagreement over what kind of a world currency system should be established and over the way in which the system might be administered so that all countries would adhere to the same rules. Although the White proposal provided a specific blueprint for both the rules and the means for administering them, some aspects engendered substantial criticism within the United States and in other countries. Each country wanted a plan that would establish rules but would at the same time be compatible with its own special economic interests.

The plan's principal objectives were firmly rooted in U.S. monetary policy of the 1930s, when the U.S. government opposed what was called "competitive exchange depreciation," and bilateral currency agreements and exchange controls that discriminated against U.S. exports. The concept of assisting other countries to stabilize their exchange rates at agreed levels is found in the Tripartite Agreement of 1936 with Britain and France. According to this agreement the three nations, later joined by three others, agreed to consult one another before changing their rates and to assist each other in stabilizing their rates.

Accepting the White plan enthusiastically, Morgenthau believed the first job was to sell the ideas to other agencies in the government and, of course, to President Roosevelt. White wanted Morgenthau to send a draft of the plan to Roosevelt immediately with a recommendation that he call a United Nations conference to consider it. However, Roosevelt did not learn of the plan until the late spring of 1942, and Morgenthau did not want the plan circulated among officials of other countries until it had been studied and found acceptable within the U.S. administration.

In May 1942, a Cabinet-level committee was established that consisted of the Secretaries of State, the Treasury, and Commerce, the chair of the Board

Raymond F. Mikesell

of Governors of the Federal Reserve System, and the chair of the Board of Economic Warfare. At the initial meeting in Morgenthau's office on May 25th, the committee established a subcommittee, the American Technical Committee (ATC), under White's chairmanship. The ATC conducted negotiations on the ISF and the World Bank within the U.S. government, and later with foreign governments, prior to the Bretton Woods conference.

Individuals involved in the ATC varied from meeting to meeting, but those attending most frequently were Lauchlin Currie and Benjamin Cohen from the White House; Undersecretary Dean Acheson, Adolf Berle, Herbert Feis, Frederick Livesey, Leo Pasvolsky, and John Parke Young from the State Department; Elting Arnold, Edward Bernstein, Henry Bittermann, Irving Friedman, Ansel Luxford, Raymond Mikesell, Norman Ness, and Harry White from the Treasury Department; Will Clayton and August Maffrey from the Commerce Department; Mariner Eccles, Walter Gardner, and Emmanuel Goldenweiser from the Federal Reserve Board; Walter Lockheim from the Securities and Exchange Commission; Hawthorn Arey and Warren Pearson from the Export-Import Bank; Frank Coe from the Foreign Economic Administration; and Alvin Hansen from the National Resources Planning Board. Hansen was a leading economist on leave from Harvard University.

Many meetings of the ATC consisted largely of questions to White, which he and Bernstein answered in considerable detail. Technical questions were directed to those of us on the staff, and all of us supplied information relating to foreign trade and payment practices. My interventions were largely limited to technical information, such as the contributions to the Fund's capital from major donor countries. Most of the questions and critical comments came from representatives of the Department of State and the Federal Reserve Board. By and large, members of the ATC knew one another well and the meetings were cordial. Only occasionally did White pound on the table or express anger at some of the questions, but he knew he had to be responsive and persuasive if he was to obtain the endorsements of other government agencies for his plan. Later on in the meetings, some ATC members introduced proposals for major changes in the ISF and World Bank plans, but only a few minor changes were acceptable to White.

U.S. Government Criticism of the White Plan

In the course of the ATC meetings, two main areas of criticism of the White plan emerged. First, the plan gave the ISF and the World Bank powers and responsibilities that went beyond foreign exchange and balance of payments issues to include international trade policy, commodity price stabilization, expansion of the world's supply of foodstuffs, and a requirement that members of the World Bank subscribe to a "magna carta" of the United Nations setting forth human rights and freedoms. Their inclusion in the White plan reflected White's and Morgenthau's desire to enhance the role of the Treasury Department in postwar planning. The State Department was already planning an international trade organization, and both the State and the Agriculture Departments were planning international commodity agreements and food relief. The "magna carta" was obviously a concern of the United Nations itself. White readily accepted the deletion of these matters from the responsibilities of the ISF and the World Bank.

The second main area of criticism had to do with the relationship between the immediate postwar problems of world reconstruction and White's international financial plan. State Department representatives worried about the balance of payments problems Britain would face immediately after the war. They questioned whether the ISF could meet Britain's financial needs, since the original White plan provided only $3 billion as the U.S. subscription to a fund that might need to provide assistance to a large number of countries. To address this concern, Goldenweiser suggested a plan developed by the Board's staff; he proposed increasing the gold holdings of the ISF by requiring that all contributions be made in gold, up to a limit of one-half or three-fourths of a country's gold holdings. The Board plan also gave members greater freedom to revalue their currency parities than White's plan did, and it gave the ISF authority to require a country to devalue its currency when its deficit reached half of its quota. Alvin Hansen suggested that international cooperation in preventing depression should receive more attention in the ISF than the establishment of international monetary rules, and that exchange rate flexibility was desirable for all but the largest countries. White, backed by Morgenthau, rejected these and other proposals to basically change the ISF.

Raymond F. Mikesell

The State Department differed with White on the timing of an international conference for negotiating the charters of the ISF and the World Bank, which White wanted to call immediately so that the two institutions could be operating at the end of the war. The State Department's position was that the U.S. government should discuss the plan with a few major countries before calling a conference. This was also Morgenthau's position when he discussed the possibility of a conference with Roosevelt. Other ATC members had views on the proposed World Bank plan that differed from the White draft, and the State Department had its own bank proposal, which was prepared by John Parke Young. However, relatively little attention was paid to the Bank in the course of the ATC meetings, in part because the Bank was less controversial. The White plan went through a number of drafts using suggestions from the ATC meetings. The plan was not formally made public until April 1943, but a number of unofficial reports were published on it.

The White plan was only one of several proposals for postwar international financial institutions—including a Canadian plan; a French plan; a plan formulated by Harvard Professor John H. Williams and known as the "key currency" approach, which had the support of the U.S. banking community; and John Maynard Keynes's International Clearing Union (ICU) plan. Only Keynes's ICU plan was considered at any length by the ATC. It was this plan that was the principal rival of the ISF in the course of the international discussions between the ATC and representatives of forty-six countries that Morganthau invited to meetings in Washington during the summer of 1943. Some of the meetings were bilateral, while others were attended by representatives from several countries. By far the most important meetings were those with Keynes and other British officials.

1943 Meetings with Keynes and the British Delegation

The meetings between the ATC and the British delegation headed by Keynes occurred from time to time during the period May to October 1943. They were very important in shaping the International Monetary Fund agreement that was approved at Bretton Woods in July 1944. The meetings were dominated by Keynes, White, and Bernstein, but I spoke occasionally, largely to supply information. My main work came after the meetings, when

I wrote memoranda for White on some of the points made by the foreign representatives and provided quantitative information relating to the issues discussed.

Much of the early discussions with the British delegation concerned the relative advantages and disadvantages of the White and Keynes plans. Both plans were made public in April 1943, but officials of both countries had been aware of the plans since late 1942. These were not simply academic discussions between two economists. The two plans, each of which had the support of the author's government, contained provisions that reflected the sometimes divergent national interests of the governments.

The major objectives of the ICU were the same as those of the ISF; otherwise, a compromise would never have been reached. Keynes favored exchange-rate stabilization and elimination of exchange controls that involved discrimination against imports from particular countries. Actually, Keynes was bound to this proposal because Article VII of the Lend-Lease Agreement of 1942 provided for elimination of trade discrimination such as that associated with the operation of the sterling area.

Both plans included temporary financial assistance to countries experiencing balance of payments difficulties. However, the administrative arrangements for providing such assistance differed substantially. The ISF proposal provided for subscriptions of gold and domestic currencies to the Fund by its members, and foreign currencies could be drawn from the Fund by countries needing assistance. According to the ISF proposal, each member country was given a quota that determined both its normal right to draw currencies from the Fund and its contribution in gold and currencies to the Fund. Countries requesting assistance "bought" the foreign currencies they needed from the Fund with their own currency, so that the Fund's holdings of a member's currency was a measure of that member's indebtedness to the Fund.

The ICU proposal, on the other hand, would have established a clearing union on the books of which each member's credits and debits would be recorded. Countries with net balance of payment surpluses would have credit positions with the clearing union, while countries with deficits would have net deficit positions. This process assured multilateral clearing: since all bilateral payment positions were reported to the clearing union, each country

Raymond F. Mikesell

had a net position with the clearing union at the end of the reporting period. Multilateral clearing means that a country can use its bilateral surplus with one country to settle its deficit with another country.

An essential difference in the two plans was the maximum amount of credit each member was obligated to subscribe for lending to other members. Under the ISF plan, the obligation of each member to provide its own currency and gold to the Fund was fixed by its quota. On the other hand, under the ICU proposal, the amount of credit each member was obligated to provide was not limited. Such credits represented the member's willingness to accept credits from the clearing union as payment for amounts owed to the member by other members. In the extreme case in which the United States was the only creditor, and each of the other members ran deficits in the ICU equal to its quota, the U.S. would be obligated to provide credits equal to the sum of the quotas of all the other members. On the basis of Keynes's suggested formula for calculating the quotas in the ICU, I estimated that the U.S. might be obligated to provide credits as much as $470 billion or more during the first decade of operation. By contrast, White suggested the U.S. quota in the ISF should be no more than $3 billion.

It was not surprising that this large potential obligation under the ICU proposal was a major source of U.S. objections. In addition, even if a limit could be placed on the U.S. obligation, ATC officials pointed out that the clearing procedure was unfamiliar to most Americans. The idea of providing credits by having countries run debits in a clearing union appeared to be creating assets without a tangible contribution. As will be discussed, a decade later the U.S. government did accept the Special Drawing Rights program, which involved much the same principle as a clearing union.

Keynes replied to the criticisms of the ICU by stating that the Treasury Department economists had used "worst case" scenarios that were highly unrealistic. He believed there would be other surplus countries, such as Canada and the oil-producing countries, not just the United States. He pointed out that the U.S. could prevent large surpluses by increasing imports and by more expansionist monetary and fiscal policies. However, midway in the negotiation, the U.S. delegation made it clear to Keynes that the ICU was not acceptable to the U.S. government. Keynes then fell back to trying to get some of the aspects of the ICU incorporated into the White plan. He did this by pointing to various technical difficulties of the White plan, which were recognized not only by Keynes but by other economists and eventually by White himself. One was the "multilateral clearing problem" that arose under the White plan, because members were not required to allow their own currencies held by other members to be transferred to a third member to settle a payment deficit. This meant that a country with a surplus with one country could not use that surplus to discharge a deficit with another. In addition, currencies drawn from the Fund could only be used for making payments to the country whose currency was drawn. For example, a country drawing dollars from the Fund could use the dollars to buy imports only from the United States. This was a senseless provision, which White thought would please Congress and make it more likely to approve U.S. membership in the Fund. The multilateral clearing problem was debated at length during the negotiations with Britain, and a number of complicated arrangements for dealing with it were suggested by Keynes and others. Because of White's unwillingness to make significant changes in the ISF plan, the multilateral clearing problem was never satisfactorily dealt with in shaping the Fund agreement at Bretton Woods. However, it never became a problem in the course of the Fund's operation. The United States has never insisted that dollars drawn from the Fund be used only for making payments to the United States. After free markets for the major currencies were established in the 1960s, members were free to use the currency of any member for making payments to any other member.

A second technical flaw, related to the first, was that potential claims on the Fund for supplying dollars were far in excess of the Fund's holdings of dollars. This would not occur in the ICU because there was no limit on a member's obligation to accept credits in the clearing union. When Keynes and others brought up this problem, White's answer was that a shortage in the supply of dollars relative to the dollars demanded from the Fund was highly unlikely to occur, but this did not satisfy anyone. Eventually, White himself came up with a solution, called the "scarce currency" provision, according to which the Fund could declare a currency to be scarce and then ration its available supply. In the event of a scarce currency situation, the Fund could authorize members to limit the use of the scarce currency to pay for imports to the extent that such discrimination against the scarce currency country was warranted by the shortage. This provision, which first appeared in the ISF draft of December 16, 1943, caused considerable embarrassment to White because U.S. critics of his plan saw the provision as approving discrimination against U.S. imports, which the Fund was supposed to avoid. Although the scarce currency clause was included in the final draft of the Bretton Woods Agreement, the Fund has never declared the dollar to be scarce.

Four other issues that involved differences between the Keynes plan and the White plan were debated at the Washington meetings: (1) the right of Fund members to maintain exchange restrictions on capital movements, (2) the conditions for obtaining credits from the Fund, (3) the rules on changes in exchange rates, and (4) freedom to change par values.

Exchange Restrictions

During the preconference negotiations, most countries objected to the requirement in the original ISF draft that Fund members abandon all controls over their foreign exchange transactions with other members no later than one year after joining, except with the approval of the Fund. Countries wanted more freedom to control their exchange markets. The ICU provided more time for eliminating exchange restrictions, and members were free to maintain restrictions on all capital transactions if the restrictions did not affect trade in commodities. Since most countries maintained some restrictions on foreign exchange transactions, the foreign delegates argued strongly that the ISF provisions be modified, especially with respect to the control of capital movements. The provision was significantly modified, first by giving every member the right to control capital movements, and second, by giving members considerable time after joining the Fund before they had to abandon exchange controls that restricted the financing of current transactions. An important debate on this issue was whether members could draw foreign exchange from the Fund while they maintained foreign exchange restrictions with other members. This was discussed but never resolved. In any case, in the final agreement at Bretton Woods, the Fund could determine whether a country was eligible to obtain foreign exchange.

Conditions for Obtaining Resources

The ISF plan provided that a member could borrow for a year up to 75 percent of its quota, provided the loan was approved by three-fourths of the members. Moreover, as noted above, the specific currency borrowed must be required by the borrowing country to make a payment to the country whose currency is borrowed. The ICU provided that countries could run deficits in the union up to one-half of their quotas without any conditions. The British delegation at the Washington meeting argued that Fund members ought to be able to obtain some credits from the Fund automatically without the Fund's approval. Otherwise, members could not regard borrowing from the Fund as a supplement to their reserves. A subsequent edition of the White plan provided more liberal drawing conditions, but the question of whether members would be able to borrow without any conditions was never resolved to Keynes's satisfaction.

In both the White and the Keynes plans, credits were to be provided mainly for meeting deficits on current accounts and not for financing capital movements. The latter requirement, which was embodied in the Fund's Articles of Agreement negotiated at Bretton Woods, has not always been enforced and has been a source of some dispute throughout the history of the Fund (International Monetary Fund, 1969, pp. 193–94). For example, in the course of the Asian financial crisis in 1997–98, some of the credits obtained from the Fund were used to finance debt repay-ment or other capital transactions. This question is discussed in later chapters.

In the original White plan, members of the Fund were required to abandon all controls on their foreign exchange transactions with other members no later than one year after joining, except with the approval of the Fund. The ICU plan clearly gave members freedom to maintain restrictions on all capital transactions. In fact, Keynes advocated the use of capital controls for some purposes for all countries, including the United States.

White accepted the right of countries to control capital movements without the permission of the Fund, but the U.S. delegation looked forward to an international monetary system in which there would be no controls on exchange transactions of any kind. Keynes favored controls on capital movements, in part because capital transferred out of the sterling area within which capital movements were completely free could give rise to a foreign exchange drain on the British treasury. Keynes also believed that large creditor countries such as the United States should use capital import controls to assist countries in preventing a flight of capital. Another issue on exchange restrictions was whether members of the Fund had to abandon exchange controls on the financing of current transactions before they could borrow from it. This issue was never resolved, but members have in fact been able to obtain credits from the Fund while maintaining restrictions on current transactions.

Conditions for Obtaining Credits

Both the ISF and the ICU provided normal limits on the amount of credits a member could obtain as determined by its quota, although provision was made for obtaining credits beyond the normal level. According to the White plan, however, any credits provided by the Fund would require approval by three-fourths of the member votes. This meant that the United States could always prevent any member from obtaining credits. Even if the U.S. had only 20 percent of the voting power, it could always obtain support from other members for an additional 5 percent of the votes. The ICU provided that a country could run deficits in the clearing union up to one-half of its quota without the approval of the ICU. Keynes argued that all members should be entitled to a certain amount of unrestricted credit so that they could regard credits available from the Fund or the ICU as a part of their international reserves, and that this would give them confidence to take the measures necessary to eliminate their foreign exchange restrictions on current transactions.

White was adamant in insisting that the Fund should be able to deny its credit to any member. His reasoning was that the Fund must determine whether its credits are being used in accordance with the purposes of the Fund, and that meant that the borrowing member was taking action to restore equilibrium in its balance of payments. Despite various language changes suggested by Keynes and others—to make at least some amount of credits unrestricted—no satisfactory solution to this problem was forthcoming. The issue was brought up again at the Bretton Woods conference and indirectly brought up by Keynes at the inaugural meeting of the Fund's board in 1946. He was concerned that the United States would have too much power in the Fund if all credits had to be approved.

Despite the intense debates on the issue, the Fund has always been liberal in permitting its members to obtain credits within the normal limits. However, the Fund has established conditions relating to a broad range of a country's economic policies for credits beyond the normal limit.

Exchange Rates

White's initial draft gave the ISF power to set the par value of each member's currency in terms of gold at the time operations began, and a member could change its par value only with the approval of three-fourths of the member votes (International Monetary Fund, 1969, p. 60). Members were obligated to keep their exchange rates within a narrow range of their par values. Since each currency's par value was to be fixed in terms of gold, this determined the parity between each currency. As the U.S. was expected to have more than

25 percent of the total vote in the ISF, foreign representatives objected to allowing the U.S. a veto on alterations in par values. The ICU provided much greater freedom for changing parities. In the Articles of Agreement adopted at the Bretton Woods conference, countries could alter their par values up to 10 percent without permission from the Fund, but changes beyond that would require approval by a majority vote. Although Keynes preferred more freedom for countries to change their par values, this was the compromise reached in the Joint Statement discussed below.

The Fund Quotas

Much of my own work during the ATC negotiations concerned the question of Fund quotas. According to the White plan, each member of the ISF would be assigned a quota that would determine (a) the maximum amount it could normally draw from the Fund; (b) the amount of its gold and currency subscriptions to the Fund; and (c) the member's voting power in the Fund. Prospective members of the Fund were very interested in what their quotas would be and how they would be determined. In the April 1942 draft of the ISF, White provided some illustrative country quotas and suggested a formula for determining the quotas. Quotas were based on the assumption that the Fund's total assets would be $5.2 billion, a figure later raised to about $10 billion. White did not want to discuss with any individual country the actual size of its quota, but he needed a formula that would provide the relative distribution of the total quotas he had in mind. He wanted the U.S. quota to be about $2.2 billion—roughly the amount available in the U.S. Exchange Stabilization Fund, which could be used without a congressional appropriation. He wanted the United Kingdom quota to be about half the U.S. quota and the Soviet Union's quota somewhat less than the U.K. quota. China's quota was to be slightly less than the U.S.S.R. quota. These were all political decisions and had nothing, in my opinion, to do with economic reality. They reflected Roosevelt's assessment of the importance of the Allied governments in the war.

In July 1943 White asked me to devise a formula that would yield his desired distribution of the quotas among these four countries. He also wanted me to use the formula to calculate the quotas for all the countries that might be expected to join the Fund, assuming total assets (quotas) of about $10 billion. This was a difficult assignment, especially since he wanted the results in two days. I quickly determined that none of the variables that might be used in the formula—such as gold and foreign exchange reserves, national income, foreign trade, or population—bore any relation to White's desired relative distribution of the quotas among the four countries. Also, any formula that satisfied White's desired distribution for the four countries would have yielded quotas completely out of line with the economic importance of a number of other countries. For example, France, which was a major economic power and much more important in international trade and finance than the U.S.S.R. and China combined, should not have a quota less than that of China. When I raised this question with White, he stated he did not care what the French quota turned out to be.

After experimenting with a number of variables for the formula, I used the following variables and the percentage of each variable used for calculating a country's quota:

National income	*2 percent*
Gold and dollar reserves	*5 percent*
Average annual imports	*10 percent*
Maximum variation in annual exports	*10 percent*

For example, if a country's national income were $10 billion, its gold and dollar reserves $500 million, its average annual imports $1 billion, and the maximum variation in its annual exports in recent years $500 million, its quota according to the formula would be $375 million. I found that, with a small adjustment, the formula yielded approximately the quotas White had stipulated for the four countries. This exercise required many calculations with a 1940s-style calculator, using a number of variables and weights for each country. If I had had access to a modern computer, I could probably have come up with a better formula. At the time I developed the formula, there were data on trade and international reserves but virtually no official data on national income other than for the U.S. and Britain. My sources for the national incomes of the thirty-four countries for which I determined quotas were based on estimates of average consumption found in country studies, estimates of wage rates and family expenditures, and extrapolations from budget and tax data. I gave countries at a similar stage of development the same per capita income. My national income estimate for China was $12 billion, less than one-fifth of U.S. national income in 1940, and my income estimate for the Soviet Union was $32 billion. I confess to having exercised a certain amount of freedom in making the national income estimates in order to achieve the predetermined quotas.

On the basis of my formula, I calculated the U.K. quota at $1.3 billion, the Soviet quota at $763 million, and China's quota at $350 million. According to the formula I developed, the French quota would have been $700–$800 million, which would have violated White's requirement that it be less than that of China.

The first memorandum on the basis of my formula for internal use by the Treasury Department, dated June 9, 1943, listed the quotas of only eleven countries and did not include France. In a much longer list prepared in the Treasury Department while I was in Egypt, China's quota was arbitrarily raised to $600 million; France was given a quota of $500 million; and the Soviet Union was boosted to $900 million. These changes reflected political rather than economic criteria.

My formula was later used as a basis for determining the quotas in the World Bank; the numbers bore little or no relation to a country's need to

Raymond F. Mikesell

borrow or contribute to the assets of the Bank. A member's ability to borrow from the Bank is not related to its quota, as is the case with the Fund, and the Bank is not dependent on capital subscriptions for making loans. Instead, the subscriptions constitute a guarantee of the Bank's liabilities if it should become insolvent. Most of the Bank's loan resources come from the sale of bonds on the international financial markets.

My formula for the ISF quotas was also later used as a basis for determining each nation's contribution to the United Nations. This occurred because the Treasury Department was asked to come up with a formula for such contributions, and my ISF quota formula was used for this purpose. Since I was overseas in late 1943, one of my colleagues searched my files for details on the formula and the data I had used for calculating the quotas. However, he used some of my preliminary data, which were different from those to prepare the ISF formula and lacked some later refinements. As a result, the U.S. share of the financial support for the UN was somewhat higher than it would have been if my revised data had been used. I think of this story when I read about congressional objection to the size of the U.S. payment to the UN, and I wonder if this error may have contributed to the problem!

My formula was also used as a basis for determining the IMF and World Bank quotas at Bretton Woods for most member countries represented at the conference. Thereafter, it was used in a somewhat revised form for new members joining the Fund. In fact, the formula is still used, but with special adjustments for individual countries. I take no pride in having authored the formula and sometimes apologize for it as my claim to infamy! It has continued to be used in large part because the Fund wanted to apply the same conditions in determining quotas for new members as were applied to the original members.

Negotiating the Joint Statement

In the course of the bilateral meetings with the British in the summer of 1943, the differences between the White and Keynes plans were narrowed, but important controversies remained that had to be reconciled as a condition for administrative and legislative approval in both countries. White believed that if both the U.S. and Britain were in agreement on plans for the IMF and the World Bank, most of the other countries would go along. (By this time the ISF was called the IMF.) Intensive bilateral negotiations between the ATC and the British delegation headed by Keynes took place in Washington, D.C., between September 14 and October 9, 1943. I missed most of these meetings because of my mission to Africa, but I was well briefed on them when I returned. The objective of these meetings was to prepare an agreed statement on the major provisions of the IMF and the World Bank (later called the Joint Statement)—a statement to be taken to an international conference organized to prepare the charters of the two institutions.

The negotiations for the preparation of the Joint Statement were in significant measure a repeat of the bilateral meetings held during the summer of 1943. Considerable time was spent on the multilateral clearing problem and on the rights and conditions of members to borrow from the IMF. The basic positions of White and Keynes were not fundamentally changed during the negotiations on these two issues. Language was found that was sufficiently obscure to enable Keynes to agree, although later on each interpreted the language differently. Agreement was reached on the conditions under which members that had borrowed from the IMF would repay their obligation to the Fund when their balance of payments position improved.

Another important issue was the transition period that would occur between the end of the war and the return of normal commercial transactions. Following the transition period, members were obligated to abandon exchange restrictions that limited payments for goods and services or involved discrimination against the products of another country. Keynes wanted the transition period to be long and indefinite, while the White plan provided that the Fund would make representations to individual members that conditions were favorable for the abandonment of its restrictions on foreign exchange transactions. There was an implication in the IMF provision that until the end of the transition period, a country's ability to obtain credits from the Fund would be limited. Keynes did not accept this limitation, but the availability of credits from the Fund during the transition period was not resolved in the negotiations. Behind the issue of the transition period was the position of Keynes and the British government generally: Britain was not prepared to join the Fund and accept the obligations on foreign exchange controls until an arrangement for a substantial loan to Britain was made. This was not revealed either in the bilateral negotiations or at Bretton Woods.

After the negotiation of the Joint Statement, a number of issues remained, and the Joint Statement was not signed by both parties until April 1944. The Joint Statement did not deal at all with the Bank proposal, nor did it cover all the issues concerning the Fund itself. However, it provided an agreed framework to take to Bretton Woods. Although Keynes had misgivings about Britain's surrendering the sterling area in favor of full multilateralism as required by the IMF, he realized that Britain was obligated to eliminate all trade discrimination by Article VII of the Lend-Lease Agreement, and this was likely to be a condition for postwar financial aid from the U.S. Therefore, he was prepared to negotiate an agreement for establishing the Fund and the Bank, even though he realized that Britain's willingness to join the Fund depended upon satisfactory financial assistance from the U.S.

One issue on the negotiation of the Joint Statement had to do with the arrangement in the IMF for multilateral clearing. Another concerned the rights and conditions for members to draw foreign exchange from the Fund, including Keynes's insistence that a certain amount be available unconditionally for members to have confidence in their ability to fulfill their obligations on foreign exchange practices. Much of the discussion on these issues was a repeat of earlier discussions. Although language was found to enable the parties to agree on the Joint Statement, the basic issues were never resolved. In retrospect, neither issue involved significant problems in the operations of the Fund. As will be noted in a later chapter, the issue on the unconditional right of members to borrow from the Fund up to a specified amount came up again at the Savannah conference in 1946. Keynes lost the battle.

Another issue was the obligation of a member to repay the Fund; it took the form of a member's repurchasing its own currency held by the Fund with gold or a convertible currency. The July 1943 ISF draft required that each member offer to sell to the ISF in exchange for its national currency "one half of the foreign exchange resources and gold it acquired in excess of its official holdings at the time it became a member of the Fund, but no country need sell gold or foreign exchange under this provision unless its official holdings are in excess of 25 percent of its quota." Keynes wanted to limit this obligation to surrender any increase in reserves to cases in which a member's reserves exceeded its quota and the member had drawn on the IMF in the preceding year. He also wanted to define reserves to include only gold and convertible currencies. White agreed to Keynes's alternative draft, but the obligation to surrender reserves has not been a significant issue in the Fund's operations.

Evolution of the World Bank

White's April 1942 plan provided for so many functions that it was difficult to differentiate between the basic roles of the Bank and the ISF or to justify the existence of two institutions rather than one. At one of the meetings I attended, Keynes stated that the titles of the two institutions should be reversed! White's view of their respective roles was clearly stated in his proposal: "The Fund [ISF] is designed chiefly to prevent the disruption of foreign exchange and to strengthen monetary and credit systems and help in the restoration of foreign trade, whereas the Bank is designed chiefly to supply the huge volume of capital to the United Nations and associated nations that will be needed for reconstruction, for relief, and for economic recovery."

The Bank was White's answer to the criticism that the ISF could not promote currency stabilization and the elimination of exchange restrictions in the immediate postwar period without postwar economic recovery. But if the resources of the Bank were to constitute a condition for achieving the fundamental goals of the ISF, why was so little attention paid to the Bank during the inter-departmental discussions in 1942 and 1943?

In April 1943, White issued a new draft of the Bank plan, which raised the authorized capital from $10 to $20 billion, with each participating government subscribing 10 percent of its national income. The Bank plan provided that the currencies loaned by the Bank could be used only for purchases in the country of their origin. In later drafts and in the final Articles of Agreement of the Bank, a clause gave each member a veto over the use of its currency loaned by the Bank, including the right to veto an exchange of its currency for other currencies. Thus, as in the case of the currencies subscribed to the ISF, there were severe limitations on the usability of the Bank's assets. I regarded these limitations as inconsistent with the policy of nondiscrimination, which the U.S. government was promoting in both the ISF and the GATT. Again, White's insistence on such restrictions was based on his belief that Congress would not approve of U.S. dollars being loaned for purposes other than buying U.S. exports. This was a parochial position not shared by officials of other U.S. agencies. So far as I am aware, the United States has never exercised this power, although it has voted against particular loans by the Bank for other reasons.

During the bilateral meetings with Britain in 1943, a draft of the Bank plan, dated September 24, 1943, was submitted, but only one day was devoted to discussing it. A major issue was whether the Bank would engage primarily in making direct loans from its resources or in guaranteeing loans made by the private sector. Keynes favored the latter because it limited Britain's obligation to supply capital to the Bank. He recommended that the capital of the Bank serve primarily as backing for loan guarantees and that its capital not exceed $5 billion, rather than $10 billion as suggested in the U.S. proposal (the $20 billion in the April 1943 draft had been reduced to $10 billion). Keynes also wanted either no gold subscription or a very small one. It was ironic that the British wanted a smaller Bank than the U.S. delegation, for White had initially expected the Bank to meet the large postwar reconstruction and recovery requirements. Keynes evidently thought that Britain had more to gain from a small Bank requiring a small gold and sterling contribution, because he did not think Britain would borrow from the Bank.

Atlantic City

Following the final approval of the Joint Statement, the Treasury Department made arrangements for an international financial conference; to be held at the Bretton Woods Hotel in New Hampshire, beginning July 1, 1944. The conference was preceded by a meeting in Atlantic City between the U.S. and

British delegations the last week in June 1944. Several other countries were represented in Atlantic City but did not play a significant role. The stated purpose of the meeting was to set the agenda for the Bretton Woods conference. However, the meetings were mainly occupied with proposed changes in the Joint Statement and with Keynes's proposal for the Bank.

Keynes wanted changes in the Joint Statement, probably in response to his discussions with Commonwealth representatives. The Treasury Department technicians, including myself, were kept busy writing memoranda, usually in opposition to any changes. Keynes wanted to limit the power of the Fund to set conditions for the use of its resources. He also wanted the voting power of the Fund's executive directors to reflect the importance of the country rather than being determined by the size of the quota. These and other issues became part of the agenda of the Bretton Woods conference.

The Atlantic City meetings devoted considerable attention to the Bank proposal. Important changes were submitted by Keynes in a draft prepared by the British and other delegations during the trip on the Queen Mary across the Atlantic. This "boat draft" emphasized the function of the Bank as guarantor rather than as a lender of national currencies subscribed to the Bank, and it provided that 80 percent of the subscribed capital could not be called for payment except to make good a default on the Bank's obligations.

White accepted the fundamental changes made by the boat draft. For the United States it had the advantage of reducing the need for dollars subscribed to the Bank, which according to the White plan had to be used to buy goods in the United States. Some doubts were expressed by the Treasury Department staff as to how important loan guarantees would be in the Bank's operations. They have not been important, and most of the Bank's loan funds have come from its borrowings in the world's capital markets.

Explanatory Note

The White plan for the Bank was rivaled by a plan written by John Parke Young and submitted to the ATC by the State Department. This plan, entitled "A Proposal for an International Investment Agency," was similar to the White plan but had several distinguish-

Raymond F. Mikesell

ing features. It proposed that loans made in national currencies could be spent in any country chosen by the borrower, and that the borrower could repay in the same currency it had borrowed. Unlike the White plan, loans to private enterprise would not have to be guaranteed by the borrower's government. Although the provision not to require a government guarantee was not accepted by the ATC, it is not required by the International Financial Corporation established as an affiliate of the Bank in 1956.

Sources

The text of both the White and the Keynes plans, together with the background material on the Bretton Woods conference, is in International Monetary Fund (1969) and in U.S. Department of State (1948). I have also drawn on Mikesell (1994).

CHAPTER 3: BRETTON WOODS

The Bretton Woods conference was not important because of what was negotiated there; basic decisions had been negotiated beforehand. Bretton Woods is famous as a symbol of international collaboration for dealing with postwar problems, in contrast with the economic chaos following World War I. While the representatives of the participating countries disagreed on many details, they agreed on the kind of postwar economic system they wanted to foster. And they created a framework for the world economy that has lasted for more than half a century.

The conference began in July 1944. Its purpose was to prepare the charters for the International Monetary Fund and the International Bank for Reconstruction and Development (the charters came to be called the Articles of Agreement). Representatives from most of the forty-five countries assembled had met in Washington, D.C., at various times during the period 1942–44 and were familiar with the White plan for the Fund and the Bank, the Keynes plan, and the Joint Statement. If documents representing agreement between the U.S. and Britain, plus acceptance by Canada, had not been agreed upon ahead of time, it is my view that a conference with this number of countries dealing with the multitude of postwar financial issues would not have gotten anywhere. Virtually all the issues that were debated prior to the conference were discussed again by three major commissions during the conference. But no fundamental changes were made in the Joint Statement, which was essentially the plan for the Fund, or in the Bank plan, which had been substantially modified by Keynes from the original White plan. Perhaps if there had been a substantial independent group with an agreed upon agenda, significant changes might have been made. But the U.S. delegation, which kept an eye on what it believed would be acceptable to the U.S. Congress, was unlikely to agree to fundamental changes. Representatives were free to criticize elements of the plans, but the conference was carefully managed by the British and the Americans.

The U.S. delegation was composed of twelve members, including officials of several government agencies and Representatives and Senators. Other delegations had delegates and advisers. In addition, the secretariat of the conference, of which Morgenthau was chair, had four vice presidents, a secretary-general, and technical and clerical personnel, for a total of more than thirty. There was no conference secretariat independent of the country representatives, and the secretariat consisted mainly of U.S. government employees who reflected the positions of the agencies with which they were associated. I was officially listed as a technical adviser to the secretariat rather than as a member of the U.S. delegation. Technical advisers came from the Treasury Department, Federal Reserve Board, State Department, and other U.S. government agencies. I was assigned to the Quota Committee, but how people were officially listed bore little relation to their participation in the conference. All of the advisers spoke freely in the three commissions where most of the discussion at the conference took place. Commission I negotiated the IMF agreement, Commission II the World Bank agreement, and Commission III discussed other international economic issues. For example, Bernstein, who was listed as a U.S. technical adviser, probably spoke more at the sessions of the conference than anyone else and certainly more than anyone on the U.S. delegation. Informality and disregard for rank characterized the conference, perhaps due to the vacation atmosphere of the hotel and environs.

Debate was limited. Where there was a "significant issue," such as the rules on changing par values or on exchange restrictions, the British and American delegates were able to influence enough votes for their own agreed upon positions. The British Commonwealth countries were heavily influenced by Britain, and the Latin American delegates tended to support U.S. positions. There were problems in dealing with the Soviet Union delegates, but many of the technical details relating to changes in exchange rates and currency convertibility were not regarded as relevant for a nation whose government controlled virtually all international transactions.

In some cases the Joint Statement was not clear or an important function of the Fund was not covered. For example, the Joint Statement made no provision for charges on the Fund's loans to members, but it was generally agreed that borrowers should pay interest. The conference had to formulate specific provisions for levying charges, and the U.S. delegation took the position that charges should increase with the ratio of the Fund's holdings of a currency to the country's quota. (The Fund's holdings of a currency increase when a member uses its own currency to acquire foreign currency.) After considerable debate, the U.S. position was adopted. Another question not dealt with in the Joint Statement was the convertibility of the large sterling balances that had been accumulated during the war by sterling area countries such as India and Egypt. White had wanted to make specific arrangements for converting these sterling balances, but Keynes would not go along. The British Commonwealth countries holding substantial amounts of sterling wanted the Fund agreement to provide for convertibility of these balances, but the British insisted that sterling convertibility should be limited to currently acquired sterling needed for making current payments—not applied to long-standing balances. The reason was that the British wanted to limit the drain on their gold and dollar reserves that would occur if the balances were converted into dollars. In this case, the British position prevailed.

White regarded the Bank as somewhat less important than the Fund, since he was mainly concerned with the postwar exchange system. Nevertheless, the Bank was expected to provide funds both for rebuilding the world after six years of war and for making an important contribution to the economic development of nonindustrial countries. White, however, greatly underestimated the financing that nations would need before it was possible to have the sort of world trading and foreign exchange system that the Fund was designed to promote.

Much of the conference dealt with issues relating to the organization and management of the Fund—such as the functions of the executive directors, the appointment of a managing director, and the location of the Fund. These were largely resolved in accordance with U.S. positions. Most of the delegates did not want the Fund to be located in Washington, D.C., but preferred New York or London because they felt that an institution in Washington would be under too much U.S. governmental influence. However, White and Morgenthau argued that the Fund should be independent of private financial centers and that locating the Fund in Washington, D.C., would help persuade Congress to approve U.S. membership in them.

None of the delegates challenged the par value system. There was dissatisfaction with both freely fluctuating exchange rates and controlled rates which could be changed for any reason, including providing a country with a competitive advantage in trade. The gold standard of the prewar period, which required that currencies be convertible into a fixed amount of gold, was not popular either, as it was associated with depressions and the sacrifice of economic policy to maintaining convertibility of the currency into gold. All the delegates recognized, however, that since the dollar had a fixed value in terms of gold, maintaining the value of a currency in terms of dollars was much the same as maintaining its value in terms of gold. Under the plan, members were given the option of defining their currencies in terms of units of gold or of dollars.

What concerned the delegates was their ability to change the par value of their currencies; in accordance with the Joint Statement, a change in the par value of more than 10 percent required the permission of the Fund. Some delegates wanted greater freedom to change the par value of their currencies, but neither the American nor the British delegation was willing to consider further changes in the provisions agreed upon in the Joint Statement.

A member's freedom to change its par value was never a problem after the Fund was established, and the par value system itself was the first of the major canons of the postwar international monetary system to be abandoned. Today the major issue is whether the value of currencies should fluctuate freely in the exchange markets or be stabilized in some way. Where countries have stabilized their currencies, they have usually been stabilized in terms of dollars.

IMF Lending Operations

The conference renewed the debate between the U.S. and British delegations over whether members had an unconditional right to obtain credits from the Fund up to the limit established by the quota, or whether all drawings from the Fund would be subject to conditions that the Fund might prescribe. Most countries favored Keynes's position that there should be a substantial amount of unconditional credit available for each country, and that the operations of the Fund should be delegated to an international secretariat that would provide credits in accordance with general rules. The conference eventually adopted the U.S. delegation's position that, before providing loan funds, the Fund's executive board would make sure the borrower adopted policies that promoted balance of payments equilibrium. But the British and most other delegations were not satisfied.

Even White might have been surprised at the Fund's subsequent history of prescribing changes in members' fiscal, monetary, and other policies as conditions for loans. The Fund has required applicant nations to alter their social welfare policies and implement administrative and legal reforms that were certainly not contemplated at the time of Bretton Woods.

The original limitations on the amount of credits available to individual Fund members have been breached in favor of credits equal to several times a country's quota, with the additional credits designed to achieve structural changes in the country's economy. The loan terms, rather than being standardized in accordance with the provision in the Articles of Agreement, have been considerably liberalized and there are special subsidized-loan programs for poor countries.

Would the history of the Fund have been different if Keynes's position on unconditional drawings within quota limits been adopted? Probably not, because the Fund has applied conditions mainly when the drawings have exceeded the normal limits provided in the Fund agreement. These conditions, which take the form of "standby" agreements, enable the Fund to influence a member's financial and other economic policies. Since the Fund has frequently allowed members to draw well beyond the normal limit (125 percent of the quota), it would have imposed conditions in such cases even if Keynes had won the argument.

Capital Transactions

Another issue revived at Bretton Woods concerned the control of capital movements. The discussion of capital movements revealed two visions of the financial structure of the postwar world: one in which all nations would exercise controls over capital coming into the country and capital going abroad, and another in which all capital transactions were free of government control. The U.S. delegation looked forward to a world in which private capital would flow freely and play an important role in the development of poor countries. Since most countries had employed capital controls through-out the 1930s and during the war, most delegates visualized a continuation of capital controls indefinitely. White hoped to see completely free markets for both capital and currencies, while Keynes believed that all countries should maintain at least some control over capital movements. One of the reasons Keynes favored controls on capital movements was that he wanted to see the sterling area maintained in the postwar period. Although he knew that sterling must become convertible for current transactions, he believed it would be a long time before Britain could permit convertibility into dollars of the billions of sterling balances accumulated in the past. In addition, the sterling area was a system within which a group of countries could allow free capital movements without creating a demand for dollars that the U.K. treasury would be required to supply. He undoubtedly saw advantages in this wide single-currency area within which trade and capital movements could take place freely.

Despite White's vision of completely free markets for foreign exchange and capital, he was opposed to having the resources of the Fund used for financing capital exports. He wanted the Fund's resources used almost entirely for financing imports required for consumption and productive domestic investment. This required that members be obligated to impose controls on capital exports if they were obtaining assistance from the Fund. This position was reflected in the Joint Statement and in Article VI of the Articles of Agreement adopted at Bretton Woods. The proscription on financing capital exports was inconsistent with the Fund's practice of assisting a member when its balance of payments disequilibrium arises from a financial crisis in the capital markets leading to substantial capital exports accompanied by pressure on the foreign exchange market. Under these conditions the Fund has at times provided assistance to members to stabilize their capital and foreign exchange markets, which in effect has meant that the Fund was financing capital exports. For example, in 1956 Britain called on the Fund for assistance in dealing with capital exports resulting from the Suez crisis, despite the fact that Britain's exports were maintained and there was no increase in the current account deficit. More recently, the financial crisis in East Asia brought several countries to request assistance from the Fund, mainly for capital market and currency stabilization. This question was not seriously debated at Bretton Woods, especially since Keynes also believed that the Fund should not finance capital exports of members. However, some delegates wanted to give the Fund the right to provide unrestricted assistance to any member experiencing a financial crisis.

The World Bank at Bretton Woods

Relatively little attention was paid to the Bank during the conference. Most delegates regarded it simply as a source of loans at interest rates lower than the relatively higher rates on private loans to developing countries. Under the charter, a major purpose of the Bank was to "promote private foreign investment by means of guarantees or participation in loans and other investments." Initially, White envisaged the Bank as dealing only with governments, central banks, UN agencies, and international banks owned jointly by member governments. Later, when a provision was added for Bank loans or guarantees to private enterprise, a requirement was added that governments must guarantee loans to private entities in these countries. Under this condition, the Bank could not play a significant role in promoting the international flow of private capital. Private enterprises did not want government guarantees because they almost inevitably involved government controls on the investments.

There was some debate at Bretton Woods, as well as in the pre–Bretton Woods discussions, about whether the Bank's loans and guarantees should be confined to specific projects, as favored by White, or whether it could make nonproject loans, a position favored by the British. A compromise position became Article III, section iv: "Loans made or guaranteed by the Bank shall, except in special circumstances, be for the purposes of specific projects of reconstruction or development." In recent years more than one-third of the Bank's loans have been for nonproject or general balance of payments purposes.

Raymond F. Mikesell

The Quotas at Bretton Woods

My chief function at the Bretton Woods conference was to serve as an adviser to the committee on quotas chaired by Fred M. Vinson (who later became Secretary of the Treasury and still later Chief Justice of the Supreme Court). I was not favorably impressed by Vinson personally or intellectually. I found him to be formal, stuffy, and lacking in ideas or initiative. I believed that the Democratic administration appointed him to high offices because of his influence on the Southern states whose support the Democrats needed. At the first meeting of the committee, attended by the representatives of fifteen countries, Vinson distributed a Treasury Department list of quotas in which a number of changes had been made from the list I originally prepared. White had negotiated some of the changes, and I made others based on new information on the variables in the formula I had used to prepare the original list. Vinson stated that the list was only a basis for discussion, and he implied that the quotas were determined by a scientific method. White had instructed me not to mention the quota formula or show it to any of the delegates, but some were aware of its existence. This created a problem: if the quotas on the list had not been negotiated or based on some formula, then on what were they based? It suggested that the quotas were simply arbitrary. White defended the quotas as being based on a scientific assessment of country data, but he refused to reveal the formula.

The reaction of most committee members to the Treasury Department list at the first meeting was strongly negative, and several demanded to know how the quotas had been calculated. Most delegates wanted a higher quota because it determined the normal amount of credit available from the Fund. The size of the quota was also regarded as a measure of a country's importance. Vinson, who had not been well briefed on the history of quota determination, was unable to defend the list, and asked me to do so. I spoke for about twenty minutes and, without revealing the formula itself, discussed the significance of the various elements in the formula and why each was taken into account in setting the quotas. After my presentation there was a long silence during which I waited for a harsh examination. The silence was broken by Louis Rasminski of Canada (later president of the Canadian Central Bank), who said he was well satisfied with my explanation and moved to accept the list. To my surprise and relief, his motion was approved. Rasminski, it turned out, had discussed the quota issue with the U.S. delegation prior to the meeting and had agreed to support the Treasury Department list. I had said in my presentation that I would be very glad to discuss their individual quotas with any of the delegates, and I particularly wanted to know any recent official figures for the variables I had used to determine the quota for their countries. Several of them came to me with the most recent estimates of national income, which I then compared with what I had used. I did make changes on several of the quotas, subject to final approval by White.

The Quota Committee unanimously approved the quotas, but China, Egypt, France, India, and New Zealand did not agree to their quotas when the report was presented to Commission I for approval. Other countries not represented on the Quota Committee—including Australia, Greece, Iran, and Yugoslavia—also objected. By the time the conference ended, China, Egypt, Greece, New Zealand, and Yugoslavia had withdrawn their reservations, leaving only the objections of the delegates from Australia, France, India, and Iran entered on the record.

The Treasury Department list gave the French quota at $450 million, which I and other staff members thought was ridiculously low, particularly given the size of Britain's quota. Following the final meeting of the Quota Committee, Pierre Mendes-France, chief of the French delegation (and later premier of France), caught me in the main hall of the Bretton Woods Hotel, where he asked about the method of quota determination and specifically how France could possibly be allocated a quota only one-third the size of the U.K. I repeated my litany on the scientific nature of the quota-calculation process and showed him the data used for France, but I did not reveal the formula. He was not prepared to dispute my data but showed anger and disgust at a process that could give France such a low quota. The French delegation represented the Charles DeGaulle government-in-exile, and it was well known that President Roosevelt and the U.S. administration were not on good terms with DeGaulle. I believe Mendes-France regarded the decision on the French quota as a deliberate insult. Because I also believed the quota was too low, I was greatly embarrassed during the confrontation and wished some senior member of the U.S. delegation would come along to rescue me.

Raymond F. Mikesell

Mendes-France's raised voice and gestures caught the attention of Secretary Morgenthau, who happened to be passing through the hotel lobby, and asked me what the problem was. Mendes-France repeated his objection to France's quota. Morgenthau then explained that President Roosevelt had wanted China's quota to rank fourth because it was a member of the Big Four. Thereupon, Mendes-France went into a rage, speaking unintelligibly, half in French and half in English. Morgenthau calmed Mendes-France by agreeing that he and other members of the U.S. delegation would meet with him. I quietly withdrew and went for a walk on the lawn and continued to shake for much of the rest of the day! France's quota was not raised in the final agreement of the conference.

Most of the controversy on the quotas could have been avoided if White had not insisted that the quotas serve three purposes: (a) subscriptions, (b) drawing rights, and (c) voting power. A number of delegates at the conference pointed out that this combination was illogical. The subscription quota should have been related to a country's reserves, balance of payments position, and national income. Its ability to draw on the Fund might have been related to the size of its international trade and the variation in its exports and imports. Voting power might have reflected the size of its economy. But White believed that the quotas should serve all three purposes.

I have no explanation for White's behavior. The lack of candor regarding quotas at Bretton Woods was unfortunate because it created considerable controversy and mistrust. White used an arbitrarily determined procedure to produce the recommended quotas and then tried to keep the formula from most of the delegates. In his remarks during the conference, White repeatedly played down the role of the formula, while insisting that the suggested quotas were determined by some scientific procedure. White also wanted the quotas in the Bank to equal those in the Fund. In particular, he wanted the total quotas to be the same for both organizations. Many delegates objected. Latin American delegations argued that developing countries should contribute less capital to the Bank since they were the ones most likely to borrow from it. The Soviet delegation refused to subscribe more than $900 million to the Bank's capital but without reducing its (already agreed upon) $1,200 million quota in the Fund. Some countries, including Venezuela, actually wanted a lower quota in the Fund. Venezuela did not expect to use the Fund's resources because of its large monetary reserves, and it did not want a quota of $15 million, 25 percent of which was to be paid in gold. In the final agreement on the Fund, countries could substitute notes for their actual currencies in making subscriptions to the Fund, and the gold subscription was set at 25 percent of the quota or 10 percent of the member's net official holdings of gold and U.S. dollars, whichever was smaller.

The Soviet delegation maintained its opposition to the $1,200 million subscription to the Bank until the last day of the conference because the government in Moscow refused to accept a subscription higher than $900 million, thereby preventing the Soviet delegation from signing the final agreement. White obtained permission from Morgenthau to raise the U.S. Bank quota from $2,750 million to $3,175 million. This, along with Canadian and Chinese increases, made it possible to meet the proposed total of $8.8 billion in subscriptions to the Bank equal to the total Fund subscriptions, while reducing the Soviet quota to $900 million. However, at the closing plenary session, Morgenthau announced that he had just received word from Moscow that the Soviet Union would accept a quota of $1,200 million, which raised the total Bank quotas to $9.1 billion as contrasted with an $8.8 billion total for the Fund. As a result, White's unexplained objective to make the subscriptions to the two organizations equal in amount was not realized.

The Soviet Union

Despite the fact that free and nondiscriminatory trade and free foreign exchange transactions were not practiced under Soviet Communism, White and Morgenthau sought the participation of the Soviet government in the Fund and the Bank and were very solicitous of Soviet views. Although the Soviet delegates had no interest in technical discussions about foreign exchange markets, they were well aware of the provisions in the Fund and the Bank charters that affected their national interests, such as the amount and composition of subscriptions, the amount of credit a member could obtain, and the obligation of members to supply information. The Russians regarded information about their gold and foreign currency reserves as equivalent to their most important military secrets. Hence, they opposed the requirement to provide such data to the Fund. They also wanted a special exemption from the provisions for changing par values because, they argued, exchange-rate adjustments were meaningless in the Communist economic system.

Although the American delegation rejected these and several other requests for exemptions, the Soviet delegation signed the final act of the conference and gave every indication that its government would become a member of both institutions. However, by 1946, when the Bretton Woods institutions were formally established, relations between the Soviet Union and the U.S. and other Western powers had become strained. I believe the Soviet government's eventual refusal to join reflected the fear that by cooperating with the West in these institutions, some Soviet officials would compromise their loyalty to communism.

At Bretton Woods, however, the Soviet delegates were quite friendly. I recall being recruited by White on two occasions for a Treasury Department volleyball game with the Russians, who soundly defeated our team. They also entered into the spirit of what was called Commission IV, the Bretton Woods Hotel nightclub, where late at night we all tried to sing one another's songs. White usually led off with what came to be called "the Bretton Woods Song":

> And when I die don't bury me at all,
> Just cover my bones with alcohol.
> Put a bottle of booze at my head and feet,
> And pray the Lord my soul to keep.

White led the song many times in my presence, not only at Bretton Woods but on other occasions after he had a fair amount to drink.

Liquidating the Bank for International Settlements

An interesting side show at the Bretton Woods conference was a resolution proposed by the Norwegian delegation that the Bank for International Settlements (BIS) be liquidated at the earliest possible date. The BIS was created in 1931 to assist Germany in making its World War I reparation payments to the Allies. Although the Germans stopped paying reparations, the BIS continued to operate as a kind of regional central bank for European banks where European bankers could meet to discuss their common problems. The reason for the resolution, which most delegations supported, was that the BIS was alleged to have cooperated with the Germans in transferring looted assets from occupied countries, including gold taken from the watches and teeth of the Holocaust victims. The U.S. delegation was split between the Treasury Department, which favored abolition, and the State Department, which regarded the resolution as a political matter that should not be decided at the conference. Morgenthau persuaded Keynes to agree to the resolution, but Keynes wanted the liquidation delayed until the establishment of the Fund because of an unexplained obligation undertaken by Britain when it joined the BIS. The final act of the conference recommended "liquidation of the BIS at the earliest possible moment."

Despite the Bretton Woods resolution, the BIS has continued to operate and prosper throughout the postwar period. Some of us at the conference, while condemning any assistance that the BIS may have given to the German government both before and during World War II, felt the resolution was rather empty since it did not specify who would liquidate the BIS and how it could be carried out. Also, no credible evidence had been provided that the BIS had in fact helped the Germans dispose of stolen property.

A Note on Personalities
Harry White

Personalities played an important role in the Bretton Woods debates and in the final outcome. I saw White in numerous meetings and on dozens of other occasions when we talked alone in his Treasury Department office. His Monetary Research staff was largely composed of former academicians, and many of us returned to universities after the war. The staff was intensely loyal to White, and he respected us as scholars and strongly supported us even when he thought we had made mistakes. I do not recall White's embarrassing any staff member by dressing him down, but he showed another side when he was involved in negotiations outside the Treasury Department. He was often brusque, even crude, in his meetings with Keynes and the British delegation.

Raymond F. Mikesell

When annoyed, he sometimes cynically addressed Keynes as "Your Royal Highness" or "Your Lordship." Lord Robbins, who participated in many of the pre–Bretton Woods meetings but was not close to White, described White well in his book *Autobiography of an Economist*:

It is true that White was not a very beautiful character. He was brash, truculent, and, I suspect, somewhat unscrupulous where his own interests were concerned. In his younger days he had been the victim of academic unemployment, possibly due to the discreditable anti-Semitism which at that time tended to affect the policies of the great university with which he had been associated; and I am fairly clear that he was determined that henceforth Harry White should not be worsted in the struggle for survival—or eminence. But that he was in any way associated with the groups in the United States who actively wished harm or wished to exploit our [Britain's] position of weakness will not stand up to examination for a moment. (Robbins, 1971).

White often expressed to his staff his hostility toward the State Department, with which he frequently struggled for power within the U.S. government. Like Morgenthau, he wanted the Treasury Department to be the center of postwar economic policy and planning. This helps to explain the comprehensive nature of the original White plan. International financial institutions were not a high priority in the State Department; without White's zeal, there probably would not have been a Fund or a Bank. The Bretton Woods institutions might not have come into being if they had not been well advanced before the end of the war, since by then there was a plethora of immediate economic problems that these institutions were not equipped to handle.

White sought to conduct his own foreign policy independently of the State Department. He dealt directly with foreign officials in Washington, and members of the Monetary Research staff in American embassies in Allied countries, including myself, secretly reported directly to White without going through their embassies. White sometimes used the press to promote his policies that were in opposition to those of the State Department. On one occasion, while I was alone with him in his office, he dictated over the phone a long, top-secret State Department statement to a reporter. I do not know the reasons for White's antipathy toward the State Department, but it was not directed at individuals since he had close relations with some of them. I believe it was a reaction to the State Department's traditional insistence that it have commanding responsibility over foreign policy.

White believed that the U.S. government should have sought closer cooperation with the Russians. Through certain members of his staff, he provided information to and discussed policy with Soviet embassy officials. These relations were later discovered by the FBI and led to White's dismissal from the government, but they were not known to most of us in Monetary Research.

Many people have asked me if White was a Communist. I am convinced that he was not. White believed in free markets and capitalism and devoted his energies to planning for a postwar world with free and nondiscriminatory trade and payments. He was, however, quite willing to deal with Communist officials to achieve his objectives. The Soviet Union shared his political objectives regarding postwar Germany, and he believed that Soviet officials would support the Fund and the Bank proposals. He did not share the pervasive fear that the Communist ideology would spread to the rest of the world, or that the Soviet Union might dominate the world by military conquest. He believed that a Communist state could operate under a system of nondiscriminatory trade rules, abiding by the trade and exchange obligations of his plan.

White's associates who were later accused of being spies for the Soviet Union—Sol Adler, Frank Coe, and Harold Glasser—never indicated to me that they were not completely loyal to the United States or that they did not believe in a democratic capitalist society. I knew them so well personally that it is difficult for me to believe they could have concealed communist ideology from me. Although they may have had some association with the American Communist movement in their youth, as did many of my college acquaintances in the 1930s, I believe that the accusations directed against them arose from White's propensity to carry on direct relations with the Soviet government outside regular diplomatic channels. If these same activities had been carried on with the British or Canadians, they would have been acceptable. White and his closest associates simply ran their own foreign ministry.

A few weeks before White's death, he and I were speakers at a conference of the American Academy of Political and Social Science in Philadelphia.

Raymond F. Mikesell

After the evening meeting on April 19, 1947, I spent a couple of hours with him in the lobby of the Benjamin Franklin Hotel. He was in a reflective mood, and we reminisced about the events leading to the creation of the Bretton Woods institutions. White had already been compelled to give up his position as the U.S. executive director of the Fund. He had been working as a consultant to the Chilean government and had recently returned from Santiago. He was scheduled to testify before the House Committee on Un-American Activities, but he spoke very confidently of being able to disprove the charges against him and appeared to look forward to the opportunity. White was charged with providing confidential information to the Soviet Union, but I have never believed he gave any information that was harmful to U.S. national interests. White did speak of his heart condition and, when we parted, he apologized for taking the elevator rather than walking the two flights to where both of our rooms were located. Some say he committed suicide to avoid testifying before the House committee. I do not believe it.

John Maynard Keynes

As a young academic who had studied and taught both *The Treatise on Money* and *The General Theory,* I was awed by Keynes and grateful that I could sit in meetings with him. Although he fought hard for positions he regarded as important for Britain's welfare, his economic arguments were academic and dispassionate. Keynes could accept philosophically the economic advantages of multilateral trade while continuing to defend a discriminatory sterling area in terms of Britain's national interest.

There was a sharp contrast between the literary quality of Keynes's ICU proposal and the legalistic formulation of the July 1943 version of the White plan. Keynes displayed arrogance in the elegant language of an educated British lord. He disliked the style and format of the Fund's Articles of Agreement. He said they were written in Cherokee, and he blamed the language on the Treasury Department's lawyers. Keynes frequently complained that Americans were too dependent on attorneys, and once suggested that "when the Mayflower sailed from Plymouth, it must have been entirely filled with lawyers."

Keynes was capable of displaying temper and once threw one of White's drafts to the floor, but he usually expressed his anger through sarcasm. He always had an air of dignity and did not join in the revelry at the Bretton Woods nightclub. I never saw him in sport clothes. Nevertheless, he was approachable. Junior members, such as myself, were able to talk privately with him, and I always found him willing to answer my questions. If we took too much time, however, Lady Keynes would tiptoe over to protect him from becoming too tired. Those of us who were privileged to shake his limp hand on the train from Savannah to Washington following a light heart attack were left with the memory of saying farewell to a truly noble man.

What Bretton Woods Accomplished

White, Keynes, and their colleagues were planning for a postwar world economy that they could not project but hoped to influence by the institutions they wanted to establish. How much influence have these institutions had, and how different would the world economy have been if they had never been created? The following paragraphs present my personal views in answering these questions.

Neither the Fund nor the Bank has functioned as expected. White's expectation that the Fund would create an environment for stable exchange rates and convertibility among the major currencies shortly following the war was not realized, mainly because of the immense problems the Fund and the Bank could not manage or finance. However, multilateralism for the European economies was partly achieved by the European Payments Union (EPU) operated by the BIS, and European reconstruction was financed mainly by the Marshall Plan rather than by the World Bank.

Most of the changes that have occurred in the functions of the Fund and the Bank that differ from those contemplated at Bretton Woods are the consequence of a world economic system that differs significantly from that expected when the Bretton Woods Agreements were drafted. Perhaps the most monumental change has been that both institutions now operate mainly as sources of financing for developing and former Soviet bloc countries. Not only did the developed countries not need financing from these institutions over the past three decades, but the Fund has played only a minor role in supervising and financing the world's payment system. Given that, it is perhaps remarkable that these institutions have not only survived but that their resources have increased substantially.

Most Western nations did not accept the obligations of the IMF agreement with regard to exchange practices and discrimination until the 1960s. After postwar reconstruction was largely achieved, developed countries found it to be in their interest to abandon exchange controls on current transactions and to stabilize their currencies, but they may well have adopted these policies even if the Fund had not existed. The Bretton Woods Agreements committed the major Western countries to long-run policies of both convertibility and exchange rate stability. By the end of the 1960s, Western currencies were intraconvertible and exchange rates were maintained in accordance with the par value system. Ironically, it was the U.S. balance of payments deficits and the concern of the Nixon administration over the drain on U.S. gold reserves that brought an end to the par value system, but currency convertibility has remained.

The history of the Fund's lending operations has contrasted sharply with Keynes's efforts to delegate the operations of the Fund to an international secretariat that would provide credits in accordance with general rules. The Fund's conditions for loans have dealt with social welfare, tax administration, legal reforms, and other subjects that were not contemplated at the time of Bretton Woods. Political factors have certainly entered into the Fund's decisions to make credits available. A good example has been the credits to Russia. Despite failure to adopt policies for promoting equilibrium and even a viable economy, Russia has received credits at the insistence of the United States because of Russia's strong military power.

Following the breakup of the Soviet Union, virtually all of the former Soviet states and countries under Soviet control (such as Czechoslovakia, Hungary, and Poland) joined the Fund and the Bank, not as Communist countries but as countries making the transition to free market and private enterprise economies. Providing for the needs of these countries greatly increased the demand for credit from the Fund and the Bank and presented them with new problems. Most of these countries were not developing in the sense that there was little industrialization or infrastructure, but they lacked the market structure and institutions for operating market economies. This situation has created a challenge for the advisory services of the Fund and the Bank, and it has required new forms of conditionality for loans. But none of the traditional policies of these institutions have been fully applicable to a country such as Russia, whose administrative system virtually broke down in 1998.

What would have been most surprising to the Bretton Woods delegates would have been the freeing of external markets for currencies and capital in the developing countries. Many of the middle-income developing countries (such as South Korea, Thailand, Malaysia, and Indonesia) have attracted foreign capital either through their securities markets or through foreign bank loans made directly to banks and industrial firms. The major problem some of these countries faced in the late 1990s has been the loss of confidence in their capital markets, with the result that foreign investors have withdrawn capital and there has been a sharp fall in the value of their currencies. They have sought assistance from the Fund, not for the purpose of covering their current account deficits as provided for in the Articles of Agreement but for financing capital exports and supporting the value of their currencies. Such assistance, which characterized the Fund's credits to the East Asian countries in 1997 and 1998, appears to violate Article VI, which forbids the IMF from making loans to finance capital exports and, in fact, requires that countries making substantial use of the Fund's resources adopt controls over capital movements. The Fund has been reluctant to ask developing countries to impose foreign exchange controls or direct controls on their capital markets, because for some years the Fund has encouraged all of its members to establish free markets. In making credits available to promote confidence in the foreign exchange and capital markets, the Fund has allowed its resources to be used for purposes that do not directly promote production and growth.

I, along with certain other economists, have opposed this trend. It is currently a subject of considerable debate among economists and public officials, and it is sometimes used as an argument against increasing the resources of the IMF. I believe the Fund should have adequate resources to perform its proper functions, but that its resources should not be used to finance capital movements to restore confidence and equilibrium for two reasons. First, loans made to support currency values and capital markets do not finance the real investments necessary to produce income for financing the loans. And second, loans to support capital markets tend to bail out foreign lenders who have taken risks for which they have expected to receive higher than normal rates of return. Bailing them out encourages risky and often unproductive investment.

Recent Policies of the World Bank

The Bank has not made a loan to any country other than a developing or former Communist country for decades. A high proportion of its loans are made for general balance of payment purposes rather than for specific projects, and the loans are conditional on the borrowing country's taking a number of measures affecting the structure of the economy. Through its affiliate, the International Development Association, the Bank makes loans to its poorest members at rates of interest well below those in private international markets. One of the original purposes of the Bank was to promote the flow of private portfolio capital, but it has not directly promoted much private investment. Its subsidiary, the IFC, has been making a significant volume of loans and loan guarantees to private enterprises in developing countries.

Given the changes in the functions of the Fund and the Bank from those envisaged at Bretton Woods, have these institutions made a contribution to expanding world trade and to the welfare of poor countries? Overall, I believe they have. However, in my view the Bank has made a much greater contribution than the Fund. The Bank has made a significant contribution to development, particularly for those middle-income countries that have adopted the policies required to achieve per capita incomes approaching those of the older developed countries. I am in accord with those critics who charge that the Fund has often prescribed the wrong medicine for its patients and has, in recent years, allowed its capital to be used for bailing out debtors and supporting overvalued currencies, rather than for promoting production and social development. On the other hand, the Fund has provided vital assistance to developing countries that have experienced short-term current account deficits, and it has contributed to the adoption of liberal economic policies by the countries it has assisted. Despite a number of failures, the developing world has benefited from the Fund. I believe, however, that it might have contributed more to development by better allocation of its resources.

CHAPTER 4:
RATIFYING THE BRETTON WOODS AGREEMENTS

Ratifying the Bretton Woods Agreements was nearly as difficult and complex as negotiating them, for two reasons. First, there was powerful opposition from the U.S. banking community and the U.S. Congress to the IMF. And second, neither the British administration nor the British Parliament was willing to join the IMF without the assurance that Britain was financially able to meet the obligation to make sterling convertible, and that it was in Britain's interest to adopt nondiscriminatory trade policy. Much of my work for the Treasury Department between July 1944 and my departure in 1946 was devoted to "selling Bretton Woods" to the American public. I made two round trips from Washington, D.C., to the West Coast, speaking mainly to university groups and foreign policy organizations, and I frequently went on quick trips as a substitute for White or Bernstein, or even Morgenthau. Speaking before university or foreign policy groups was easy, since they accepted the idea of U.S. participation in international affairs. Occasionally when I spoke with groups dominated by bankers or isolationists, there was not just stiff opposition, but personal attacks on White and Morgenthau, who were sometimes charged with being leftists or, in White's case, pro-Communist. This occurred at a civic organization in Hartford, Connecticut, when at the last minute I was asked to speak in place of Secretary Morgenthau. I simply told the banker who made a personal attack on White that it was improper for him to raise such issues with a guest speaker who, as a minor Treasury Department employee, could not properly deal with them.

Some opposition to the Fund and the Bank stemmed from a dislike of any kind of foreign aid, especially that provided through international institutions. Many believed that the U.S. had met its obligations fully with Lend-Lease aid during the war, and that we were not responsible for reconstruction. The banking community strongly opposed the IMF on grounds that it might interfere with domestic financial policies. Instead, it favored a substantial loan

Raymond F. Mikesell

to Britain, conditional on making sterling convertible and adopting a nondiscriminatory trade policy.

The Anglo-American Financial and Commercial Agreements

Despite the elaborate planning to put new economic institutions into place before the end of the war, there was little attempt within the U.S. government to forecast or plan for the balance of payments conditions likely to exist at the end of the war. Administration officials disagreed among themselves about the nature of the immediate postwar financial problems that Europe would face when Lend-Lease was terminated. Although it was implicitly assumed throughout the debate on the Fund that Britain would need substantial assistance if it were to meet its obligation to eliminate payment discrimination, no specific proposal was developed by the U.S. government. In Britain, both the leaders and the public believed that Britain had a right to substantial American assistance in view of Britain's six years of sacrifice in the common cause. Yet the British made no formal proposal until the fall of 1945, following the termination of Lend-Lease.

This proposal, which resulted in the Anglo-American Financial Agreement negotiated in 1945–46, was tied to Bretton Woods in two ways. First, the British Parliament was unlikely to ratify Bretton Woods in the absence of a satisfactory U.S. loan. Without such a loan, Britain would have had to compete with forty other countries for the limited number of dollars available from the Fund and the Bank. In addition, it was expected that drawings from the Fund would be sharply restricted during the transition period during which members would be unable to meet their convertibility obligations. In the absence of a loan, Britain would have little incentive to commit to the obligations of the Fund, and Britain did not expect to borrow from the Bank. Second, without the U.S. loan and an accompanying commitment by Britain to sterling convertibility, there was little chance of reducing trade discrimination against dollar goods during the next decade. Failure to reduce trade discrimination would have greatly embarrassed the Truman administration. Officials of the State, Treasury, and Commerce Departments and members of the Federal Reserve Board and the Export-Import Bank had assured audiences throughout the country that the establishment of the Fund would guarantee the elimination of discrimination against American exports. I was among those who gave such assurances.

The Loan Negotiations

Formal negotiations with the British delegation led by Keynes began in September 1945. The British asked for $6 billion, which Keynes hoped would be a grant rather than a loan. It was made clear to the British that the U.S. Congress would not agree to a grant, and that the U.S. administration believed Britain could meet the obligation of making sterling convertible with half the amount requested. At the end of the negotiations, the U.S. offered a loan of $3.75 billion with generous repayment terms. Under the loan agreement, Britain agreed to make sterling earned from current transactions by all countries freely convertible. This meant, in effect, that sterling could be sold on world exchange markets for dollars or other currencies, and Britain was obliged to maintain the par value of sterling. Britain also agreed not to apply exchange restrictions to payments for U.S. products authorized for import into the United Kingdom. Another provision in the agreement supported a U.S. proposal for an international trade agreement, which served as a basis for the establishment of the General Agreement on Tariffs and Trade.

The Debate within the U.S. Government

Fred Vinson became Secretary of the Treasury shortly after Truman became president, and White lost much of the influence he had under Morgenthau. Several projections of the British balance of payments deficits were made by the Treasury and the State Departments and by the Federal Reserve Board, with a view to determining the gap that needed to be filled in the early postwar period for Britain to restore her economy. These projections were based on estimating 1938 British imports and exports to the 1946–50 period. They depended heavily on a number of assumptions about British domestic policies and production and about world trade patterns—all of which were radically changed by the war. The projections of the British deficit differed widely, and officials tended to choose whichever figure best suited their policy preferences with respect to assisting the British.

During 1945 and 1946, the Monetary Research Division was deeply divided over the need for a British loan. My own position, based on an analysis of Britain's balance of payments, favored a loan larger than Britain

Raymond F. Mikesell

actually received. Initially, White did not take a public position regarding the loan, but he made it known within the Treasury Department that he opposed the loan. Bernstein, along with most of us in Monetary Research, strongly favored the loan. We were convinced that without the loan the British Parliament would not ratify the Bretton Woods Agreements. White's opposition to the loan is difficult to understand. Prior to Bretton Woods, he recognized the need for substantial aid to Britain and other European countries during the transition period. In March 1944, he recommended to Morgenthau a reconstruction loan of $5 billion to the Soviet Union. In 1945, however, White told the Senate Banking Committee that Britain would not need a postwar loan if Bretton Woods were approved.

I recall White telling me that the British did not need the loan because they had accumulated an abundance of gold and foreign exchange for dealing with their postwar obligations. He also said that Britain could meet the Fund convertibility and nondiscriminatory obligations within a reasonable period of time if it immobilized most of the sterling balances. He suggested that a large loan or grant to induce Britain to meet those obligations would undermine public support for the Bretton Woods institutions. Was White's position based on an objective appraisal of Britain's needs, or did it reflect his concern for the passage of the Bretton Woods legislation? He surely must have been aware that the loan was a condition for Britain's membership in the Fund.

This led to a rift within the Treasury Department. Bernstein openly disagreed with White's statement to the Senate Banking Committee that Britain did not need a loan. At the time of the loan negotiations, Secretary Vinson appointed White to chair a technical committee that would prepare the Treasury Department's position, but White held only one meeting. According to Bernstein, White tried to keep Vinson from knowing that Bernstein and Luxford, who were members of the committee, favored the British loan. These men therefore wrote a memorandum to Vinson stating that Britain should have a loan large enough to meet her Fund obligations, and the loan should not be conditioned on the early convertibility of sterling balances. Bernstein was appointed Assistant to the Secretary of the Treasury for International Affairs and put in change of the Treasury Department's participation in the loan negotiations and the subsequent presentation to Congress.

Following completion of the loan negotiations in December 1945, in which White played almost no role, he supported the loan agreement and gave a very convincing analysis of why Britain needed it. One explanation of White's shift in position is that he wanted Congress to believe the loan was unnecessary before it ratified the Bretton Woods Agreements. This suggests he was being dishonest with Congress. However, I am convinced that White believed that Britain did not need the loan and that Britain would ratify the Bretton Woods Agreements without the loan.

In contrast to the negotiations on the Fund and the Bank, the Treasury Department did not play a dominant role in the British loan negotiations. The amount of the loan, $3.75 billion, was a compromise between the State Department's $5.0 billion figure and Vinson's $3.5 billion. Most of the negotiations had to do with the commercial obligations in the loan agreement. Here, the State Department took the lead, largely under the direction of Will Clayton, Assistant Secretary of State for Economic Affairs.

The Role of Congress

Hearings in both the U.S. Senate and the House of Representatives on the British loan began with testimony by Secretary Vinson, but government testimony below the Cabinet level was mainly by officials from the State Department and the Federal Reserve Board. There was no other testimony by the Treasury Department, and there was little organized opposition to the British loan in the hearings. The New York banking community, including a representative of the American Bankers Association, strongly supported the loan, as did the U.S. Chamber of Commerce. But New York bankers did not support the Bretton Woods Agreements—somewhat ironic, given that a major purpose of the loan was to make Bretton Woods possible. Senator Robert Taft, a leading conservative, made critical comments about the loan and reminded the Senate Banking Committee that White had testified during the Bretton Woods hearings that Britain did not need a loan, but Taft no longer had the support of prominent opposition witnesses. Richard Gardner has suggested that the deterioration in political relations with the Soviet Union played a major role in congressional approval of both the loan and the

Bretton Woods Agreements. He refers to an appeal by Republican Senator Vandenberg that the loan would provide political support against Soviet influence in Europe.

Congressional approval of both the British loan and the Bretton Woods Agreements was achieved because the Democratic majority in Congress wanted to support a strong request by Roosevelt, and because a large portion of the American public favored U.S. participation in international political and economic affairs. Voting against the British loan or membership in the IMF and the World Bank was regarded as an expression of isolationism.

The U.S. Public and the British Loan

U.S. public reaction to the British loan may be characterized by extreme puzzlement and considerable disapproval. A poll taken in June 1946 gave the loan only 10 percent unqualified approval. Most people believed the Fund and the Bank would meet Europe's postwar financial needs; that was what they had been told by those of us who were writing and speaking in favor of Bretton Woods. The arguments for the loan—that Britain needed it to make sterling convertible and to avoid discrimination against U.S. exports, and that the loan was necessary to induce Britain to join the Fund and the Bank—were not persuasive. The first argument suggested we were paying twice for nondiscrimination. The second suggested Britain was blackmailing us.

Some observers were willing to accept the loan as compensation for British sacrifices during the war and an important contribution to economic collaboration and world peace. Others, however, who remembered Britain's discriminatory trade policies before the war, questioned her willingness to abide by fair-trade rules. They suggested that we might be strengthening Britain and the sterling bloc at the expense of future U.S. trade.

I recall dealing with statements of this kind while lecturing on behalf of the British loan. Bankers asked why we had not negotiated a commercial and financial agreement with Britain rather than setting up the Fund. They also asked whether our other wartime allies would ask for loans, and whether this was just the first in a series of loan requests. Those of us who were sent out to win support for the loan assured our audiences that Britain's need was unique. But the skeptics were right. The British loan was just the beginning.

Moreover, Britain maintained sterling convertibility for only a few months and did not restore convertibility until 1960 after having benefitted from Marshall Plan aid.

The Inauguration of the Bretton Woods Institutions

The conference held in Savannah, Georgia, in April 1946 for the inauguration of the Fund and the Bank should have been accompanied by a high degree of international cooperation and optimistic outlook. But it wasn't. The Bretton Woods conference had been concerned largely with debating ideas, but the Savannah conference focused mainly on organizational and administrative matters, including the procedure for electing the executive directors, the duties and salaries of the executive directors, the selection of the managing director of the Fund and the president of the Bank, and the location of the Fund and the Bank.

The chair of the conference, Secretary of the Treasury Vinson, made it clear that the basic decisions had already been made by the American government and implied that it was futile to challenge them. Despite informal agreements between the U.S. and British governments on most of the matters listed above, there was wide disagreement on how the Fund would operate. White wanted control of the Fund to be in the hands of a board of directors whose members represented their governments and who would be continuously involved in decisions on exchange rates, drawings, and other matters concerning the Fund's relations with member governments.

White's position and that of the U.S. administration generally reflected the desire to have the Fund heavily influenced by the United States in order to promote the U.S. objectives of stable exchange rates, nondiscrimination in trade, and international financial equilibrium. This position contrasted sharply with that of Keynes, who wanted the day-to-day operations to be in the hands of an international secretariat with only an occasional executive board meeting on general Fund policies.

The final Articles of Agreement were not wholly clear concerning the Fund's management. It stated that "the executive directors shall function in continuous session at the principal office of the Fund and shall meet as often as the business of the Fund may require." This provision had been a compro-

Raymond F. Mikesell

mise and begged the question of whether the business of the Fund required daily, monthly, or annual meetings. Keynes believed that the executive directors should be high officials of the countries they represented and should meet only occasionally to determine general policies, while the managing director and his staff should carry out the Fund's routine operations.

These two views of the Fund's operations were reflected in the debate over salaries of the executive directors. If the executive directors were going to meet only two or three times per year and were to be high-level government officials, the salaries would not be a significant factor in attracting competent people for the positions. But if they were to serve full time as the U.S. government wanted, compensation was important. The U.S. delegation recommended an annual salary of $30,000 for the managing director, a salary of $17,000 for each executive director, and $11,500 for their alternates.

Considering the fact that the salaries were not subject to income taxes by any government, at that time the recommended salaries were higher than those of U.S. Cabinet members and much higher than salaries of British officials. Keynes expressed the view in the open meeting that the salaries were monstrous, while the Americans argued that high salaries were necessary to attract competent people to such important positions. In Keynes's view, salaries that were out of line with those of top government ministers would create administrative difficulties.

In an effort to settle the issue, a small meeting was arranged involving Keynes, White, E.G. "Pete" Collado, and me. White had been designated the U.S. executive director for the Fund, and Collado the U.S. executive director of the Bank, so each had a personal interest in the salary issue. Therefore, I believe it was a mistake to put White and Collado on the salary committee, although I feel sure that both were guided in their arguments by the principle involved, namely, what should the functions of the executive directors be? At this meeting Keynes behaved rather emotionally and implied that White was promoting the "outlandish" salaries for his own personal gain. To his credit, White did not reply to this personal attack. I felt considerable embarrassment in the meeting watching two people I admired in an emotionally charged argument.

The U.S. position prevailed, but Keynes was obviously bitter because he saw that the Fund would operate quite differently from what he had hoped. Keynes's desire to have the Fund operated by international civil servants reflected his desire to make drawing rights largely unconditional and in accordance with rules rather than being subject to the judgment of a political body. It is somewhat surprising that Keynes continued to hold this position, since the U.S. position had already been established in the Joint Statement and in the Articles of Agreement. Why, then, did Keynes continue to argue the point at Savannah? In discussing this question, Roy Harrod, in *The Life of John Maynard Keynes*, stated "that it has been represented to me by Professor Mikesell and Mr. Bernstein that Keynes ought to have realized at Bretton Woods that it was the intention to make drawing rights conditional and must have realized it at the Savannah meeting." Keynes evidently believed that the matter was still open for discussion at Savannah.

It was expected that White would be named managing director of the Fund, but two developments prevented this. First, a Federal Bureau of Investigation report alleged that White had participated in a group providing information to the Soviet Union, an allegation that eventually led to his resignation as U.S. executive director of the Fund. Second, the U.S. government decided that an American should be president of the Bank and a European managing director of the Fund, and that the U.S. could not properly ask that Americans occupy both positions. It was Keynes's candidate, Camille Gutt, who was elected managing director. It may be noted, however, that before the decision in favor of a European managing director, Keynes had favored White for the position. He believed White would provide competent technical leadership and be able to protect the independence of the Fund from subversion by politicians.

Keynes was also disturbed that both the Fund and the Bank were to have twelve executive directors and twelve alternates. With considerable justification he asked what all these people would do. In practice, the large number has been a boon for retired government officials desiring a high salary with little work in Washington, D.C., or a political plum bestowed by successful prime ministers. The surplus executive directors might have been used by both the Fund and the Bank to reduce the need for staff people. But since few

Raymond F. Mikesell

of the executive directors possessed the special skills, such as economics, engineering, and accounting, required for loan appraisal and financial advice, the abundance of directors has simply increased the need for clerical personnel to serve the directors rather than reducing staff requirements.

Keynes was bitterly disappointed that the Bretton Woods institutions would be located in Washington rather than in New York, where they might be less influenced by American politics. And he was apparently disappointed by much more. Harrod states that Keynes was "deeply distressed by the proceedings at Savannah, and it was his doctor's opinion that his distress at the meeting was directly responsible for his death a few weeks later."

The Savannah conference was a triumph of American power but a dismal demonstration of American diplomacy. Vinson angered many of the foreign delegates by forcing through the American positions with little regard for normal conference proprieties. He expressed displeasure at Keynes's opening speech, which invoked the "good fairies" to watch over the "Bretton Woods twins" and expressed hope that a "bad fairy" would not condemn the institutions to become political instruments. Vinson regarded the reference to a bad fairy as an attack on American politicians in general and on the secretary of the Treasury in particular.

The Savannah conference witnessed dissension among the Americans as well as between the Americans and the British. Vinson and White did not get along well, perhaps because Vinson knew of the FBI report on White. Relations between Bernstein and White, who had been very close for years, had become strained, in part because of Bernstein's disagreement with White on the British loan and on the future of Germany.

Perhaps as a reflection of the general atmosphere at the conference, Bernstein had a distressing personal confrontation with my close friend, Roman L. Horne, who had been appointed acting secretary of the Fund pending the election of a managing director. Horne controlled the funds made available by the U.S. government to finance the Savannah conference. Bernstein had asked Horne to authorize the use of these funds to pay for a dinner party Bernstein gave for several delegates, but Horne refused on grounds that he was not authorized to use the funds for this purpose. At a chance meeting between Horne and Bernstein at the conference when

I happened to be present, the two exchanged insults. Horne, who was under great pressure, completely lost his temper and hit Bernstein on the nose, knocking him down and breaking his glasses.

Another source of tension within the U.S. government, which may have had some influence on the Savannah conference, was that White did not get along well with some of the State Department representatives who played leading roles at the conference. Morgenthau and White, for example, had proposed plans for the deindustrialization of Germany in a treaty that would have kept Germany economically weak for a long period. They did not trust the German people and wanted to punish them for the Holocaust. The State Department and the European governments wanted an economically strong Germany that would be closely integrated economically and politically with the rest of Europe. They believed this to be the best way to prevent Germany from starting World War III.

Bernstein and several of us in the Monetary Research Office objected to White's position on Germany, and with Morgenthau's retirement in 1945 there was no one with any influence in the Treasury Department to promote a weak Germany. I embraced the idea of a highly integrated Western Europe in which no one country would have the economic resources for military dominance.

Retrospective on the Savannah Conference

Much of the dissension at the Savannah conference might have been avoided if the delegates had realized that both the Fund and the Bank were to become institutions almost entirely devoted to promoting the development of poor- and middle-income economies. Providing financial assistance and advice to developing countries has required comprehensive involvement of the two institutions in the domestic problems of the aid recipients. Conditional agreements and close monitoring are required rather than rules defining automatic rights to financial assistance. There has been no need for an institution to employ rules on exchange rate stability in order to prevent competitive exchange depreciation, since such tactics have rarely been used since before World War II. As to the issue of whether the operations of the Fund should have been in the hands of international civil servants as Keynes wanted

Raymond F. Mikesell

or under the control of politically appointed executive directors, the existing system has resulted in substantial control by the managers of both institutions rather than by the executive board. However, the managers have had to conform to the governmental policies of the major industrial countries, especially the U.S.

In recent years the Bank has had more popular approval than the Fund, although the latter has received more publicity. The Fund has been widely criticized by a number of economists as well as politicians for its unsuccessful efforts to deal with the East Asian financial crisis. It has been charged that not only has the IMF wasted public funds by helping countries support their currencies and capital markets, but it has encouraged countries to take monetary and fiscal actions that caused economic recession and hardship on the poorer classes who have been unable to buy food and other essentials. In addition, the Fund has been criticized because its loan activities have duplicated those of the World Bank. It has been suggested that the Fund either be liquidated or merged with the World Bank. Questions have also been raised about the desirability of maintaining the Fund because its original purpose of supervising the international monetary system is no longer relevant.

Recent Experience with Bretton Woods Institutions

My direct relationship with the Bretton Woods institutions has been to serve as a consultant to the World Bank during the summer of 1971 and again in 1992–94. My first work with the Bank was mainly concerned with formulating an index of economic and social development, which included not simply per capita output and trade but indicators of social progress, such as health, education, income distribution, and the reduction of poverty. My more recent work has been with the Bank's Environment Department. My main assignments were preparing memoranda on the environmental assessment of projects and participating in the Bank conferences on environmental issues.

In July 1994 two conferences were held to celebrate the fiftieth anniversary of Bretton Woods, and I participated in both. The more exciting was the conference at Bretton Woods itself, where the few survivors from 1944 could relive the physical as well as the intellectual environment of the conference.

The second conference, held at the State Department, was much more formal. The latter conference was organized by the Bretton Woods Committee, a private Washington, D.C.–based organization headed by Paul A. Volcker, former chair of the Federal Reserve Board. In anticipation of the anniversary, I wrote a monograph titled *The Bretton Woods Debates: A Memoir*, which was published by the Princeton University International Finance Section. This proved to be the most popular document I have ever written, judging from the number of comments I received.

During the Bretton Woods memorial conference at the State Department, Paul Volcker gave a reception for those of us who had been at Bretton Woods. I believe there were only five surviving economists and each of us was given special mention by the secretary. He also provided pen and pencil sets engraved with our names on a gold-colored plate. The next week I received a congratulatory letter on my participation (and survival) from the White House signed "Bill."

My participation in the activities associated with the Bretton Woods Agreements was perhaps the most important in my career. It provided personal contacts with a number of scholars and government officials whom I would otherwise have never met, and it has been the source of a great deal of information for my research and teaching. I continue to receive inquiries from reporters and scholars all over the world regarding the conference. This interest has increased over the past few years as a result of the recent activities of the Fund in dealing with the East Asian crisis.

Sources

Much of the material in this chapter is based on my own memoranda, none of which was circulated in the Treasury Department. The quotation on page 70 is from Harrod (1951). Other sources include Black (1991), Gardner (1969), Harrod (1965), Rees (1973), and Robbins (1971).

Raymond F. Mikesell

CHAPTER 5: CURRENCY MISSION TO SAUDI ARABIA

After retiring from a full-time position at the Treasury Department to teach at the University of Virginia in the fall of 1946, I became a regular consultant to the State Department and spent one or two days a week in Washington. It was a hard schedule: leaving Charlottesville on a 6 a.m. train and returning home at 8:30 p.m., sometimes twice a week, but the work was so fascinating I could not give it up. It also fit well into my research interests, since I was writing a book on U.S. economic policy and shortly thereafter one on foreign exchange practices.

In retrospect, on weekdays at least, I neglected my family, consisting of my wife, Desyl, and twin boys born in 1942. However, nearly every weekend was spent hiking in the Blue Ridge Mountains near Charlottesville, and both Desyl and I were active in the Unitarian Church and sang in the choir. I worked more than fourteen hours a day in a normal week—teaching, writing, and consulting. I did get an hour or so of vigorous exercise every day, either playing tennis or running. Why did I work so much? It certainly was not for lack of money. I had a good university salary, a beautiful home on five acres of land with no mortgage, and more than $100,000 in other assets, largely accumulated from profits in the stock market. The reason for my crowded schedule was that I loved everything I was doing. I enjoyed working with graduate students, especially on their dissertations. I have always been a compulsive writer and found it difficult to refuse invitations from foundations and academic friends who edited journals or book series. My consulting assignments in Washington and abroad were so exciting that I could not turn them down. Much of my life has been so rich in enjoyable tasks that retirement has brought more frustration than acceptance of relatively affluent leisure. Fortunately, I can continue to give papers at conferences, provide an occasional lecture at my university, and do professional writing.

Some of my work at the State Department had to do with formulating U.S. policies regarding the International Monetary Fund and the World Bank. The State Department's recommendations were transmitted to the U.S. executive directors via the National Advisory Council on International Monetary and Financial Affairs, whose meetings I frequently attended. Most of the IMF loans, and the conditions the Fund attached to the loans, were considered by the council, which was chaired and dominated by the Treasury Department. I sometimes expressed opposition to an IMF credit when it appeared to violate the conditions stipulated in the IMF Articles of Agreement. I found that few people paid any attention to such legalities, in part because they were unfamiliar with them. I recall opposing a loan to Yugoslavia, whose government policies and economic conditions provided no possibility of restoring balance of payments equilibrium. But President Tito's break with the Soviet Union led to strong State Department support for IMF assistance. As I review the IMF operations over the past few years, I find that political interests remain the strongest factor in loan decisions.

I advised State Department officials on a range of Middle East problems, mostly dealing with foreign aid. Nearly all the Middle Eastern countries received some aid from the United States along with assistance from the World Bank. Foreign aid was motivated less from a desire to help these countries develop than to promote U.S. influence, secure our investments in petroleum, and keep the Arab states from attacking Israel. My background in the Middle East led to an invitation to serve as a member of a financial advisory mission to Saudi Arabia—mounted in response to a request from the Saudi Arabian government for financial advice in modernizing its primitive monetary system. I was greatly attracted to the opportunity of working in this country about which little was known by most people except for the exploits of T. H. Lawrence during and after World War I.

Prior to World War I, Saudi Arabia was largely under the control of Turkey but it emerged from a loose confederation of tribal communities to become a kingdom in 1932, under King Ibn Saud. During the 1930s, the new nation had almost no exports. Its foreign exchange income came mainly from the annual visit of thousands of foreign Muslims to the holy city of Mecca. Just as sudden wealth changes lives and creates complex problems

Raymond F. Mikesell

within families, sudden wealth brought revolutionary changes to Saudi Arabia, whose tribal government and traditional social customs had difficulty adjusting to modern economic realities. Between 1943 and 1948, annual government revenue, mainly from oil, rose nearly tenfold to about $60 million (equivalent), and to over $100 million in 1951.

U.S. petroleum activities in Saudi Arabia date from 1933, when Standard Oil Company of California (SOCAL) obtained a concession along the east coast of the country. This was followed in 1939 by a supplementary concession which covered much of the rest of the country. Commercial oil production began in September 1938. Standard Oil of New Jersey, Socony Vacuum, and Texas Gulf later joined SOCAL in the ownership of the Arabian-American Oil Company (ARAMCO), which operated the concession.

Beginning in 1943, the U.S. government developed close relations with the Saudi government and provided various forms of assistance, including lend-lease supplies of civilian goods, technical assistance, and loans for economic development. Not only were Saudi Arabia's large oil reserves being developed by U.S. firms, but unlike most of the other Arab nations in the region, the country was not under British economic and political hegemony. Although the Saudi government sought to remain independent of Western control, it turned to the United States for financial advice.

Saudia Arabia's Monetary Problems

Prior to the development of the petroleum industry, Saudi Arabia's monetary system was primitive and inadequate for a modern developing economy. It had a metallic currency system consisting of silver coins and British gold sovereigns, a budgetary system that made little distinction between the king's household and the government administration, and no domestic credit or foreign exchange system. There was no paper money, and payments by check against demand deposits were rare. Financial transactions were governed in part by the teachings of the Koran, which, in addition to forbidding the payment of interest, forbade certain other monetary arrangements. The official currency was the Saudi riyal, a silver coin first circulated in 1933, for which the government lacked exclusive legal tender privilege—allowing the coins to be minted abroad and brought into the country.

The generally recognized standard of value, however, was not the riyal but the George V gold sovereign. Its value tended to fluctuate widely in terms of both riyals and other British sovereigns, such as the Queen Victoria sovereign, which had an identical gold content but was subject to discount by as much as 20 percent because of the religious prejudice against portraits of women! The rate of exchange between the riyal and the gold sovereign varied with the relative demand for and supply of the coins. Since neither the riyal nor the sovereign was freely coined, their exchange ratios bore little relation to that between the values of equivalent amounts of gold and silver bullion in world markets. There were also restrictions on coin and bullion imports from neighboring countries such as India. The volatile and uncertain rates of exchange between the domestic currencies, and between the domestic currencies and the major foreign currencies, made paying for imports difficult and costly.

Saudi Arabia's currency system created problems for the pilgrims to Mecca. They were exploited in various ways, one of which was to require them to buy silver riyals with sovereigns at a rate that undervalued the sovereign in comparison with the rate of exchange between gold and silver in world markets. In 1943–44 the government guaranteed a minimum riyal-sovereign ratio of forty to one, which required the government to control the supply of riyals. In the fall of 1943, the government received a large shipment of riyals that had been coined in the United States from silver on lend-lease to Saudi Arabia from U.S. Treasury stocks. This gave the government better control over the supply of riyals. Later, under an arrangement with the British Treasury, pilgrims from nearby countries were permitted to pay in advance in their own currencies a large part of the cost of the visits, and the British then paid the Saudi government in sterling exchange. The erratic monetary situation also caused difficulties for ARAMCO. Under the concession, the royalty rate was fixed in terms of sovereigns, but the foreign exchange value of the sovereign in terms of dollars and sterling fluctuated widely. This condition made their royalty payments in dollars uncertain. There was obviously a need to overhaul the Saudi Arabian monetary system.

The Eddy-Mikesell Mission

Both the Saudi government and ARAMCO were anxious to establish a currency system that would provide a stable foreign exchange value of the domestic currency and a more convenient domestic payments system. Government officials and the business community recognized that trade and financial payments under the existing system were costly and time-consuming. ARAMCO wanted a system in which its royalty payments to the government and its wage and other expenditures could be in a currency that maintained a fixed relationship to the dollar income. During the mid-1940s, informal discussions were held with Saudi government officials on the possibility of sending American experts to give advice on its currency and foreign exchange situation. But nothing came of it until July 1948, when Judd Polk, the U.S. Treasury Department representative in Cairo, visited Saudi Arabia and talked with both government and ARAMCO officials. The government wanted a currency system consisting of both riyals and sovereigns with a fixed rate of exchange between them. Polk told government officials that an attempt to maintain a fixed link between the two currencies would inevitably fail. He advised the government to invite one or more foreign consultants to study the Saudi currency system and make recommendations.

Late that summer, Robert Brougham, financial vice president of ARAMCO, proposed that George Eddy, senior economist of the U.S. Treasury Department's Office of International Finance, accompany him to Saudi Arabia to advise the Saudi officials on monetary reform. The State Department wanted a competent financial adviser sent as well, but Paul H. Nitze, deputy assistant secretary for Economic Affairs, recommended that Eddy not go to Saudi Arabia with Brougham. He wanted the mission to be a U.S. government mission rather than a private one. He said Eddy should go instead as a representative of the Treasury Department to conduct informal discussions with Saudi officials concerning their monetary problems, and that he should be accompanied by one or more representatives of other agencies, including the State Department. I was working with Nitze at the time, and since I had experience in the Middle East, he recommended me as the State Department representative to accompany Eddy. I was acceptable to the

Treasury Department for membership in a two-man mission, and the University of Virginia gave me a three-week leave.

Eddy and I arrived in Jidda on the Red Sea coast in late October 1948 and were given offices at the American legation. Jidda was a typical Arab city, where one sees more camels than autos and the few women on the streets were in *purdah* (not just veils). Five times a day the Muslim call to prayer could be heard from the top of a mosque, and the faithful would either enter the mosque or bow down wherever they were. Most of the diplomatic missions were in Jidda rather than in the capital city of Riyadh. It was especially important for us to work in Jidda: the office of Minister of Finance Sheikh Abdallah Sulayman and his deputy, Sheikh Mohammed Suroor, was located there. Although our salaries and transportation were paid by the U.S. government, our advice and reports were to be our personal opinions as individuals and not official recommendations of the U.S. government. Neither the State nor the Treasury Departments wanted the Saudi government to feel any obligation to accept our recommendations, nor did they want the U.S. government blamed if our recommendations proved harmful or inadequate. Also, they did not want to deal with any U.S. political objections that might arise from our recommendations.

Shortly following our arrival we were introduced to the minister of finance, Sulayman, and his deputy, Suroor, both of whom were dressed in formal Arabian robes. Because neither spoke English, we had to rely on translators; this took a good deal of time because we had to be sure that what we said was understood. We met with Suroor for two or three hours nearly every day we were in Jidda, and occasionally Sulayman would join us for a short time. We met in Suroor's palace in a large room with a high ceiling and skylights, but we were never taken on a tour of the palace or given an opportunity to see members of his harem. During our discussions, a servant would appear from time to time offering bitter Arabian coffee containing cardamon, while Suroor smoked his huba huba (waterpipe). Despite our frequent meetings, we never felt close to Suroor, who was very courteous but always formal. This was true of all the Saudi Arabian officials we met. We also had to be careful to be sure our statements were not misunderstood. Our meetings and dinners with American officials at the legation were very relaxed, and we learned a great deal about the country from them.

Mohammed Suroor was born a black slave. His family had been brought to Mecca from northeast Africa as household servants. When Suroor's father was later freed, his son was brought up in the Sulayman household. He was a brilliant student and later served as secretary to Abdallah Sulayman before being made deputy minister. In 1954, following Sulayman's retirement, Suroor was named minister of finance, making him the highest ranking nonroyal person in the country.

Saudi leaders hoped to establish a monetary system in which both the riyal and the sovereign would be in circulation, but they wanted a fixed rate of exchange between them. In order to keep the traditional system of the two currencies intact, they hoped to tie both the sovereign and the riyal to the dollar at a fixed rate. At that time the dollar was convertible into gold at $35 an ounce, but the dollar price of the sovereign fluctuated in world markets because sovereigns were no longer being coined and were valued in world markets in part for their value as collectibles. At the official U.S. price for gold of $35 per ounce, the gold content of the sovereign was worth only $8.24. However, sovereigns had been selling in world markets at $12 to $14 per sovereign in response to demand from collectors.

In our initial discussions with Suroor, we used a number of examples to illustrate why it would be impossible to maintain fixed ratios for the riyal, the sovereign, and the dollar. Suppose, we argued, the government ties the riyal to the sovereign at fifty to one and to the dollar at twenty-seven U.S. cents per riyal. This set of rates could remain stable only so long as the sovereign stayed at $13.50 (twenty-seven cents times fifty). Now let us assume that the world price of the sovereign rose to $14.50. In that case a money dealer with fifty riyals could get only $13.50 by exchanging them for dollars at the official rate of twenty-seven cents each. But by exchanging fifty riyals into sovereigns at the official rate of fifty to one and exporting the sovereigns, he could get $14.50. The dollars would be brought back into the country for the purchase of more riyals, which would be exchanged for sovereigns at the official rate. This could continue until the supply of sovereigns in the country was exhausted.

On the other hand, if the outside market price of sovereigns declined to $12.50, anyone with fifty riyals could change them into dollars at twenty-seven cents each (for a total of $13.50), and buy sovereigns abroad at $12.50 each. The sovereigns could then be imported and exchanged into fifty riyals per sovereign, and the dealer would make a profit of $1 or nearly four riyals on each sovereign. This could go on until the government had no more dollars to maintain a rate of twenty-seven cents per riyal. The principle we were illustrating is known as Gresham's Law.

It was also possible that ARAMCO might start paying royalties in dollars rather than in sovereigns—which they could do under the petroleum agreement. In this case, the government would have to acquire sovereigns from abroad at higher and higher prices in order to maintain a fixed riyal-sovereign rate. We pointed out that ARAMCO had the option of paying royalties in dollars, and this option might be used when the sovereign rose in world markets above $12 per sovereign. We therefore recommended that the riyal be tied to a single strong foreign currency: the dollar, because it was the world's most stable currency and its value was maintained at a fixed relationship to gold.

Despite our arguments, Suroor would always revert to a device he believed might enable the Saudi government to overcome Gresham's Law and achieve the government's goal of a bimetallic monetary system. We soon felt we were teaching a class in which the students forgot each day what we had said the day before. We were reminded that in the previous century, bimetallism had strong political support in the U.S. Prominent leaders, such as William Jennings Bryan (who twice ran for president), refused to accept the time-tested truth that a fixed ratio of silver to gold coins could not be maintained in the face of fluctuating ratios of gold and silver prices in the world's bullion markets.

Although we told Suroor that it was advantageous to tie the riyal to the dollar, we were aware that officials of the British government advocated tying the riyal to sterling and keeping their monetary reserves in sterling. In favoring the dollar, we pointed out that because of exchange controls within the sterling area, there were different kinds of sterling—Iraq sterling, Dutch sterling, Egyptian sterling, etc.—and that the sterling held by different countries was being exchanged at a discount from the official dollar value of sterling at $4.03. Tying the riyal to sterling would create a Saudi sterling that might sell at a discount in terms of dollars. Also, since most of its oil income would be in gold or dollars, if the Saudi government held its monetary reserves in sterling, it would be acquiring a weak currency in exchange for a strong one.

If the government were to set the value of the riyal in terms of the dollar, what should the rate be? The market rate at the time was about twenty-five cents. Whatever the official rate, it would need to be supported by the government's standing ready to buy or sell riyals against dollars. We would have preferred that the riyal be made a token currency with a low silver content or even a paper currency, but the government wanted to maintain the tradition of a metallic currency with full metal value. The government would need to have a sufficient supply of both riyals and dollars to maintain whatever riyal-dollar rate was chosen. We did suggest it was advisable to have a spread of 1 percent between the government's buying rate for dollars and the selling rate for dollars, say, 25.25 cents and 25.00 cents, in order to cover the cost of minting riyals.

Maintaining a fixed rate was complicated. If the dollar value of the riyal were too low relative to the market value of its silver, dealers would melt down the riyals, export the metal, and use the dollars from the sale to acquire more riyals. On the other hand, if the dollar price of the riyal were too high relative to the international market price for silver, merchants would have an incentive to convert riyals into dollars for investing abroad, and this would drain the country's foreign exchange. Whether the official price of the riyal is too high or too low depended in considerable measure on changes in the world price for silver. While we recommended that the Saudi government neither institute an exchange control system in which foreign exchange transactions would be regulated nor put restrictions on the internal exchange of riyals for dollars or dollars for riyals, we did suggest that the government take reasonable precautions against large-scale exports of riyal coins for their silver content.

We also recommended increasing the use of bank checks for payments of substantial size in order to reduce the burden of counting and transporting coins, and allowing merchants to pay custom duties with checks drawn on reliable banks in the country. Finally, we recommended that the government open deposit accounts in riyals in domestic banks against which it could issue checks when making payments.

Following our initial meetings with Suroor and Sulayman, Eddy and I sent a telegram to the State Department on November 4, 1948, outlining our proposed recommendations and requesting Washington's approval. We favored supporting the riyal with dollars at around twenty-eight cents—but without exchange controls—and leaving the sovereign rate to be determined by the open market. We also favored a paper riyal, convertible into silver riyals and supervised by a currency board. The paper currency would be backed by (1) dollars, (2) gold bars, (3) riyal coins within limits, (4) sterling currency limited to one year's receipts, and (5) sovereigns. The sovereigns should be sold within thirty days of receipt to avoid market loss. We did not receive the requested reply to our recommended program while I was in Saudi Arabia, and I do not believe Eddy received it after I left. The U.S. government did not want any responsibility for our recommendations.

Recommendations on a Paper Currency

Although there had been discussions about a paper currency in Saudi Arabia for several years, because of traditional opposition it was a delicate subject that we did not initiate. But Mohammed Suroor asked us to give our views on the subject. We, of course, favored the idea, first, because conducting transactions in coin is highly inefficient and costly when large sums are involved, and second, a paper currency gives the government better control over the supply of riyals than is the case when new coins need to be minted or riyals retired and melted into bullion.

We first pointed out that because a very large proportion of the purchases by consumers and business people in the country were for imported goods, a paper currency should be readily convertible into foreign exchange and, therefore, should be backed by ample foreign exchange reserves. This would be consistent with past practice, because riyals and sovereigns were acceptable all over the world and could be readily converted into foreign exchange. We recommended that the reserves behind Saudi paper currency should be equal to at least 100 percent of the paper outstanding in order to avoid an inflationary

Raymond F. Mikesell

expansion of the currency. In addition, paper money should be convertible into silver riyals as well as into foreign exchange. Maintaining the dollar value of the riyal would depend on controlling the supply of riyals—not on the price of silver. Thus, any increase in the supply of paper money should be accompanied by an increase in reserves of both dollars and the government's holdings of silver riyals.

We suggested that it would be important to give workers the right to choose whether they were paid in paper money or riyals and to provide facilities throughout the country for the free exchange of one into the other. Otherwise, a discount market for paper money might develop in certain areas of the country. We pointed out that it was important that bank deposits be convertible into foreign exchange, and that additional foreign exchange reserves would need to be maintained by the government to assure convertibility. This would mean that both paper currency and bank deposits should be backed 100 percent by foreign exchange or by supplies of riyals. However, since the bulk of the Saudi government's income was in the form of foreign exchange or gold sovereigns, providing for reserves should not be a problem.

We made some suggestions regarding the design and denominations of a paper currency. Saudi Arabia had some experience with paper currency. A large amount of Indian rupee currency was in circulation on its east coast, and it was accepted by ARAMCO and the U.S. Consulate. Also, American oil workers were exchanging their dollars for rupees in Bahrain. We pointed out that it would be better to have the dollars changed into paper riyals, thereby keeping the dollars in Saudi Arabia.

In the course of our meetings with Mohammed Suroor, a question arose as to whether the paper U.S. dollar might provide a means of facilitating domestic money transactions, at least until a paper Saudi riyal was introduced. Since we had recommended that the riyal have a fixed relationship to the dollar, why not have the riyal readily convertible into dollar bills at the same fixed rate? Suroor expressed considerable interest in having the dollar circulate. After I left Saudi Arabia, Eddy wrote a long memorandum on how a dollar currency might be introduced and made acceptable for all domestic payments, including payments to the government. He emphasized that everyone in the country should have the option of being paid in riyals or dollars. Some Saudi officials thought the U.S. government should supply the paper dollars for circulation in their country without cost, since as long as they were not used for payments for imports they would not be a drain on the U.S. economy. However, we explained that since the dollars were potential claims on the U.S. economy and could be used by anyone in the world receiving them, the U.S. could not make them available except in exchange for drafts on deposits in U.S. banks. Using dollar currency would relieve the Saudi government of printing charges for riyals, and the use of dollar currency would reduce the number of riyals the Saudi government would need to have minted as coins. We said that if dollar bills were to circulate in Saudi Arabia, U.S. coins should not be used. Rather, we suggested the use of token riyal coins, which would not contain more than a fraction of the silver the coins represented. U.S. dollar bills could be obtained by Saudi banks by drawing drafts on their deposits in American banks, or by drafts on the government's dollar deposits. There would be a cost of exporting the dollar bills to Saudi Arabia, but this cost would be less than 1 percent of the face value of the bills and much smaller than the cost of minting silver or printing paper riyals. The government took no action on introducing dollar currency, probably because of objections within the government to the use of any paper currency, but it did allow ARAMCO to import American currency to pay its American staff.

Following our mission, the government was able to hold the riyal at about twenty-five cents in the exchange market. Maintaining this ratio depended upon the government's control over the supply of riyals. However, when a shipment of sixty million riyals, coined abroad on orders from the Saudi government, began to arrive in the spring of 1949 the new riyals flooded the market. This caused the riyal value to fall below twenty cents and led to smuggling of a large volume of riyals into India, where the value of silver was much higher. The government could have maintained the twenty-five cent rate by restricting the supply of riyals but did not do so.

Despite our recommendations against the government's trying to maintain a fixed relationship between the riyal and the sovereign, Saudi officials turned for advice to Christian Delaby, manager of the Banque de L'Indochine in Jidda. He persuaded the government to order from abroad two million Saudi gold sovereigns, a new coin equal in weight and fineness to the British sovereign. Delaby's idea was to link the riyal to the new gold coin, probably at forty to one, and hold the riyal to about twenty-six or twenty-seven cents. It is reported that after receiving the new gold sovereigns, the Saudi government was confused about what to do with them; the plan to stabilize the riyal in relation to the new gold sovereign was not successful. Indeed, it could not have been, in view of the changes in the world values of silver and gold.

Following our mission, there were other visits by foreign financial specialists, including a representative from the British Treasury who proposed a monetary unit equal in value to the pound sterling in early 1949. This proposal had been rejected earlier and was not acted upon. Meanwhile, the inconvenience and cost of Saudi Arabia's chaotic currency and foreign exchange system continued. Currency reform was delayed until December 1959, when a new paper riyal was given a value of four and one-half to the dollar and made freely convertible into dollars (as we had recommended). After the establishment of the Saudi Arabian Monetary Agency in October 1952, monetary matters came more or less under the control of the agency, but it was several years before it achieved a viable monetary system for the country.

Visit to Dhahran

Before I left Saudi Arabia, Eddy and I were flown across the country to visit the ARAMCO headquarters in Dhahran. As we flew at night over the desert, we saw the bright flames produced by the gas flared from the oil wells. We wondered whether this enormous energy could be captured to supply a portion of Middle East energy needs but were told that the cost of storing and transporting the gas was too high. We were royally treated by ARAMCO officials, who spent considerable time describing their currency problems under the Saudi monetary system, with royalties payable in gold sovereigns, laborers paid with silver riyals, American and other foreign employees often paid in dollars, and many transactions on the east coast made with Indian rupees. We were given very comfortable air-conditioned quarters with the refrigerators well stocked with beer, wine, liquor, and various luxuries not available elsewhere in the country. At that time the Saudi government permitted foreign ARAMCO employees to have alcoholic beverages; later, possession of alcoholic beverages anywhere in the country was made illegal and punishable by high fines and/or imprisonment. However, ARAMCO employees could spend their weekends and vacations in Bahrain, a few miles offshore in the Persian Gulf, where most any form of libation was available. We spent a relaxed weekend in Bahrain as guests of ARAMCO.

Advice on Taxation

Originally our mission was expected to last only three weeks. Since my leave from the University of Virginia was limited to that time, I left Jidda on November 11, 1948. However, as the Saudi officials wanted to discuss a number of additional financial topics with us, Eddy was given permission by the Treasury Department to remain in Jidda until February 1949. During that time he prepared a summary report of our recommendations to the Saudi government in both our names titled "A Program to Improve the Monetary System of Saudi Arabia."

Although the issues of taxation and government expenditures were outside the terms of reference of our mission, Eddy was drawn by the Saudis into a discussion of the taxation of ARAMCO. He was asked what kinds of taxation arrangements were in use in other petroleum-producing countries. In the course of his answer, Eddy mentioned an income tax in addition to royalties and rental arrangements. In 1952 the Saudi government decreed a 50 percent income profits tax to be applied to ARAMCO in place of the royalty. Since, according to U.S. tax legislation, any income tax paid to a foreign government is directly credited against U.S. income tax liabilities, the result was to eliminate ARAMCO's obligation to pay any income tax to the U.S. government. This action was regarded as scandalous by some congressmen; although the Saudi Arabian income tax was not proposed until long after Eddy left the country, he was accused of contributing to its enactment. Eddy was called to testify before a congressional subcommittee on monopoly. There he was charged with deliberately recommending to the Saudi government the use of an income tax, which would eliminate or greatly reduce any U.S. tax on ARAMCO's income. Actually, all he did was give the usual explanation of the effects of various types of taxation on the Saudi Arabian government income without discussing its implications for U.S. income taxes.

Eddy's work was so appreciated by the Saudis that he was given a valuable pearl necklace before he left Saudi Arabia in February 1949. But he had to surrender the gift when he returned to Washington, D.C., because of regulations against U.S. government officials accepting gifts from foreign governments. I received a wristwatch and a beautiful set of royal robes, which I have managed to keep.

Eddy's career at the Treasury Department was terminated when he was dismissed in 1953 as a Communist sympathizer. The charge was based on the fact that Sol Adler, his roommate at Harvard a number of years before, had been charged with being a Communist. This was ironic because Eddy was a registered Republican and I had always found him to be quite conservative in his economic and political views. The dismissal was one of the most outrageous acts in the McCarthy period. Eddy sued the U.S. government and was reinstated by the Treasury Department with full back pay a year or two later. He resigned the following day and, as far as I know, never again worked for the U.S. government.

How Should Our Currency Mission Be Appraised?

Measured according to short-term results, our mission was a failure. None of our recommendations were put into practice until several years afterward, and satisfactory reform did not occur until more than a decade had passed. Our advice to Saudi officials might be regarded as useful education for them, although our principal recommendations had been made earlier by Judd Polk and repeated by other financial advisers after we left. Change takes place slowly in a traditional theistic monarchy. Most of the credit for eventual currency reform was due to the 1951–52 financial mission headed by Arthur N. Young, whose advice resulted in the Saudi Arabian Monetary Agency in October 1952. But effective reform required centralization of authority in a single institution. It was several years before the Monetary Agency, which repeated a number of past mistakes, was able to put into operation a reasonably satisfactory currency system.

Our oral advice and written reports to Saudi officials contained a number of sound recommendations, the most significant of which was tying the riyal to the dollar and eliminating the attempt to tie the riyal to the sovereign. In a negative sense, I think we had considerable influence in preventing Saudi Arabia's currency from being tied to sterling, which at the time was not freely convertible into dollars. This could have resulted in discrimination against U.S. exports and higher prices to Saudi consumers. Saudi Arabia's large oil revenue in dollars made it possible for the riyal to be fully convertible into all currencies. Our mission was well received by Saudi officials, and I think it tended to strengthen the influence of the U.S. government in the country. However, our recommendations were based on what we believed were the best interests of Saudi Arabia.

Personally, participation in this three-week mission was a delightful educational experience. I learned that traditional practices do not readily give way to economic reasoning, especially when strongly supported by political oligarchy. It also served my academic interests by providing the empirical basis for my first book (in collaboration with Hollis B. Chenery), *Arabian Oil: America's Stake in the Middle East* (1949). And it helped to establish my credentials as a Middle East specialist in the U.S. government, leading to my participation in other U.S. government activities in the area. My partner, George Eddy, who devoted nearly three months to the mission as contrasted with my three-week tenure, did not feel rewarded; he expressed great disappointment and frustration in what he regarded as a failed mission. We needed to learn that government officials adopt recommendations from foreigners only after they come to believe the advice was really their own idea.

Sources

Much of the information in this chapter is based on the Eddy-Mikesell report (1948) and on Young (1983).

Raymond F. Mikesell

Chapter 6: Palestine

A substantial amount of my early activity in government dealt with Palestine and the creation of the state of Israel—an exciting and emotional experience. My participation in these events provided some historical background of considerable relevance to the tumultuous conflicts in the area today. My first visit to Palestine was in late 1942, while serving as U.S. Treasury representative to the Middle East. The only purpose of my trip to the Levant, which included Lebanon and Syria as well as the British Mandate of Palestine, was to survey economic conditions and prepare a report for the Treasury Department. While in Palestine I wanted to meet with both Jewish and Arab leaders as well as U.S. and British government personnel. However, I did not receive much cooperation from the U.S. delegation for meeting nongovernment people, especially the more militant Jews from whom I was eager to learn of their plans for a future Jewish state.

I was amazed at the degree of violence which at that time took the form of terrorist acts by Jews and Arabs against one another and by both against the British military. The British had lost a number of their military personnel and some were anxious for Britain to be free of the burden of the British Mandate. Other military personnel favored a different solution. I had dinner with one British officer who suggested that every other day ten Jews be rounded up and shot and that on alternate days ten Arabs be rounded up and shot! Arms were being smuggled in for use by the militant Jewish leaders despite British efforts to keep them out, and preparations were being made for a Zionist takeover of Palestine.

Before World War I, Palestine had been under Turkish rule but since then was under a British Mandate. The Balfour Declaration of 1917 promised the establishment of a national home for Jewish people in Palestine. But the British, in accordance with the McDonald White Paper of 1939, had restricted immigration of Jews into Palestine and announced Britain's intention to establish a Palestine state in which Arabs and Jews would share local control. Both Jews and Arabs denounced the 1939 white paper since each wanted to control all of Palestine. The U.S. administration was divided between those favoring an independent Jewish state, which would absorb a large number of the Jewish refugees following World War II, and those wanting to maintain good relations with the Arab states, particularly Saudi Arabia. However, Jewish interests were politically strong in the U.S. and exercised substantial influence on both the Congress and the administration.

The division within the U.S. government over the future of Palestine made it difficult to reach a satisfactory agreement with the British on the political status of the area. The British wanted U.S. financial and military assistance for implementing a solution to the problem that would satisfy the Arab states while eventually carrying out the Jewish immigration promise of the Balfour Declaration. The approach of Britain's Labor government (under Prime Minister Clement Attlee and Foreign Minister Ernest Bevin) had been unsatisfactory to President Harry Truman. Truman insisted upon the immediate admission of 100,000 Jewish refugees into Palestine—which the U.S. was willing to help finance—but he refused to consider any form of U.S. military involvement. U.S. participation in keeping order in the area would very likely have meant fighting Zionists, and this would have been political dynamite in the U.S. British limitation of Jewish immigrants into Palestine was severely criticized by many U.S. congressmen; some senators had earlier threatened to vote against the $3.75 billion loan to Britain because of British actions in Palestine. Truman assured the American Jewish leaders he would abide by the promises made by Roosevelt and the Democratic Party to support the Balfour Declaration and the admission into Palestine of as many Jews as could be settled there.

Early in 1946, Bernstein asked me to serve as his deputy in the Research Department of the International Monetary Fund. This was a difficult decision for me, because such a position would have elevated my professional standing and given me an after-tax salary of twice what I could hope to receive from a university. I turned down the offer in favor of a professorship at the University of Virginia starting in the fall of 1946. I wanted very much to return to academic life and felt that if I did not do so then, I might never return.

Meanwhile, I accepted an invitation to serve as an economic adviser to the Joint Anglo-American Cabinet Committee (JCC) on Palestine which met in London during July and August of 1946. I was still an employee of the Treasury Department, while the committee was under the jurisdiction of the State Department. This placed me in a somewhat awkward position; the Treasury Department attaché in London, along with other Treasury Department officials, expected me to report on negotiations that were regarded as secret by the State Department. I also knew that the Treasury Department had no respect for the confidentiality of State Department secrets.

My fellow economic adviser to the committee, Henry Villard (on leave from Hofstra College in New York), was chosen by the State Department, although I believe he never regarded himself as a State Department employee. Villard was the grandson of the nineteenth century railroad magnate Henry Villard, who made a financial contribution to the inauguration of the University of Oregon in the 1880s. There was a gigantic picture of him in Villard Hall on the University of Oregon campus. When my friend Henry Villard visited me in Oregon, he said the family had been looking for that picture for many years and was glad to know where it was. Villard and I got along very well and were in agreement on all the advice we gave.

Although both Morgenthau and White had left the Treasury Department, leading Treasury Department officials, both Jews and non-Jews, continued to favor the Jews in the Palestine conflict. The State Department was more concerned with keeping the Arab states cooperative and supporting U.S. economic interests in the Middle East.

The Anglo-American Committee of Enquiry

Differences in the approaches to the Palestine problem by the two governments led the British government in October 1945 to propose an Anglo-American Committee of Enquiry (AACE). Truman accepted the proposal with some reluctance; he believed the AACE was a tactic to delay large-scale admission of Jews (which he favored). The AACE, created in December 1945, was asked to examine the political, economic, and social conditions of Palestine as they bore upon the problem of Jewish immigration and settlement. It was to make recommendations to the two governments for meeting the immediate needs arising from the condition of the Jewish refugees, and for the provision of facilities for their immigration to and settlement in countries outside Europe.

The AACE consisted of six Americans and six Britons appointed by the two governments. None were members of the Truman administration and only one member, British lawyer Bartley C. Crum, had any special familiarity with Palestine. The major recommendations of the AACE report issued in April 1946 were: (1) immediate admission of 100,000 victims of Nazi and Fascist persecution into Palestine; (2) Palestine should be neither an Arab nor a Jewish state, and the interests of Christians, Muslims, and Jews should be fully protected by international guarantees; (3) the government of Palestine should be continued under the British Mandate or a United Nations trusteeship; (4) the mandate or trustee should give equal importance to the economic, educational, and political advancement of Arabs and Jews, and it should take measures designed to bridge the gap between the two groups by raising the Arab standard of living; and (5) immigration of Jews beyond the 100,000 recommended would be contingent upon making sure that the rights of other sections of the population were not prejudiced.

The AACE report failed to resolve the differences between Truman and Prime Minister Attlee, and it did not provide a plan for the implementation of a unitary state based on nondiscrimination and equality in social services. British government officials argued that the admission of 100,000 Jewish refugees should take place only after hostilities had stopped and both Jewish and Arab leaders had agreed with the recommendations. In addition, they requested that the U.S. provide financial and military assistance for the implementation of the program. Truman, on the other hand, insisted on the immediate admission of 100,000 refugees and stated that while the U.S. would be prepared to provide financial assistance for transporting and housing the immigrants, it would not become involved militarily. In commenting on the AACE report, Truman praised the admission of 100,000 Jews into Palestine, safeguarding the holy places sacred to Moslems, Christians, and Jews, and the guarantee of civil and religious rights. But Truman did not pass judgment on the recommendations regarding the future government of Palestine.

The reaction of the American Jewish community to the AACE report was mixed. While some denounced the report, others believed Truman should be urged to accept what was favorable to Jews in the short run and not commit the U.S. to the long-range political policy recommendations of the report. Denouncing the recommendation for the admission of 100,000 Jews, the Arab governments would be satisfied with nothing short of Palestine becoming an Arab state. Since the Arabs outnumbered the Jews, a unified Palestine governed on the basis of a majority vote would have meant Arab control. Zionism had less political support in Britain than in the United States. The British government wanted to maintain its military presence and strong political influence in the Middle East, which required a Palestine plan that was acceptable to the Arabs.

The Joint Anglo-American Cabinet Committee

In light of the differences between the U.S. and U.K., the British proposed that a high-level group chosen by the governments make recommendations on a number of economic and political issues relating to Palestine. The suggested agenda for the JCC included:

1. Finding new homes for Jewish displaced persons outside Palestine;

2. Transporting, maintaining, and housing 100,000 Jewish immigrants in Palestine;

3. Financing the capital assets necessary for productive employment for the immigrants;

4. Determining the rate at which 100,000 immigrants could be absorbed without creating widespread unemployment;

5. Determining the nature of the administrating authority in Palestine—single state, or two or more states, or direct administration by the United Nations;

6. Recommending measures to bridge the gap now existing between Jewish and Arab standards of living, and increase facilities for education of the Arab population;

7. Determine the principles for regulating future immigration into Palestine and for preventing illegal immigration.

This was an enormous agenda for what turned out to be a series of meetings held in London between July 12 and 24, 1946. Truman was somewhat reluctant to agree to another Anglo-American committee, since he regarded the British request as another effort to delay the admission of 100,000 Jews. But he finally agreed. Truman assigned the secretaries of war, treasury, and state to the U.S. delegation, with the actual discussions with the British to be conducted by alternates. Henry F. Grady, representing the State Department, chaired the U.S. delegation; Goldthwaite H. Dorr represented the War Department; and Herbert D. Gaston the Treasury Department. Gaston was a former assistant secretary of the Treasury Department and currently headed the Export-Import Bank. The British team was headed by Norman Brook and included Sir Douglas Harris and Harold Beeley. Herbert Morrison was appointed secretary of the JCC prior to its first meeting in London. In addition to Villard and me, several staff members were appointed by the American and British governments.

Villard and I both played active roles in the deliberations of the JCC. We were regarded as advisers to the JCC as a whole and not simply to the American delegation. We wrote a number of memoranda on economic issues that were circulated to all members of the JCC, but some of these memoranda had strong political overtones since it was impossible to separate economic and political questions. Neither Villard nor I was Jewish or pro-Zionist. Gaston tended to reflect the Treasury Department position on Palestine, while Grady and Dorr favored the State Department's position. Working closely together during the London discussions, Gaston, Villard, and I were in agreement on all major issues.

A basic issue for the JCC was whether planning for Palestine should be based on an eventual unitary state, as recommended by the AACE, or on partition. British government policy had shifted back and forth on this issue in the past. The Royal Commission report of June 22, 1937, known as the Peel Commission, had recommended the partition of the country into an Arab state and a Jewish state, except for enclaves under the British Mandate for Jerusalem, Bethlehem, and Nazareth. The British government expressed agreement with the Peel Commission report, which was followed by the Palestine Partition report of 1938 (British Command Paper No. 5854).

It proposed a modified partition scheme under which fiscal policy for the two states would remain in the hands of the British Mandate. Foreign Minister Ernest Bevin was against the creation of a fully independent state but recognized the advantages of separate states with limited autonomy.

Douglas Harris of the Colonial Office had earlier proposed the creation of two semiautonomous provinces to administer their local affairs, but this recommendation had been rejected by the AACE. When he submitted the same proposal to the American delegation of the JCC upon our arrival in London, it was quickly accepted by Grady and adopted with little change in the JCC report on Palestine. The territorial plan in the JCC report provided for the division of Palestine into four areas: an Arab province, a Jewish province, a district of Jerusalem, and a district of the Negev—with the latter two under the jurisdiction of a United Nations trustee. The Jerusalem district was to include Jerusalem, Bethlehem, and their immediate environs. The Jewish province would include eastern Galilee, most of the Plains of Estraelon and Jezreel, the Beisan area, Haifa, the Plain of Sharon (excluding the town of Jaffa), and a portion of the southern coastal plains. The Jewish province would hold 451,000 Jews and 301,000 Arabs, while the Arab province would hold 815,000 Arabs and only 15,000 Jews. The Jerusalem district was about equally divided between Arabs and Jews. The provincial governments would have the power of legislation and administration over agriculture, fisheries, forests, land registration, land sales and settlement, education, public health and other social services, trade, industry, local roads, irrigation, and public works. They would have the power to limit the number and determine the qualifications of individuals who applied for permanent residence in their territory, but they were not to impose obstacles to free interterritorial transit or trade. The provincial governments would have the power to appropriate funds, levy taxes (excluding customs and excise taxes), borrow within the province, and, with the consent of the central government, borrow abroad.

Powers reserved for the central government, controlled by the UN trustee, included control of foreign exchange and currency, licensing of imports, relations with international bodies such as the United Nations, the International Monetary Fund, and the World Bank, customs and excise taxes, defense, foreign relations, police, prisons, courts, railways, harbors, ports, telegraph, civil aviation, and broadcasting in Palestine.

The JCC endorsed the AACE recommendation of the admission of 100,000 Jews but accepted the British condition that this immigration should take place when "it is decided to put the constitutional proposals into effect." This somewhat ambiguous statement actually meant that the plan must be acquiesced to by both Arabs and Jews before the admission of 100,000 Jews. The JCC report recommended that once the proposals were adopted by the U.S. and British governments, they should be presented to the Arab and Jewish representatives as bases for negotiation at a conference to be convened by the British government. The final paragraph of the JCC report read as follows:

> We are not able at this stage to make recommendations regarding the course to be adopted if the conference with Arab and Jewish representatives led to the conclusion that the introduction of the policy proposed would be so violently resisted by one or both of the two peoples in Palestine that it could not be enforced. In that situation further consultation between our two governments would be necessary.

Villard and I seriously doubted that the plan would be acceptable to either the Jews or the Arabs, and therefore would not be implemented. The JCC report endorsed most of the other AACE recommendations. It also presented a financial program for the absorption of the 100,000 Jews; the bulk of the funds would be provided by reparations, contributions from world Jewry, and loans raised in Palestine. Fifty million dollars would come from the U.S. government for the Arab program and a capital program for development of Palestine would be financed by loans. The report stated that the "U.S. delegation proposes, in the event that finance from other sources such as the International Bank is not available, to recommend that the President seek legislation authorizing the making of loans through an appropriate agency for the development of the Middle East region, including Palestine, of up to 250 million dollars."

The JCC report endorsed the AACE proposal for a UN trusteeship for Palestine following a sufficient degree of acceptance of the constitutional plan by both Arabs and Jews. However, it was unclear whether the administering authority under the trusteeship would be Britain or the UN itself. Since the

British government planned to maintain military bases in Palestine, Britain evidently expected to be designated as the administrative authority under a trusteeship. A draft of the terms of a possible trusteeship for Palestine was prepared in the U.S. State Department and transmitted for use by the JCC.

The report of the JCC came to be called the Morrison plan, since he prepared the initial draft prior to the arrival of the American delegation in London. As far as I am aware, no member of the U.S. delegation saw the Morrison draft prior to our arrival in London, and there was little opportunity for the staff to study it and offer alternatives. Villard, Gaston, and I preferred provincial autonomy to the unitary state recommended by the AACE, because we believed one group or the other would completely dominate a unitary state. However, we were also concerned that under the Morrison plan the provinces would not have sufficient power to function as viable economic units. The central government was given complete control over imports and foreign exchange, customs duties and excise taxes (which were the principal sources of government revenue), and immigration. The central government's permission was required for foreign borrowing and for certain types of development projects. Villard, Gaston, and I argued for greater economic independence for the provinces so that they could plan and implement development programs and so that the Jewish province could regulate immigration in line with its ability to absorb immigrants into the economy. We believed that, given the expected large flow of capital from international Jewry, Palestine could absorb hundreds of thousands of Jews while achieving a relatively high rate of economic growth. This, of course, has proved to be the case. We believed that the central government was likely to determine Jewish immigration on the basis of political negotiations with the Arab states rather than on the basis of economic absorptive capacity.

We wrote memoranda on the Palestine economy and government finance from sources largely prepared by the Palestine government and Jewish organizations with which we were in contact. We argued that the Morrison plan grossly overstated both the financial requirements for covering the net current cost to the Palestine government and the development outlays associated with the plan that would have to be covered by government loans and grants from abroad. This was important for U.S. acceptance of the proposal, since Truman could not commit more funds from the U.S. government than were likely to be appropriated by Congress. Villard and I showed that, based on experience, the receipts of the central government would cover the required current expenditures, and the necessary capital to support immigration would be provided from private external sources. The British delegates argued that large development expenditures would be necessary to reduce the per capita income gap between the Jewish and Arab provinces as recommended by the AACE, and that such capital was unlikely to be provided by private external sources. Our answer was that if educational and other social services were equal, Arab income should grow, but no amount of external assistance could guarantee income equality.

Villard and I argued that the territory allotted to the Jewish province was too small to provide a land base sufficient to support large Jewish immigration. We proposed that the Jewish province should include at least the area recommended by the Peel Commission plus the Negev, a large desert area with substantial development potential but a small population.

Villard and I presented a memorandum showing that Palestine's land, water, and mineral resources were sufficient to permit the immigration of many more than the 100,000 Jews contemplated, and that the possibilities for expanding the country's manufacturing, agriculture, and foreign trade were very great. However, we were never able to get the British delegation to seriously discuss our arguments that immigration would not require large subsidies from the U.S. or the U.K. government, and that much of the needed external capital could be provided by nongovernmental loans serviced by Palestine. The British opposed large-scale immigration because it would have been unacceptable to the Arabs.

Finally, we protested delaying the immigration of 100,000 Jews pending acquiescence to the constitutional plan by both the Arabs and the Jews. In a strongly worded memorandum to the members of the JCC, Henry Villard pointed out that this condition was at variance with President Truman's request for the immediate admission of 100,000 Jews into Palestine. Herbert Gaston also opposed this condition, and rightly believed it was likely to lead Truman to reject the committee's report.

Grady and members of the British delegation proved unwilling to take the time to explore these and other important issues before final agreement on the report. Grady was under pressure from the president and from Secretary of State Byrnes to complete the committee's work as soon as possible. Tension in Palestine and Britain's problems with Egypt and other Arab countries gave a sense of urgency to Bevin, who was anxious that a British program on Palestine be shared (and financed and implemented militarily) by the U.S. government. Our interventions in the JCC subcommittees, where much of the substantive discussion took place, seemed to be regarded as needless interruptions in the process of completing the report. I recall an occasion when I proposed that the provinces should have the right to control the allocation of import licenses within the limits of the foreign exchange made available to them by the central government. This led to an extensive argument with Sir David Whaley, a member of the British delegation's staff. I was strongly supported by Herbert Gaston, but Dorr called me aside and asked me not to fight too hard on this point since the debate was holding up the work of the subcommittee. On several occasions Dorr argued in favor of granting certain economic powers to the central government rather than assigning them to the provincial governments. He believed that providing too much autonomy to the Jews would lead to the rejection of the JCC plan by the Arabs.

Although the deliberations and official documents of the JCC were supposed to be top secret, little went on without the knowledge of people in the Jewish Agency, an organization financed by Jewish groups to promote a Jewish state. Deliberate leaks to the press played an important role in the reception of the Morrison plan in the U.S. As a Treasury Department employee, I discussed the work of the JCC with the Treasury Department attaché and his staff in the American embassy in London, just as I am sure Grady discussed the deliberations of the committee with Ambassador Averill Harriman and his staff. The Treasury Department attaché in turn reported directly to the Treasury Department in Washington, and people in the Jewish Agency were informed in one way or another—all without the knowledge of the State Department. This may sound strange, but, as I have noted, throughout the war and early postwar periods, the Treasury Department's Monetary

Research Office under Harry White and his successors conducted its own foreign service independently of the State Department. All official cables had to go through the American Embassy, but there were unofficial means of communicating between Treasury Department officials abroad and in Washington. One of the memoranda I sent to Harold Glasser, then head of the Monetary Research Office, was transmitted to the Jewish Agency and now resides in the Central Zionist Archives in Jerusalem.

A major leak occurred with the publication, on the front page of the July 16, 1946, *New York Herald Tribune*, of the details of the provincial autonomy scheme prepared by Morrison, including the proposed Jewish and Arab sectors. The reporter obtained the story from the London office of the U.S. Treasury Department attaché. Grady was furious at the leak and blamed the American staff. For some reason, Henry Villard was widely believed to be the culprit, but I can testify to his innocence. Publication of the partition plan played a major role in mobilizing American Jewish leaders against the plan, which in turn influenced Truman's decision to reject it. The Jewish community was not prepared to accept any proposal that did not provide for full Jewish autonomy.

When the JCC finished its work on July 24, 1946, Bevin announced he would call a conference of Arab and Jewish leaders to discuss the report, which was signed by all members of the JCC. I was surprised that Gaston signed the report, but he believed it provided a basis for discussions with moderate Jewish leaders. Some of the American delegates and staff went to Paris to consult with Secretary Byrnes (who was attending the Paris Peace Conference) and to meet with people in the Jewish Agency and with other Jewish leaders. Gaston and I attended several meetings with Jewish leaders, including Nahum Goldmann, Eliezer Kaplan, David Ben Gurion, and Oscar Gass, whom I had known when we both worked in the U.S. Treasury Department. We found the Jewish leaders divided over the Morrison plan as a basis for consultations with the British. Moderate leaders, such as Goldmann and Kaplan, were willing to accept the British invitation; more radical Zionists, including Ben Gurion (who became Israel's first prime minister), were opposed to discussions with the British, except on the basis of outright partition. The minimum conditions under which the moderate Jewish leaders would have been willing to acquiesce (without violent opposition to the plan) were given to the U.S. government as follows:

1. Jews must be free to nominate their own representatives, which meant that some of their leaders, then detained by the British in Palestine, must be released.

2. Movement of the 100,000 Jews must begin at the time the negotiations with the British are initiated.

3. The area of the Jewish province must be sufficient to permit economic development for a large immigration. As a minimum, this is the territory provided in the Peel Report plus the Negev.

4. Jews must be given control over immigration into the Jewish province.

5. There must be greater political and economic autonomy for the Jewish province with the exact nature subject to negotiation.

6. The plan must include the promise of complete independence within a stipulated period.

During our meeting in Paris, Goldmann and Gass told us of conversations they had with some British members of parliament and with the British minister of health, Aneurin Bevin, who was a pro-Zionist member of Attlee's cabinet. Gass stated that the British were surprised at the complacency of the American negotiators and the ease with which the British delegation was able to reach agreement on its program. Goldmann said that Foreign Minister Bevin told him the decision to move the 100,000 Jews was a British cabinet decision, and that they would be moved regardless of the attitude of the Arabs and Jews with respect to the report as a whole. If this was Bevin's position, he certainly did not make it clear to the American government.

After spending a week in Paris, where I attended the Paris Peace Conference as an observer and visited museums and cathedrals, I was ordered back to Washington to consult with the Undersecretary of the Treasury, Edward Foley, who was sympathetic with the Zionist cause and wanted a first-hand briefing on the JCC report. Being recalled to Washington was a great disappointment to me, because I had been scheduled to visit several European capitals and make a report to the Treasury Department on financial conditions. About the time of my return, Truman called all of the American members of the JCC to meet with the AACE members. I briefed the top

Treasury Department officials, including Secretary John W. Snyder, on the work of the JCC. Snyder worked closely with Dean Acheson, who as acting secretary of state was involved in the formulation of U.S. policy on Palestine.

Meeting with Acheson in Washington, Nahum Goldmann of the Jewish Agency told him that while the report of the JCC as announced by Morrison in the House of Commons was unacceptable to the Jews as a basis for discussion, he was prepared to discuss a proposal for the establishment of a viable Jewish state in an adequate area of Palestine under the conditions listed above. Goldmann told Acheson that if these conditions were met, a majority of the Jewish leadership might be induced to support what could be called a variation and extension of the Morrison plan. In a telegram to Averill Harriman, U.S. ambassador to Britain, Acheson suggested that the U.S. government could give moral support and financial assistance to a plan along the lines that Goldmann proposed, and he authorized Harriman to discuss it with Attlee and Bevin. There is no indication whether Acheson cleared this approach with Truman. However, Attlee did not agree to Acheson's suggestions. When Attlee called the conference to discuss the Morrison-Grady proposal, only the Arabs attended. Little was accomplished since the Arabs continued to denounce the concept of a Jewish state and large-scale Jewish immigration.

Truman's Reaction to the Morrison-Grady Plan

When the Morrison plan was received by Truman and Secretary of State Byrnes on July 25, 1946, the immediate reaction was disappointment over the timing of the admission of the 100,000 Jewish refugees. There followed on July 26 a teletype conference between Byrnes in Washington and Grady in London. It began with the following question to Grady: "What did you do to secure British consent to starting 100,000 immigrations immediately instead of starting when plan agreed to?" Grady was again advised that Washington would not agree to any arrangement that departed from the immediate admission of the Jewish refugees, and that waiting for an agreement on the general plan might delay immigration for months or years. At the conclusion of the teletype conference, it was decided that Grady, Gaston, and Dorr would meet with Secretary Byrnes in Paris on July 29, when the American delegation would advise Bevin that there had not been sufficient time to consider the plan and make a recommendation to President Truman. Following the meeting in Paris and the receipt by Byrnes of a statement by Prime Minister Attlee, Byrnes sent a telegram to President Truman on July 29 recommending that the president agree to the recommendations of the JCC report, including the delay of the immigration pending completion of discussions with Jews and Arabs on the new proposal. Byrnes's message to the president closed by stating that he believed "the plan proposed is the best solution of this difficult problem that can now be secured."

Truman found the delay of the immigration unacceptable, and Acting Secretary of State Acheson delivered this message to the British ambassador in Washington. Truman stated that "in view of the extreme intensity of feeling in centers of Jewish population in this country, neither political party would support this program at the present time and the President's statement, therefore, would be wholly personal and most misleading." The president referred to that portion of the program that required him to recommend to Congress legislation granting aid of $50 million to Palestine and providing loans of up to $20 million for Middle East development. Attlee was, of course, disappointed that the president could not support the program, but he stated he was going ahead with the consultations with the Arabs and Jews on the proposal.

When I returned to Washington, I gave a copy of the Morrison plan (classified Top Secret) to my superior in the Monetary Research Office. A few days later, excerpts from the document appeared in Drew Pearson's column, "The Washington Merry-Go-Round," in *The Washington Post*, including material that had not been previously leaked to the press. I believe this action was deliberately taken by people in the Treasury Department who wanted to sabotage the JCC plan. The leak, together with the failure of the president to make a public statement on the proposal, sparked widespread denunciation by people sympathetic to Zionism—including several congressmen. A telegram dated August 12, 1946, from Acheson to Ambassador Harriman in London stated that

> premature leaks from London re contents recommendations incorporated in Morrison plan, gave groups in this country opposed to the plan opportunity to mobilize so much public sentiment against it, the Cabinet Committee and President felt they could not agree accept recommendations, at least

until they had studied and discussed them in detail. . . . During discussions it has become clear it would be unwise for President to give his formal support to plan in its present form. President feels that in view of opposition to the plan, he would not be able to prevail on Congress to agree to financial contributions for its implementation nor to rally sufficient public support to warrant undertaking by this government to give Plan in its present form moral backing."

On the same date, Truman sent a message to Attlee stating that "the opposition in this country to the plan has become so intense that it is now clear it would be impossible to rally in favor of it sufficient public opinion to enable this government to give it effective support."

Subsequent Developments on Palestine

Truman failed to exert strong leadership on the Palestine issue. He was reluctant to endorse any concrete plan for Palestine. But on October 4, 1946, (the eve of Yom Kippur), he issued a weak endorsement of partition, suggesting a revision of the Morrison plan together with the immediate admission of 100,000 Jews into Palestine and the liberalization of Jewish immigration to the U.S. and other countries. Within the U.S. government influential officials were concerned about the reaction of the Arab states to a policy that favored the Jews. Both the Defense Department (which feared an Arab threat to the oil supply and to the Suez Canal) and the Office of Near Eastern and African Affairs in the State Department were strongly against partition or the creation of a Jewish state. American oil companies with investments in the Middle East feared their interests would be jeopardized by U.S. support of Zionism. Roosevelt had made a promise to King Ibn Saud of Saudi Arabia that he would consult with the king before taking any action on Palestine that would affect the Arabs, and Truman felt bound by this pledge. These considerations undoubtedly played a role in Truman's reluctance to adopt a definitive U.S. position on Palestine and take measures to implement it. Although Truman had a strong humanitarian interest in the refugee problem, he was frustrated with the complex issues arising from the Jewish-Arab conflict and with the fact that any policy he chose was likely to lead to political embarrassment.

The diplomatic debate on Palestine next shifted from Washington-London to the United Nations. On May 15, 1947, the UN General Assembly established the Special Committee on Palestine. A majority of the committee members endorsed the partition of Palestine into an Arab state, a Jewish state, and an international city of Jerusalem—with Britain in control of the entire country for two transitional years and allowing 150,000 immigrants into the Jewish state during the two-year period. The General Assembly approved the Partition Plan on November 29, 1947, but the Arabs found it unacceptable because they insisted on a unified state under majority Arab control. Again the U.S. government was divided on the issue of partition and on the nature of the UN trusteeship. After a year of debate over the future of a land marked by terrorism and civil war, the U.S. administration agreed to partition and "a temporary trusteeship established under the Trusteeship Council of the United Nations." However, the issue of Palestine was settled not by the United Nations but by the triumph of the Jewish military forces over the Arab forces in Palestine. The British military forces abandoned Palestine in April 1948, and the Jews wiped out the Arab forces, including those sent in by some of the Arab governments. Truman officially recognized the state of Israel on May 14, 1948.

Was the Outcome Inevitable?

After nearly five decades of conflict, including three wars and constant civil strife, would a different JCC plan and implementation by the two governments have made a difference? One is tempted to conclude that the Arab-Jew conflict is one of those problems for which there can be no permanent solution. But the current Middle East peace talks appear to be moving toward the creation of a semiautonomous Arab state alongside Israel. What if two viable states had been created on the basis of a 1946 Anglo-American agreement that both the U.S. and U.K. had been willing to defend militarily and support financially? The basis for such an agreement can be found in the discussions in August 1946 between Goldmann and Acheson. I suggest that the following conditions might have made possible a lasting solution to the Palestine problem:

1. *The appointment of a stronger and more enlightened American delegation to the JCC with a mandate from Truman to formulate with the British a realistic partition plan.* The Arab states would not have agreed to any partition plan at

the time, but there is a good chance they would not have attacked a Jewish state with the U.S. and Britain guaranteeing the territories of both the Arab and the Jewish states.

2. *Complete secrecy of the deliberations of the JCC and of its report, pending formulation of a U.S. policy for supporting and carrying out the plan.* This would have enabled Truman to present a comprehensive program to important political leaders and thereafter to the country before extremists mobilized popular opinion against the plan.

3. *A commitment by the U.S. government to share with the British the burden of defending both the Jewish and the Arab states, pending creation of a UN trusteeship with ample power to maintain peace.*

My experience with the JCC was a high-level education in diplomacy. I was asked to supply advice as a professional economist but became involved in complex political differences not only between the British and American members of the JCC but between Americans who differed on U.S. policy objectives. Villard and I provided sound economic analysis and advice on the potential absorptive capacity of Palestine for Jewish immigrants with Western backgrounds. Palestine could have provided a prosperous homeland for a million or more Jewish refugees alongside a much higher level of living for the Arabs than they are likely to realize for many decades in the future. I believe I was wrong in making the JCC report available to my Treasury Department colleagues, who may have used the material for propaganda rather than for promoting an agreement such as that reached by Acheson and Goldmann. Perhaps the political forces in the U.S. and Palestine were so strong that no agreement would have been possible. In any case, the experience with the JCC was valuable for my mission to Israel in 1952 and 1953, where I was also confronted with political issues overlaying my function as an economic adviser to both the U.S. and the Israeli governments.

Source

U.S. Department of State (1946).

Chapter 7: Israel's Debt Crisis of 1952–53

My missions to Israel as a representative of the U.S. Department of State during the summers of 1952 and 1953 combined work as a professional economist and an amateur diplomat. I was engaged at the highest level I have ever regularly worked with any government—with the prime minister and the minister of finance. What I accomplished, however, is shrouded in the sloppy financial accounting of the Israeli government and the veiled dealings between the Israeli officials and Jewish leaders in the U.S. and elsewhere. For example, my major task was to help Israel avoid bankruptcy by defaulting on her foreign loan obligations, but I never knew how close the country was to default or whether the international Jewish community would have bailed out the new nation at the last minute. I do not know whether Teddy Kollek was right in telling a friend of mine some forty years later that I was one of the saviors of Israel, or whether I was used by the officials in order to secure more U.S. aid. It is likely that no one knows. In any case, I believe my account represents a previously unpublished addition to Israel's history.

The Purpose of the Mission

For several years after the birth of Israel in 1948, the country's political and economic security were highly tenuous. Israel's territory between Tel Aviv and Jerusalem was quite narrow, exposing the main road (which I had to travel nearly every day in 1952) to Arab snipers, and a portion of Jerusalem was under Jordanian control. The U.S. government did not provide assistance to Israel until its existence was officially recognized by the United Nations. The first U.S. grant aid was in 1951, but the U.S. Export-Import Bank made two loans totaling $135 million to Israel in 1949–50. During these years, Israel received about $60 million annually from the United Jewish Appeal and another $50 million from purchases of state of Israel bonds. Because Israel exported very little, the cost of reconstructing the country after the civil war and of providing for the large inflow of Jews from Europe and Africa greatly exceeded its sources of financing.

Regular U.S. aid began to flow with a grant of nearly $65 million voted by the Congress for the fiscal year ending June 30, 1952. In 1952 Congress approved a grant of $70 million for refugees and about $3 million for technical assistance under the Mutual Security Administration (MSA) program for the fiscal year ending June 30, 1953. Private loans and grants, mainly from American Jewish organizations, totaled over $600 million during the period from mid-1948 to mid-1952. Nevertheless, Israel's imports exceeded its capacity to pay in every year between 1948 and 1952. The Israeli government financed a large portion of the deficit by means of short-term borrowing, which by early 1952 had increased to over $100 million. As early as 1951, the government was experiencing difficulty in meeting its short-term debt obligations.

In the spring of 1952, Israel's ambassador to the United States, Abba Eban, approached the State Department for assistance in funding Israel's short-term debt. Since Israel had virtually no foreign exchange reserves, there was a danger that the government might be forced to default. This request presented the U.S. with a dilemma. If Israel defaulted on her external obligations, it would be more difficult for her to attract private Jewish financing, such as the sale of state of Israel bonds. In addition, a default might lead the Arab states to be more aggressive toward Israel. On the other hand, the U.S. government did not want its assistance to be used to finance short-term debt, since this action would provide an incentive to both the Israeli government and lenders to increase short-term lending to finance additional imports. The U.S. government wanted its aid to be employed for investment goods that would contribute to Israel's development and to the achievement of economic self-sufficiency rather than for increasing imports for consumption. In April and May of 1951, portions of the MSA grant to Israel for fiscal 1951 were made available in free foreign exchange for short-term debt repayment, but the U.S. government did not want to provide further assistance in this form.

In dealing with Israel's financial problems, both the State Department and the American Embassy in Tel Aviv were handicapped by the absence of adequate information on economic conditions in Israel and on the financial operations of the government. In May 1952, the State Department asked me to go to Israel to obtain this information and to prepare a report with recommendations on how the U.S. government should respond to Israel's request for assistance on its short-term debt problem. At the time I was working two days a week at the State Department while serving as professor of economics at the University of Virginia in Charlottesville. While I could scarcely qualify as an expert on Israel, there were few specialists on that country in the State Department. Moreover, most State Department specialists on the Middle East tended to be pro-Arab and, therefore, might have been unacceptable to the Israeli government. Some of the Israelis knew of my work with the Joint Anglo-American Cabinet Committee and my position on Jewish immigration. I believed that Jewish refugees should have been freely admitted to all countries, including the United States, and I did not regard Israel as a convenient dumping area for the refugees. However, I knew that many Jews wanted to go to Israel and that its rapid development was necessary for a homeland to both provide a relatively high standard of living and defend itself against Arab countries that wanted to destroy it. Since I was to work closely with Israeli government officials in a professional capacity, it was important for them to have confidence in me. This was made clear to the State Department by the U.S. ambassador to Israel, Monnett Davis, who had urged that a financial specialist be sent to Israel by the U.S. government. A meeting with Ambassador Abba Eban was arranged for me in the Israeli Embassy, following which the ambassador readily accepted my appointment to work with his government in Israel.

Meetings in Washington

Shortly before I left for Israel in June 1952, Ambassador Eban called on Henry Byroade, Assistant Secretary of State for Near East Affairs, to request further assistance with Israel's short-term debt problem. On this occasion, Eban did not request a release of U.S. government funds for meeting short-term debts but proposed funding from two other sources. One was an Export-Import Bank loan to consolidate Israel's existing debt; the other was the U.S. Exchange Stabilization Fund. Byroade immediately rejected the latter as inappropriate and expressed serious doubts regarding the appropriateness of an Export-Import Bank loan for this purpose. (The Export-Import Bank was established to promote U.S. exports, and loan refinancing was not consonant with that purpose.) Byroade told Eban that the answer to his request for assistance would have to await my report. Eban replied that he had met with me and that the officials of his government were prepared to cooperate fully with me. The following day Eban returned to Byroade's office with Moshe Sharett, Israel's foreign minister, to discuss Israel's short-term debt problem. Sharett emphasized the urgency of the matter since it threatened Israel's solvency; he suggested that before going to Israel I make an interim report that would—he hoped—recommend some immediate relief. Stating that the U.S. could not assist Israel unless it had more information, Byroade expressed doubt that any report could be made until after I had completed my work.

With typical Israeli persistence, Eban and Sharett called on Acting Secretary of State David Bruce with the same request for funding the short-term debt, then estimated at $124 million. By then I had already left for Israel. Bruce told them I was sent there to try to find an answer to Israel's financial troubles, and that no answer to the request would be forthcoming until I had made my report. In a memorandum to President Harry Truman, whom Sharett was to meet on July 1, 1952, Bruce recommended that Sharett be told "(1) the subject is now under study by Dr. Mikesell, who is on his way to Israel; (2) that any action will depend in part on the nature of his findings; and (3) that Israel should by no means assume that a favorable reply is a foregone conclusion."

Before leaving for Israel, Byroade told me that while the U.S. wanted to assist Israel regarding its current financial crisis, it did not want to provide continuing assistance over a long period of time. Bruce said I should deter-mine whether Israel's policies were directed toward achieving independence from U.S. government aid. I was continually reminded of this position in the course of my missions to Israel. The reason for the State Department's desire to provide development assistance rather than assistance for meeting Israel's short-term debt was that it wanted to promote self-sustaining growth in Israel. However, State Department policy was not in accord with the political forces in the U.S. that strongly supported continued U.S. aid to Israel, and the Israelis were well aware of these forces. Jewish political leaders and others highly supportive of Israel were quite influential in the Democratic Party, and they believed that the U.S. government must not allow the Israeli government to fail. Israeli leaders went to them with demands for assistance; the American supporters in turn lobbied congressmen and the White House, where there were strong supporters of the Israeli cause. Under these circumstances it became difficult for the State Department to carry out a program directed toward promoting Israel's development. The undercutting of State Department policies by these political forces greatly limited what I was able to do on my missions to Israel.

1952 Mission

When I arrived in Tel Aviv in late June, I immediately called on our ambassador, Monnett Davis, who told me that my mission was so important he wanted to have constant contact with me. Davis invited me to live with him and his wife in the ambassador's residence during my stay. I accepted, but living with the ambassador made it necessary for me to make a one-and-one-half hour drive from Tel Aviv to Jerusalem nearly every morning on a long winding road almost within sight of Arab territory. The U.S. government, along with other governments and the United Nations, did not recognize Jerusalem as the Israeli capital and they have continued to maintain their embassies in Tel Aviv to the present time.

In the course of my efforts to obtain information for my report, I met frequently with Teddy Kollek, at that time the director general of the prime minister's office (and later mayor of Jerusalem), and with Ehud Avriel, director general of the Ministry of Finance. I also met frequently with Levi Eshkol, the minister of finance, and David Ben-Gurion, the prime minister, and other cabinet officials. I recall several pleasant evenings in Ben-Gurion's home—listening to stories about the fight for Israel's independence, how arms were secretly (and illegally) shipped to Palestine by Jewish interests in the U.S., and about the war with the Arabs following the British withdrawal.

Ben-Gurion was an impressive man. His piercing eyes were set between a row of unkempt white hair on either side of his bald head. Although he talked a great deal, he was willing to listen—at least for a short time—without intervening. I found him pleasant and polite in social gatherings and at his home, but I also experienced his wrath when any of his views about Israel were criticized. His wife tried to prevent him from getting too tired or emotionally excited by joining us whenever our discussions became heated.

Ben-Gurion insisted that Arabs who chose not to fight against the Jews were not driven out of Palestine but left on their own accord. (This, however, was not true for many of the 700,000 Arabs that left Palestine in 1948.) He said he was eager for the Arabs who remained to become citizens of Israel without discrimination.

I had met Ben-Gurion briefly in Paris in 1946 when I was an economic adviser to the Joint Anglo-American Palestine Commission, and I had known Kollek when he was with the Israeli Embassy in Washington. One of Kollek's principal jobs in the U.S. was arranging clandestine shipments of military supplies to Israel. Kollek and I became very close friends and continue to correspond to this day. Kollek took me on a tour of Israel, including the Negev and the coastal cities. We spent two days in a kibbutz on Lake Tiberias, from which I could see the Golan Heights, which was then a part of Syria. I was conscious of the fact that Syrians at times sent shells into the kibbutz from the Golan Heights. I was impressed with the large community buildings in the kibbutz and with various amenities, such as being able to have dinner in a garden on the shore of Lake Tiberias. I visited other kibbutzim that were less elegant, but social life was similar in all of them. The practice of communal life in the kibbutz was carried much further than in U.S. communities with which I was acquainted. For example, children spent a relatively small amount of time with their parents but were regarded as belonging to all members of the kibbutz.

To prepare my report, I needed a great deal of information on Israel's international transactions that the government either did not have or was reluctant to give me. Given the substantial amount of foreign assistance, why were short-term credits needed to finance imports? Were new credits being obtained and was net indebtedness rising? Who were the creditors and how likely were they to refuse to extend the credits? My first problem was to determine the minimum amount of free foreign exchange the government would need to meet its short-term debt obligations and maintain essential

Raymond F. Mikesell

imports for at least a year, provided it did not increase the existing amount of short-term debt. My second problem was to determine how imports could be reduced without hardship on consumers or hampering the development projects the U.S. wanted to promote.

Israel's complex system of foreign exchange controls and import licensing complicated my analysis. Under the foreign exchange control system inherited from the British Mandate, with certain exceptions, foreign exchange receipts from exports and other sources had to be surrendered to authorized foreign exchange dealers, usually banks. Israel had no central bank until 1954. Foreign exchange expenditures required government authorization, either for specific imports or for a class of imports. Import allocations were made to various ministries and private organizations, and the Ministry of Finance adjusted those allocations to anticipated receipts. But the allocations did not stipulate how the imports were to be paid for—cash, credit, or barter—so that it could not be determined in advance how much authorized foreign exchange was required for import allocations. A foreign exchange budget linking the two was not introduced until late in 1952. Import licenses were normally issued only for "necessary" imports, but this was modified by a system of "imports without payment," meaning that the imports might be provided by foreign investors or paid for by residents holding foreign deposits. Such imports could be luxury goods available for sale on the market or capital or intermediate goods used in production. There was also an arrangement whereby exporting firms were permitted to use a portion of their foreign exchange receipts to buy raw materials and capital goods required for export production. This seemed to make sense, except that in practice there was little relationship between the imports licensed under this system and actual production for export. The production facilitated by the imports might have been sold in the domestic market.

The Ministry of Finance stated that Israel's imports were roughly equal to its annual receipts from exports plus grants and long-term capital imports. If this were true, it might be expected that Israel's liquidity requirements for the year were equal to its short-term debt obligations for that year. However, reliable supporting evidence was lacking. An analysis of the relationship between Israel's imports and means of payment other than short-term credits was hampered by the variety of means of paying for imports noted above, and by the existence of multiple exchange rates for valuing imports. Balance of payments data were valued in Israeli pounds, but to be meaningful it was necessary to convert the data into dollars. In 1952 there were three principal exchange rates for the Israeli pound: (1) the official parity of $2.80 applied to imports of essential goods and to the conversion of export receipts for specified goods; (2) a rate of $1.40 per pound applied to the conversion of foreign currency received by public or semipublic institutions, foreign diplomatic missions, and specified categories of government loans; and (3) $1.00 per pound applied to most other transactions. Not until the end of 1953 was the official rate adjusted to $1.00 per pound and the other rates abolished. In the absence of balance of payments data useful for financial analysis, I sought to compare future maturing obligations with expected free foreign exchange receipts for different periods during the year and to learn which short-term obligations were likely to be extended for another year.

Some of the indebtedness was to Jewish merchants who were unlikely to bring legal action if not paid on time, but other creditors might have taken action leading to an official Israeli default. In some cases even cooperating members of the American Jewish community would not have been able to extend maturing debts; to do so would have caused them to become insolvent. The Israeli government was securing one- or two-day loans from Jewish firms in New York, and these funds constituted the working capital of the firms. Such obligations were then paid by borrowing daily from other Jewish firms. This practice is similar to writing checks in excess of your bank balance and expecting to cover the deficit before the checks are received by your bank for collection.

Balance of payments estimates reported by the Ministry of Finance showed that Israel's 1951 import surplus was covered by a variety of transfers consisting of foreign government and private grants, long-term loans, private remittances, and short-term loans. But the import surplus exceeded total reported transfers by more than $100 million. The inability to account for more than $100 million in imports financed in 1951 was due both to the government's poor system of accounting for imports and the method by

Raymond F. Mikesell

which they were paid. This meant that the government was not exercising proper control over its international transactions. The same system was in operation during 1952. In order to determine Israel's external financing requirements to avoid default on its obligations, I needed an accurate accounting of how its imports were being paid for. However, such information was not forthcoming. The discrepancy between imports and means of payment may have arisen from imports financed by transactions that were not reported, or been caused by different valuations of the Israeli pound. Without full information on the balance of payments, I had to rely on estimates of the amounts of maturing obligations in 1952 and assume that no additional borrowings would mature in 1952. This was the basis for my estimate of Israel's liquidity requirement for 1952.

In reviewing the trade data for the early months of 1952, it appeared that imports had declined by about 10 percent, while exports were running higher. I was assured by the Ministry of Finance that this trend would continue, and that estimates of receipts from foreign loans and grants were higher than for 1951. I became convinced that, for 1952 at least, Israel's import surplus could be covered without additional net short-term borrowing. Based on information received from Israeli officials on estimated monthly foreign exchange receipts and the obligations that had to be met to avoid default, I estimated that Israel needed about $25 million in free foreign exchange over the year beginning in mid-1952. This estimate was based on the assumption that for the year beginning in mid-1952 there would be no net increase in short-term credits.

The Long-Term Outlook

An important question for the future was how the large import surplus could be reduced, since there was no certainty that the current flow of grants and loans would continue in future years, and Israel should be working toward self-sufficiency. Government data showed that real gross domestic product (GNP) grew by 23 percent between 1950 and 1951, but relatively little of the additional output appeared to be directed to producing exports and to substituting domestic production for imports. This was indicated by a 5.6 percent rise in real per capita consumption and a similar decline in per capita domestic capital formation. In other words, Israelis were spending more but not creating additional productive capacity. Between 1950 and 1951, imports for private consumption grew faster than the increase warranted by immigration. This information showed that Israel had not been making progress toward becoming less dependent on foreign assistance. I wanted to know which Israeli policies were responsible for the situation.

The Role of Inflation

I thought it likely that the high rate of inflation (running at an annual rate of 70 percent in mid-1952) was contributing to the import surplus by stimulating the demand for imports and reducing the incentive to produce for export. By contrast, according to the official price index, prices rose only 10.5 percent in 1951 and were stable in 1950. I needed to know the reason for the rapid increase in prices during the first half of 1952 and whether inflation was likely to continue at this rate. To assist me in analyzing domestic financial conditions, I contacted Don Patinkin, professor of economics at Hebrew University. Patinkin was well known in the U.S. for his economic writings, and I was amazed that he was not working with the government, at least as a consultant. To my surprise, officials of the Ministry of Finance were not aware of his work and reputation. Patinkin agreed to assist me but did not want to go on the U.S. government payroll. An arrangement was made for him to be paid by the Israeli government, and for copies of the memoranda he prepared for me to be given to the Ministry of Finance. This was satisfactory to me since I wanted the government to have his findings.

Patinkin's analysis showed that, over the period February 1950 to March 1952, money supply increased by 62 percent, an amount roughly equal to the increase in government internal debt. However, in 1950 and 1951 inflation was suppressed by price controls and by a substantial increase in imports. Because of the elimination of price controls and rationing in 1952 and the depreciation of the pound in February 1952, inflation was high. During 1952 the government stopped inflationary financing, reducing the rate of increase in the money supply. Patinkin therefore concluded that the inflationary forces had largely been removed and that the rate of inflation would decline. Also, the public was increasingly willing to hold money rather than simply run out and spend it. I was convinced that current monetary policy in Israel was reducing the rate of inflation in the second half of 1952. This was evidenced by a reduction in the rate of increase in the cost of living between June 1952 and June 1953. Imports valued in dollars declined from $426 million in 1951 to $393 million in 1952; coupled with the increase of exports from $67 million to $87 million, this led to a decline in the import surplus from $362 million to $306 million. A further decline to $263 million followed in 1953. Some of the decline in the import surplus may have been a consequence of the reduction in inflationary pressures in 1952 and 1953.

Consumer demand was also enhanced by increases in real wages negotiated by Israel's powerful unions. Real wage rates in manufacturing rose sharply in 1951, declined in early 1952 due to a surge in consumer prices accompanying devaluation of the Israeli pound, but regained the 1951 levels by mid-1952 and continued to rise thereafter. In spite of large immigration, real per capita consumption rose between 1950 and 1953 by nearly 6 percent; it leveled off, then rose sharply again in 1954. Per capita GNP also rose in 1951 by about 4 percent, but consumer saving as a percentage of national income failed to rise between 1950 and 1951. These figures suggested that while the Israeli economy was growing with the aid of capital imports, capital investment financed by saving was insufficient to put the economy on the road to independence from foreign assistance. I concluded that government policies were contributing to the rapid growth in consumption and to the low level of domestic savings. Patinkin agreed that per capita consumption levels were rising in Israel due in part to the strength of the labor unions in pushing up wages and in part to the government's fiscal deficits. The rise in per capita consumption rather than immigration alone prevented Israel from reducing its dependence on foreign assistance during this period.

The 1952 Report

My investigation convinced me that Israel was currently limiting imports to her means of payments (other than short-term borrowing) and that there was a liquidity problem in the form of a need to cover maturing short-term obligations with free foreign exchange during certain periods in the coming year. Thus I decided to recommend that the U.S. government make available

$25 million to cover Israeli's maturing debt, subject to an agreement by the government to reduce its net short-term indebtedness. The only source of U.S. funding available for Israel's short-term debt was the MSA grant for fiscal 1953. But MSA funds were intended to pay for imports approved by U.S. aid administrators, not to repay debt obligations incurred from past imports. The latter use of MSA funds would have violated congressional intent in authorizing these funds. On the other hand, an Israeli default would have reduced the flow of private funds needed for a viable economy, which was the purpose of U.S. assistance. I suggested that the problem could be handled by using MSA funds to pay obligations created by purchasing commodities in the past that might have been acquired under the current MSA program, and by falsifying the dates on which the purchases were made. Although I do not recall all the details, some of the debt financing was handled in this way. I was not responsible for the way my recommendation was carried out, and I am unaware that any auditor of MSA transactions reported the action. Sometimes it is necessary to violate the letter of the law in order to realize the fundamental purpose of the legislation. In any case, I never regretted my recommendation.

On July 25, 1952, I met with Ambassador Davis, Reeseman Fryer (assistant administrator for Near East and Africa in the MSA), and Bruce W. McDaniel (director of the MSA mission in Israel). I outlined what I thought should be in my report. We all agreed that Israel was facing a financial crisis arising from being unable to meet its maturing short-term debt obligations to foreign banks and other creditors. We also concurred in the conclusion that present conditions resulted from an almost complete disregard for elementary financial principles, including failure to establish a system of accounting controls and a foreign exchange budget. Therefore, any emergency assistance to Israel should be given only as a part of a coordinated program with commitments to financial reform from the Israeli government. Without such conditions U.S. assistance would merely delay inevitable insolvency. We agreed that the financial burden for any solution should be shared by American Jewish organizations and by the creditors who greatly benefited from U.S. aid to Israel. Following this meeting, Davis and I went to see Ben-Gurion for the purpose of (1) impressing upon him the importance of preparing a balanced foreign currency budget; and (2) getting his support for the adoption of, and adherence to, a realistic domestic budget. Ben-Gurion agreed with our advice but, as we discovered later, the minister of finance failed to implement it.

In my report, which the embassy sent to Washington just before I left, I recommended that $25 million of the MSA grant for fiscal 1953 be made available to pay selected short-term obligations; that the Israeli government agree not to enter into new short-term obligations; and that the Israeli government establish a foreign exchange budget and system of accounting that would enable the Ministry of Finance to know its financial position at all times. The basic provisions of my report were agreed to by the Israeli government, and the funds were made available.

There was considerable interest in my report and recommendations in the U.S. government. Averell Harriman, who was at that time director of the Mutual Security Agency, wanted to see me immediately upon my arrival— even before I returned to Charlottesville. Although suffering from jet lag and eager to see my family, I agreed to go to Harriman's office at 5 p.m. Harriman liked to work late and I did not see him until nearly 6:30 p.m. I briefed him and answered his many questions until after 8 p.m. He quizzed me on the details of Israel's financial condition and complemented me on my report. Despite the fact that he was a former Secretary of Commerce and member of a distinguished family, Harriman was very informal and not in the least overbearing. He was quite sympathetic to the Jewish cause but understood well the problems I faced in obtaining information and negotiating with Israeli officials. I was favorably impressed with Harriman as a competent administrator and a compassionate person dedicated to social welfare.

1953 Debt Negotiations

By December 1952, Israeli officials were again requesting the use of MSA grant funds to settle their short-term debts. The U.S. Embassy informed them they should assume responsibility for handling their debts and that re-funding without basic fiscal reform would make conditions worse in the future. In March 1953 the Israeli government approached the newly elected Eisenhower administration for assistance in debt refinancing. It requested $70 million in grant funds to meet debts estimated at $98 million, with payments falling due from April 1, 1953, through May 30, 1954. It was argued that this grant was needed to prevent a default, which would cause immediate termination of all bank and commercial lines of credit and a disruption of the flow of consumer goods and raw materials. Israel further requested a $118 million MSA grant for fiscal 1954. However, a State Department analysis indicated that MSA aid of $50 to $60 million should be adequate to provide for an austerity living standard with $10 to $20 million for modest capital development.

On June 9, 1953, having found that approximately $6 million in MSA funds remained for fiscal 1953, Eban requested that his government be permitted to use this money for debt retirement rather than for the regular program. Byroade, who continued for a time in the Eisenhower administration, said he would do what he could under existing authority, but the desirability of this action was debated at the State Department. The U.S. Embassy's position was that an advance of $6 to $7 million would buy only a few weeks' time. Nevertheless, Secretary of State John Foster Dulles agreed to the use of the $6 million for short-term debt financing, and this was approved by Harold Stassen, the new director of the Mutual Security Agency. Like his predecessor, Dulles was subjected to strong pressure by the Jewish leaders in the U.S. and did not want the Republican Party blamed for allowing the Israeli government to become bankrupt.

Since I was familiar with the problems, the State Department asked me to undertake another investigation of Israel's financial problems during the summer of 1953. Ambassador Davis also wanted me to examine the conditions under which Israel might make progress toward independence from foreign aid. However, most of my time in Israel on this visit was again occupied with the short-term debt problem.

In June 1953 Israel's total debt was estimated at $386 million, of which $111 million matured in the twelve months from April 1953 through March 1954. Although the State Department was very anxious to avoid a default and resulting condemnation from the American Jewish community for reneging on the bipartisan commitment to support a Jewish homeland, the Republican administration under Eisenhower and Dulles was less willing to accede to the demands of the Israeli government than Truman's administration had been.

One reason was that the Republican Party, critical of the large foreign aid programs sponsored by the Democrats, had made campaign promises to reduce them. Another reason may have been that there was evidence Israel's debt position was somewhat less precarious in mid-1953 than a year earlier.

When I arrived in Israel in the summer of 1953, Davis was still ambassador but not in residence, and Francis H. Russell was charge d'affaires. I did not have the close relationship with him I had had with Davis and did not live at his residence. Most of the time I stayed at a pleasant resort motel near Tel Aviv, but some nights were spent at the historic King David Hotel in Jerusalem; there my room overlooked the wall between Israel and Jordan, with troops stationed on either side of the wall. One evening while staying at the Tel Aviv Motel, I was invited to have dinner with a group of Americans touring Israel. The dinner was served in an open area near a dance floor, and I was fortunate to be seated next to Helen Gahagan Douglas, a former congresswoman who had recently been defeated by Richard Nixon in an election for the Senate. I had met Ms. Douglas several times before, and we had a great deal to talk about. She was a beautiful woman who looked radiant under the full moon above us. When the orchestra began playing we danced several numbers together. Frankly, I was feeling very romantic, but instead of light conversation she began telling me the methods Nixon had used to beat her in the election. Among other things, he called dozens of people and asked them to call others to tell them that Helen Douglas was a Communist. Our minds were not on the same wavelength, but I often remember that beautiful evening.

Although I continued to have warm relations with Kollek, I did not get the same degree of cooperation from other Israeli officials that I had in 1952. The reason may have been that they believed I supported a less liberal U.S. policy toward Israel in my 1952 report than they had hoped. The change in attitude of the Israeli officials was also recognized by the MSA mission and the embassy. Shortly after my arrival, I met with embassy representatives, and we discussed the policies on assistance to Israel imparted to me by the State Department. Although I was asked to prepare a report on Israel's financial condition, I did not have the latitude of recommending any assistance for dealing with short-term indebtedness. The principal purpose

of my mission was to make clear to the Israeli government the position of
the State Department and the MSA that Israel must reduce the rate of growth
in its consumption and devote more resources to expanding exports and
reducing its dependence on foreign aid.

Later, I met with Eshkol and people from the MSA and the embassy.
Minister of Finance Eshkol insisted on talking about assistance for repaying
the short-term debt, but we stated that using MSA program funds for debt
repayment would not contribute to Israel's long-term viability. Furthermore,
we reminded him that Section 105 of the MSA appropriation for fiscal year
ending June 30, 1954, provided that "none of the funds provided by this Act
nor any of the counterpart funds generated as a result of assistance under this
or any other act shall be used to make payments on account of the principal
or interest on any debt of any foreign government or on any loan made to
such governments by any other foreign governments." Thus the release of
MSA funds for debt service was a clear violation of U.S. legislation. We also
reminded Eshkol that Washington had made a definite decision against an
Export-Import Bank loan to Israel for debt re-funding. At this meeting we
emphasized that Israel should be maximizing productive investments and
minimizing consumption, attaining internal economic stability and reducing
inflation, and consulting with the MSA mission on foreign exchange
and development budgets with a view to reducing Israeli dependence on
foreign aid.

Eshkol, whom I never found especially friendly or tactful, was obviously
resentful. He seemed to believe that there were important officials in Washington who were much more friendly to Israel than those of us in the embassy
and the MSA. Defending Israel's past deficit financing policies, he implied
that Israel would continue to borrow as much as possible in a manner determined by statesmen motivated by faith in Israel and not by "financial experts,
bookkeepers, and statisticians."

The embassy immediately sent a telegram to the State Department
describing the meeting. The department was naturally disturbed by Eshkol's
remarks, particularly by his intention to borrow as much as possible, since it
seemed to be in conflict with the government's agreement to reduce its short-
term indebtedness. A telegram from the State Department asked whether

Eshkol had the support of then Prime Minister Ben-Gurion. I believed he did because Eshkol appeared to be speaking for the government rather than giving his personal views. A few days later I received a telegram from the State Department requesting that I convey to Ben-Gurion the U.S. position regarding Israel's economic policies. I read the telegram at a meeting presided over by Ben-Gurion. He replied that if he and his colleagues "had followed Mikesell's advice on economic policy, there never would have been an Israel." I was disturbed by this personal attack on the "messenger."

It seemed evident that the MSA mission was not going to have much influence on Israel's economic policies as long as the Israeli officials thought they could override the mission's decisions by contacting U.S. government officials in Washington, D.C. Therefore, the embassy recommended that all discussions on financial problems take place in Israel. The State Department and the MSA agreed with this recommendation. They also stated that the U.S. government did not consider itself committed to guaranteeing the Israeli government against default, and that the ambassador might inform the Israeli government of this position. At a meeting between Harold Stassen (director of the MSA) and Israeli Embassy officials in Washington on July 22, 1953, Stassen told the ambassador that he wanted all negotiations on financial aid to take place in Israel. However, this did not prevent continued end-runs to Washington by Israeli officials.

The U.S. mission's desire to discuss financial problems in Israel rather than in Washington, D.C., ran into another difficulty. The embassy wanted the discussions held in Tel Aviv, while the foreign minister wanted them held in Jerusalem. This reflected the refusal of the U.S. government to regard Jerusalem as the capital of Israel. Relations between the MSA mission and Israeli officials were further complicated by a delay in fiscal 1954 assistance to Israel. The MSA Appropriation Act of Fiscal 1954 did not make an allocation to Israel or to the Arab states; it was simply a sum of about $100 million for the Middle East. Allocation of assistance to Israel in turn was delayed by the Israeli government's refusal to comply with an order by Vaughn Bennike, chief of staff, United Nations Truce Supervision Commission, to stop diverting water from the Jordan River—an order fully supported by the U.S. government. Following the Israeli government's agreement on October 27, 1953, to

suspend work on the Jordan River project and to cooperate with the UN
Security Council's efforts to reach a solution to the water problem, President
Eisenhower announced that $26 million in economic aid would be made
available to Israel for the first six months of the current fiscal year.

Shortly after I left Israel, Foreign Minister Sharett and Kollek presented
embassy officials with another debt crisis—due they said, to lower-than-
expected United Jewish Appeal cash receipts, a tightening of private credit
sources, and the uncertainty created by the suspension of U.S. aid. However,
embassy officials concluded that the government should be able to avoid
default and did not recommend a cash release. On November 20, 1953,
Israeli officials asked Stassen directly for $20 million in cash from the $26
million MSA allotment. The embassy recommended against the release of
cash, and the secretary of state notified Stassen that he agreed with the
embassy. But the Israelis did not stop. On November 30, 1953, Stassen
delivered to Dulles a message stating that his office was convinced Israel
needed $9 million of the $20 million requested to meet indebtedness for
avoiding default. The release was authorized.

Back in the United States during these negotiations, I was satisfied with
taking no responsibility for this action. I had become convinced that no
additional short-term debt should be covered with MSA funds. I believed that
economic reform was essential for Israel's long-run progress and financial
stability, and that continued short-term financial bailouts were delaying
reform. Despite the many cries of alarm by Israeli officials, Israel did not
default and was able to achieve a relatively high level of consumption, although it remained heavily dependent on external assistance.

Visit to Ethiopia

Before returning from Israel I received a cable from Reeseman Fryer, an
assistant director of the MSA, with whom I had been working closely and
whom I greatly admired for his knowledge of the Middle East. Fryer requested that I make a quick visit to Addis Ababa, Ethiopia. There had been
some problems with the MSA mission there, and he wanted a first-hand
account of what was taking place. I was glad to do so since I had always
wanted to visit Ethiopia. I had the impression that by the time I arrived the

problems had been solved, but I did prepare a full report for Fryer. At my hotel in Addis Ababa, I became acquainted with a couple of aviators attached to the local U.S. locust eradication program. When they asked if I would like to have a bird's-eye view of the surrounding area, I took them up on the offer. The country's very deep gorges are fascinating, but about fifteen minutes into the flight I experienced one of the greatest frights of my life. The single engine motor cut out and the pilot flew low over the native grass-hut villages near the edge of a deep gorge to look for an emergency landing site. Fortunately, he got the engine restarted and was able to get us back to the airport. Except for flights related to my work with mining companies, I always declined such opportunities after that.

Conclusions on Missions

If there are lessons to be learned from this experience, they are more political than economic in nature. If Israel had been a member of the International Monetary Fund in 1952–53, it might have been able to obtain IMF assistance. But Israel would have been required to negotiate a standby agreement committing it to monetary and fiscal reforms designed to move the country toward balance of payments equilibrium and growth. The U.S. government was not equipped to monitor such a program. Moreover, with an import surplus more than five times its exports, no short- or medium-term financial program designed for balance of payments equilibrium would have been possible. What was required was a ten-year (or longer) development program for greatly increasing investment and production for exports. The U.S. government sought to differentiate between Israel's liquidity needs and financing her annual import surplus. This distinction was artificial because imports were not determined by a foreign exchange budget designed to match imports with normal means of payment. Rather, imports were only limited by the amounts that could be obtained by any means, including short-term borrowing. The debt crisis was created as a means of increasing imports. A better course might have been to allow the Israeli government to be fully responsible for its short-term debt, and for the U.S. and other donors to provide assistance in support of a long-term program designed to achieve specific development objectives. In my view, this policy should be applied to all developing countries.

On my return to Washington, D.C., I had the feeling that my mission had failed. The conclusions of my report had been overruled without discussing them with me, and I had failed to convince Israeli officials of the desirability of promoting long-range development instead of maximizing imports for consumption. Later, I realized that I had done my job as an economist and that I could not be responsible for political events that determined the outcome. I was convinced I had made a contribution by analyzing Israel's short-term debt problem; my recommendations were in the interests of Israel as well as supporting U.S. policy.

Despite the disappointment, I did enjoy the work in Israel and learned much that proved useful both in my later consulting activities and in teaching and writing. Israel fascinated me. Few scholars or reporters had the opportunity I did for traveling about the country with Teddy Kollek and spending many evenings in the homes of the prime minister and other high officials.

The experience taught me the importance of having a strong central bank to control domestic credit and foreign exchange transactions and a system of budget control, independent of political interference. My Israeli experience also taught me a great deal about how decisions were made in the U.S. government. I admit to acquiring a good deal of cynicism about the competence and honesty of all governments.

A Personal Experience with McCarthyism

An event that occurred a month after my return discouraged and disillusioned me with regard to the Eisenhower administration, even though I served that administration until leaving for Oregon in 1957. I had taken leave from the University of Virginia for the fall of 1953 to serve as a member of the faculty of the National War College (now the National Defense University) until December of that year. However, I spent a couple of hours each week with MSA officials giving advice on developments in Israel. (Stassen had fired the very competent Reeseman Fryer and replaced him with someone much less knowledgeable about the Middle East.) One day I was told by a very embarrassed MSA official with whom I had been meeting that I had been dismissed by Stassen as a consultant to the MSA. I had held that position for several years, but I had not been on the MSA payroll since returning from Israel. In addition to serving on the faculty of the War College, I was spending half my time in the White House as a consultant to the Presidential Commission on Foreign Economic Policies (Randall Commission). I drew pay only from the War College, but I put in a large amount of overtime for the government.

My colleagues in the MSA told me they had asked Stassen why I was dismissed, and this is what they had been told: Stassen had nothing against me personally, but he had promised Vice President Nixon that he would help carry out a pledge to fire hundreds of Communists from the government— mostly staff members hired by the Democratic administration. Since I would not be directly hurt by the dismissal, he added my name to the list of those dismissed from the MSA. This is an amazing story, but I have no reason to believe it is not true. I have a number of friends who were also dismissed from the government as leftists or Communists on no evidence whatsoever. The treatment by Stassen disturbed me greatly. I was able to check with an FBI agent regarding any adverse information in my file, but he found none. As a youth I had been a member of Norman Thomas's American Socialist Party, but Thomas was fiercely anti-Communist and, as far as I am aware, the FBI did not regard this as a black mark on my record.

Sources

The principal sources for this chapter are my unpublished memoranda prepared in Israel and U.S. Department of State (1986).

CHAPTER 8: ACTIVITIES IN LATIN AMERICA

My interest in Latin America dates from a Spanish class in high school. I have made more trips to Latin America than to any other region outside the United States.

When I was eighteen I spent a summer traveling by ship to Central America and Colombia. I had read a fascinating article in the *National Geographic* on the San Blas Indians, an isolated tribe in the border area between Panama and Colombia which had been little influenced by Western civilization. I was determined to visit the tribe but had no idea how to do so as the area had no tourist facilities.

On landing in Colon, Panama, I was told at the local YMCA to visit a small tienda whose proprietor owned a coconut-buying boat that went to the region. I learned that his boat was leaving at midnight, and it would take me on a two-week trip for $20. The captain and chief engineer (who was also the cook) of the fifty-foot sailboat were Jamaican blacks, and the person in charge of buying the coconuts was a native Panamanian. It was perhaps the most pleasant and exciting trip of my life. When the boat stopped at San Blas Indian villages for coconuts, I could see the way people in the area lived before any contact with Europe. There were no signs because no written language was in general use. The homes were small hovels made of local vegetation, but there was a large meeting area with a roof. Some of the men were busy gathering coconuts by climbing trees and throwing them down. Most people were partially naked, but the chief whom I met with some ceremony wore a shirt. Coconuts were paid for largely in trade goods such as canned foods and simple utensils. There were many monkeys in the village who seemed to be part of the population. Unfortunately, I could not view the tribe's dances and social life in the evening because of a firm rule that no nonmember was permitted to spend the night in the village, and boats were required to move well offshore. I wish it had been possible to converse with these people, but no one on the boat was familiar with their language beyond that necessary for business transactions. If my father had not wanted me to study engineering in college, I might have become an anthropologist as a result of this visit.

After returning to Colon, I boarded a ship for Baranquilla, Colombia, and from there took a river boat up the Magdalena River to Bogota, Colombia, which at that time had retained its old Spanish character more than any city in Latin America. The previous summer I had spent more than a month in Spain, so that my Spanish was fairly good.

Association with Latin American Universities

More frequent visits to Latin America began after World War II, when I began serving as a consultant to the Organization of American States (OAS) and the State Department on Latin American problems. I visited these countries to attend conferences, give lectures, and do research. As an academic, I made a special effort to visit Latin American universities. Several of my early trips were financed and arranged by the State Department's Cultural and Educational Exchange Program. I gave many lectures and seminars at universities in Argentina, Brazil, Chile, Colombia, Costa Rica, Ecuador, Guatemala, Peru, and Venezuela. In the early years I gave these lectures in Spanish, but my Spanish suffered because university, government, and business officials I met with preferred to speak in English; in some cases more than half my audience knew English far better than I knew Spanish. On one occasion, as I walked out of the room after I had given a rather poor lecture in Spanish at a university in Quito, Ecuador, I heard one student saying to another, "If he had just spoken in English I think I could have understood him." I should not have tried to lecture at all since my wife and I had arrived early that morning from Guayaquil, Ecuador, which is at sea level, while Quito is 11,000 feet high. A U.S. Embassy official met us at the airport with a list of speaking engagements for that day, which included a mid-morning meeting with government people, a business luncheon meeting, a mid-afternoon meeting, and a 6 p.m. lecture. Just before the evening lecture I nearly passed out—due mainly to not having time to acclimate to the altitude. I revived with the help of oxygen sent by the embassy.

I never learned Portuguese, so my lectures in Brazil were simultaneously translated and delivered to members of the audience through headphones. On one visit I lectured in Rio de Janeiro, where I had an excellent translator who knew a good deal about economics. I was also scheduled to lecture for five days at the University of Brasilia, 500 miles from Rio. I was accompanied by a translator and two people who set up the speaking equipment. I had an audience of about forty people, about half of whom were university faculty members and the other half government officials. My assistants arranged for simultaneous translation, but no one in the audience put on headphones; they simply listened to my English presentation. The same thing happened at the afternoon presentation. My three assistants took an evening plane back to Rio. Their services were not needed because nearly all the faculty members and many of the government officials, who had gone to graduate schools in the U.S. or Britain, found it easier to listen to my English than to a Portuguese translation. In giving short talks in the course of conferences in Latin America as a representative of the State Department or of the OAS, I usually spoke in English. Nearly all the Latin American representatives knew English, and both languages were used without translation at the conferences.

During later visits to Latin American universities, I sought to establish student and faculty exchange relationships between them and the University of Oregon. When I came to Oregon in 1957, I obtained a grant from the Ford Foundation, to be administered by the university, for the purpose of establishing such relationships and particularly to provide an opportunity for our Ph.D.s in economics to spend a year in a Latin American university doing research for their dissertations. I also encouraged faculty members and graduate students at these universities to apply for graduate work at Oregon. I established relationships with the Universidad de los Andes in Colombia, the University of Chile, and the Universidad de los Andes in Merida, Venezuela. In the case of the Merida university, the Ford Foundation granted several hundred thousand dollars to the University of Oregon to establish a research and teaching program. This program, which lasted for three years, involved sending Department of Economics and Business Administration faculty members to Merida to teach and direct research programs. The program also provided funds for Merida faculty members to attend the University of

Oregon for advanced degrees. Although I directed the program from Eugene, I made two or three trips every year to Merida to participate.

On one speaking trip, the American Embassy in Bogota asked me to give a talk at the embassy, followed by a reception in my honor at the ambassador's residence. When asked if there were people in Bogota I would like to invite, I provided the names of two of my former students (who were with Colombia's Central Bank) and my friend Lauchlin Currie. Currie was President Franklin Roosevelt's economic assistant in the 1940s and later an economist with the World Bank. He had attended meetings with me on international financial matters at the Treasury Department and was also at Bretton Woods. As with many other liberal economists, Currie was under surveillance by the FBI and on McCarthy's list of Communist sympathizers, mainly because he was a friend of Harry White. While I do not believe the FBI had anything on Currie himself, he was subpoenaed by the Committee on Un-American Activities to testify while he was on a World Bank mission to Colombia. Since Currie expected to be asked to testify about his friends, he refused to return to the United States and remained in Colombia, later becoming a Colombian citizen. He headed an economic consulting agency and had held important positions in the Colombian government.

When I told the economic counselor at the embassy that I wanted Currie at the reception, he looked at me strangely but said he would be glad to invite him. Although Currie was perhaps the most prominent economist in Colombia at the time, he had never been invited to the American Embassy, which frequently held meetings to which they invited economists to review economic problems. The reason was, of course, that he was a victim of McCarthyism, and the people in the embassy lacked the courage to invite him. Currie was well received at my talk and the party. He told me later that from then on he was a frequent visitor to the American Embassy for seminars and social occasions. It is well to remember how long McCarthy's influence poisoned American relationships!

I continued to correspond with and occasionally visit Currie until his death in the early 1980s. I particularly remember his beautiful and charming Colombian wife, who bore his child when Currie was in his early fifties. The divorce from his American wife at the time he was subpoenaed probably had something to do with his decision not to return to the United States or to Canada, the country of his birth.

The Inter-American Development Bank

The U.S. has had a long-standing interest in Latin America, but there was a special reason for its concern during the late 1950s. Since U.S. foreign policy was largely dominated by a desire to prevent the spread of Soviet Communism, anti-U.S. sentiment fueled by poor economic conditions led the Eisenhower administration to seek ways of promoting closer ties with the region. There were official visits to the area in 1958 by Vice President Nixon, Secretary of State Dulles, Secretary of the Treasury Henderson, and by the president's brother, Milton Eisenhower. Their reports led the administration to believe that special economic programs were urgently needed for our foreign policy objectives. The Latin American community wanted aid to help establish a regional development bank to be controlled by Latin Americans but financed by the U.S. and other developed countries.

Prior to 1958 the official position of the U.S. was that the World Bank should be the principal source of multilateral loan assistance for all developing countries. However, since the World Bank was largely controlled by developed countries, it was not regarded by Latin Americans as an organization in which their views were represented. Perhaps more important, it did not satisfy the political objective of having a Latin America–controlled development bank. In August 1958 the U.S. government announced that it was prepared to consider establishing a more satisfactory regional development institution.

During the late 1950s, I was serving as a consultant to the OAS and had attended meetings at which the Latin American desire for a regional bank was discussed. Sometime in early 1958 the executive director of the OAS Economic and Social Council asked me to outline a structure for a regional Latin American bank that might be acceptable to both the Latin American and the U.S. governments. Since I was engaged in a number of activities of higher priority, I put this request on the back burner. One day in early August 1958, I learned that Secretary Dulles had proposed a Middle East regional bank to provide loans to both Israel and Arab states. I wondered at the time how the United States could offer to sponsor a Middle East regional bank and not be responsive to the desires of the Latin American republics for a regional development institution. The next day I received a call from the OAS asking what progress I had made on the earlier assignment and requesting that I complete the study as soon as possible.

In preparing the regional bank study, I drew on a proposal for an inter-American bank made by the Inter-American Economic and Social Council of the Pan American Union in March 1949, as well as on other sources. After working for a month, I submitted a plan to the OAS for an inter-American development bank. After some minor changes, my study was submitted to an OAS committee organized in 1959 to prepare a plan for the regional bank.

Called to Washington, D.C., in January 1959 to serve as an adviser to this committee, I fully expected the committee to discuss my proposal. However, the day after discussions began, the Treasury Department submitted its own plan, which was patterned after the charter of the World Bank; the Treasury Department spokesman made it clear that this plan would be the basis for discussion. My own plan was preferred by many committee members because it gave less power to the Bank's executive board, which probably would be dominated by the United States. The committee approved the Treasury Department plan, and following approval by the U.S. Congress, the Inter-American Development Bank (IADB) was established in February 1960. Members included all Latin American countries except Cuba; the U.S. had 40 percent of the subscribed capital, which entitled it to 40 percent of the votes on the board of executive directors. Since the U.S. could usually obtain votes from a few other member countries on any issue it felt strongly about, the U.S. had an effective veto over all loans. However, the individual loans made by the IADB were usually determined by agreement among the Latin American executive directors. There was an understanding that each member was entitled to a certain portion of the total loans made. I believe that inter-American politics played a much more important role in the allocation of the IADB funds than did the economic priority of the projects.

I served as a consultant to the IADB for several years. My work consisted mainly of writing memoranda on topics related to IADB policy and attending conferences or working groups in Washington, D.C., and in Latin America. Inter–Latin American trade, promotion of private direct investment, balance of payments of member countries, and domestic problems of Latin American countries—especially inflation—were the principal topics on which I worked.

In spite of numerous studies, special trade conferences, and organizations, the IADB did little if anything to promote regional objectives. Almost no regional planning went into the selection of loan projects, and the distribution of loans was made on political grounds rather than in response to a conscious program of regional economic development. Nor has the Bank made a significant contribution to the liberalization of the Latin American economies, including the removal of barriers to foreign investment and trade. I found that the officials of the IADB were careful not to question the economic policies of the Latin American governments whose representatives were, after all, their employers. Economic liberalization in Latin America since the early 1980s has arisen from within the intellectual and business community and, in some cases, been promoted by conditional loans from the World Bank and the IMF. As for promoting the foreign policy interests of the U.S., the Latin American countries were undoubtedly grateful to have their own development institution despite the dominant role played by the U.S. executive director, who is appointed by the U.S. Treasury Department. However, the U.S. government might have had more political influence in Latin America if it had provided equivalent amounts of bilateral assistance. The problem with regional institutions is that, like all public institutions, they have layers of management and organizational services that duplicate the functions of the world institutions designed for the same purpose. Each executive director is given a staff consisting mainly of people from his own country. This cost can only be justified if there are uniquely regional functions that can be provided. The IADB could have made contributions to regional integration but failed to do so.

Latin American Economic Integration

Much of my work as a consultant to the State Department, OAS, and IADB concerned regional integration, especially intraregional trade. Regional economic integration has been a goal in Latin America for more than 100 years. Latin American economists have long realized that national industrialization based solely on domestic markets is costly, and that for many agricultural and manufactured products regional markets are required for efficient production. Although some actions were taken to develop regional markets among the Central American countries in the early 1950s, concrete steps toward the creation of a Latin American common market began in 1957 with the establishment of the Working Group on the Latin American Regional Market by the United Nations Economic Commission for Latin America (ECLA). The Working Group, with which I later became associated, established the principles and guidelines for the Latin American Free Trade Association (LAFTA) created by the Montevideo Treaty in 1960.

To understand the deliberations of the Working Group and the subsequent formation of LAFTA, it is important to know something about the economic philosophy of the Latin American political leaders, especially Raul Prebisch, director of the Central Bank of Argentina before Peron and the head of the ECLA. As with most developing country governments in the period following World War II, Latin American government officials and the economists who advised them believed strongly in governmental economic controls and national planning. Economic planning was regarded as the key to development during the early post–World War II period. This was not only true of the intellectual and government leaders in the developing countries. Many of the economists in the foreign aid agencies of developed countries and in the World Bank shared this view of development. These agencies often recommended, and in some cases insisted, that the recipients of financial assistance prepare detailed five- or ten-year devel-opment plans for achieving target rates of economic growth. The external assistance agencies favored neither a system of controls on production and domestic trade nor controls on foreign trade. National economic plans were to be carried out by macroeconomic poli-cies—the allocation of government expenditures, tax policy, and controls over the allocation of foreign aid. Nevertheless, the governments of the developing coun-tries were expected to play a major role in the economies. Not until the 1970s did external aid agencies emphasize the desirability of free markets and private enter-prise for achieving development.

Prior to the 1980s, nearly all Latin American countries maintained comprehensive controls over domestic and foreign trade, over production through credit allocation and allocation of imports, and government ownership of major industries. Both privately owned and government-operated industries were often subsidized either directly or indirectly, and there was special promotion of import-substituting industries. Price controls were widely applied not only to essential consumer goods but also to farm products, often at the cost of depressing agricultural prices in favor of urban consumers. Foreign exchange was monopolized by the government by requiring exporters to surrender their foreign currency receipts to the central bank. Foreign direct investment was controlled mainly to avoid competition with domestically owned private firms and state-owned enterprises. Mineral development was often reserved for state enterprises and foreign investment in the resource industries forbidden. Competition was frowned upon as inconsistent with achieving government objectives. Despite the fact that nearly all governments formulated long-range national economic plans, frequently with the assistance of foreign advisers, the plans were largely paper documents without specific instruments for realizing them. They were published by governments for political reasons but usually forgotten after the election.

Leading Latin American economists such as Prebisch argued that only through comprehensive government controls could national economic and social goals be achieved. Competitive free enterprise was distrusted as a failed system advocated by international firms that sought to profit at the expense of poor countries. Prebisch formulated a hypothesis that the traditional dependence of developing countries on raw material and food exports could not generate development because the long-run terms of trade for developing countries move downward: world prices of resource-based exports tend to decline relative to prices of manufactured imports. For developing countries, the solution to this problem was to become as self-sufficient as possible in manufacturing and to restrict resource exports by creating international cartels dominated by developing countries. Domestic investment should be directed toward producing substitutes for imports rather than raw materials for export. Latin American governments were strong supporters of international commodity agreements designed to raise international prices of materials and food. Efforts to establish international commodity agreements were supported by the United Nations; in some cases the governments of developed countries also cooperated.

Raymond F. Mikesell

Within this somewhat hostile environment, the Working Group on a regional market sought to establish the principles for a free trade area (FTA) and, ultimately, a common market with common tariffs on imports from outside the region. The contradictions are obvious. There cannot be free external trade without free trade in the same products within a country. Government controls on domestic trade—such as price and production controls—would constitute controls on external trade as well. For free external trade to exist, the exporter should be able to market competitively without restriction in both the foreign and the domestic markets. If a government agency is the sole buyer of a product, the agency should be able to buy from a domestic or foreign source in accordance with competitive price advantage. This principle is set forth in the General Agreement on Tariffs and Trade (GATT) as applied to purchases by government agencies.

The foreign exchange control systems of the Latin American countries were incompatible with regional free trade, since there cannot be free trade without the unrestricted ability of importers to obtain the foreign exchange required to make payments within the region. The Working Group paid little attention to these contradictions between free intraregional trade and controlled domestic markets. Measures for establishing an FTA were recommended by the Working Group without considering the inconsistencies.

February 1959 Working Group Session

The Working Group's first session held in Santiago, Chile, in February 1958, created broad guidelines for the establishment of a regional Latin American market. Further details were to be formulated by a second session in Mexico City during February 1959. There was no representative from the United States at the 1958 session—only distinguished Latin Americans from individual countries and the ECLA secretariat. An official of the U.S. State Department suggested to a UN official that the United States would welcome the opportunity to send an observer to the second session of the Working Group, since the U.S. government was intensely interested in Latin American efforts to achieve economic integration and in the kind of intraregional trade agreement that might be established. But this was to be a working session. ECLA wanted neither observers nor U.S. government participation. The State

Department did not want to participate officially in the creation of a treaty for establishing an organization that was likely to sanction discrimination against U.S. trade.

A State Department official suggested that a nongovernmental U.S. citizen might participate in the meeting, and that any position he took would not necessarily represent that of the U.S. government. This was acceptable to the ECLA. Because I had worked on Latin American integration for the State Department as well as for the OAS, I was asked to participate in the Mexico session of the Working Group in my private capacity as professor of economics at the University of Oregon.

I doubt that Prebisch was pleased with my selection since, although I had published papers in favor of a Latin American free trade area, my views on the national policies of Latin American countries were directly contrary to his. I also had views on the structure of an FTA that were contrary to the principles established by the first session of the Working Group held.

Although I realized that I would be in disagreement with Prebisch, I knew some of the other members of the Working Group whose economic philosophies differed from Prebisch, and I hoped to win them over to some of my views. Personally, this was a great opportunity for a scholar with a special interest in Latin American problems to gain information and experience. When my wife and I arrived in Mexico City, we were greeted by officials of the Mexican central bank and attended a reception by our host, Rodrigo Gomez, head of the Central Bank of Mexico.

The chair of the group was Galo Plaza, former president of Ecuador and a well-known Latin American leader. Other members included Jose Garrido Torres, Brazil's director of the Department of Currency and Credit; Flavian Levine, head of Chile's leading steel company; E. M. Delfino, president of the Buenos Aires stock exchange; and Carlos Lleras Restrepo, a senator from Colombia. I had met Torres and Levine previously and became friends with some of the other members, who entertained me in their homes when I later visited their countries. Another member, Juan Pardo Hereen, entertained my wife and me at his beautiful estate in the Peruvian Andes, where a number of llamas grazed on his large front yard. We were also entertained in the homes of both Torres and Levine in their own countries.

Galo Plaza was fair and nondiscriminatory in giving all participants an opportunity to speak. However, the meeting was dominated by Prebisch and the other ECLA secretariat members, who sought from the beginning to dictate what the Working Group would recommend. The secretariat's draft of the Working Group's report became the agenda for the meeting. Instead of eliminating all customs duties and nontariff equivalents on trade among members within the FTA, the secretariat draft proposed an agreement whereby each country would reduce its average duties applied to specific categories of goods gradually over a period of ten years, with a further percentage reduction to be agreed on thereafter. No date was set for the complete elimination of barriers to intraregional trade, and there were so many exceptions to the principle of "most favored nation" (MFN) treatment as to make the application of the MFN treatment meaningless. (MFN treatment requires that there be no discrimination in the treatment of imports from different members of the trading group.) Regional MFN is a basic condition for an FTA and a condition required by the GATT for FTAs. Otherwise, the countries forming the FTA would be in violation of the GATT trade rules.

One exception to the MFN principle in the Working Group draft report was its advocacy of the use of "industrial complementarity agreements"— bilateral agreements negotiated between countries for reducing trade barriers on the products of particular industries. Another exception was special concessions granted to exports of members in the early stages of industrial development. A third exception provided that existing preferential concessions might be continued after the FTA was signed. There were special concessions for countries in trade disequilibrium with the region as a whole, allowing them to slow down the rate of tariff reduction. All of these exceptions were designed to provide a weak regional trade agreement, which was compatible with existing domestic policies of the governments that the ECLA represented.

In the secretariat's draft, there was no mention of the GATT, to which several of the Latin American countries were signatories and which provides strict rules for the negotiation of an FTA. When I raised the issue, I was told that the Working Group would not be guided by what countries or agencies outside Latin America might think.

I was permitted by the chair to speak to each of the provisions of the secretariat draft as they were taken up, as were all the other participants. I argued from the beginning that the secretariat's draft violated the traditional principles of FTAs, especially since it lacked a definitive schedule for removal of all barriers to intraregional trade. I stated that the draft contained too many exceptions and special concessions and violated the MFN principle. I said the secretariat proposal represented an agreement for a preferential trading area rather than either an FTA area or a common market.

I got some support from Levine, Torres, Hereen, and Gomez for the trade principles I was expressing, but this support was never carried through to the point of challenging the secretariat's draft. While there was bickering over details among the members, they failed to support constructive alternatives to the secretariat's provisions. They were simply not willing to challenge Prebisch and the ECLA secretariat in any effective way, since each member was concerned about the political reaction to his position in his own country.

Torres of Brazil was as guilty of this as any other, but he accused members of the Working Group of acting like representatives of their governments rather than like experts who were supposed to develop principles to guide the drafting of an actual agreement. Torres chose to appear as a liberal free trader as long as it did not contradict the national interests of his country. His schizophrenic behavior became rather obvious to everyone, and some of us kidded him on social occasions.

I felt I had a great deal in common with Levine of Chile. As a businessman he appreciated the advantages of trade and competition, but he would not take a stand against Prebisch and seemed at times bored with the whole business. Pardo Hereen of Peru agreed with me in urging more liberal trade policies, but he was not forceful or effective. Lleras of Colombia sought to present the image of a scholar by arguing on fine legal points, but by and large he seemed to have little interest in liberal trade policies. D'Ascoli of Venezuela was very protectionist minded and reflected the highly protectionist trend of the new Venezuelan government. Delfino of Argentina had little to say and generally went along with Prebisch.

Gomez of Mexico was greatly interested in expanding markets in the region for Mexico, but he did not translate this interest into an appeal for

Raymond F. Mikesell

trade liberalization. He spoke only occasionally as an elder statesman, usually agreeing with Prebisch. As the pleasant and charming host of the conference, he took the Working Group on a weekend trip to Acapulco as guests of the Central Bank. The bank has a large lodge at Acapulco, and we were given front seats for the famous cliff diving performance.

I had limited success in modifying a few points in the ECLA draft, such as eliminating the provision based on the principle of equilibrium of each country with the group as a whole. I prepared a statement on adjustments for balance-of-payments deficits; it was circulated by the secretariat and accepted by the group, but then largely eliminated by the secretariat in the final report.

By Wednesday of the final week of the conference, widespread disagreement on many fundamental aspects was evident. Torres even suggested that the secretariat not attempt to formulate recommendations for a draft treaty, but rather present the various views of the Working Group on specific issues. There was considerable support within the group for this position, but Prebisch insisted that the Working Group must present a draft treaty. He did state that a commentary on individual positions would be prepared by the secretariat after the conference. This meant that anything the secretariat wanted to report would be passed on to those drafting the final treaty for the regional trade arrangement. The Working Group then went sightseeing until Friday morning, when we were supposed to review the secretariat's draft.

On Friday morning we were presented with a thirty-five-page document, including seventeen pages of commentary the Working Group had not seen before and which now was to be part of the Working Group report itself. When we met at 10:30 a.m, Prebisch announced to my utter amazement and consternation that he had arranged a press conference at noon to present the final report (with such minor changes as we might care to make). I was not even able to read the entire document, since I read Spanish slowly, and I also wanted to participate in the discussion. The previous understanding that the document would reflect different views within the Working Group was completely violated, and we were asked to agree to the commentary which we had not seen before that morning. Torres and I protested, but the rest accepted quite meekly.

I gave a short speech stating that this document would be regarded outside Latin America as a recommendation for a preferential trading area, and I explained in some detail why it would be so regarded. Prebisch repeated again that the Working Group should not be governed by what the rest of the world might think of it. I asked that a statement be placed in the introduction to the effect that members of the Working Group were not in unanimous agreement on all provisions of the document, but this was rejected. I then stated that I would have to insist on a statement in the document before it went to press to the effect that I could not agree with all the provisions. Prebisch agreed to include my reservations in the final report, although he was quite angry with me. The press was called in and given copies of a "revised document" with only a portion of the changes that had been agreed to at the meeting just concluded, and there was no mention of my reservation. I asked for copies of what was given to the press and was told they would be sent to my hotel that afternoon. Copies arrived at about 8 p.m. that evening.

The final report contained an annex in fine print (and with my name misspelled) with a watered-down version of my statement. It failed to state specifically that I was unable to agree with all the provisions of the report released to the press, and it did not include all my specific objections. The Working Group report stated that an effective common market would require the creation of a payments-and-credit regime to facilitate financing intraregional trade, especially since most intraregional trade was not expected to be financed with convertible currencies such as the dollar. I agreed with this position but made some suggestions regarding the nature of the payments system. Prebisch was quite interested in my views on this issue; I had a long talk with him after one of the meetings and prepared a short memorandum at his request. He maintained that the kind of arrangement I envisaged was consistent with his own views. However, the report did not deal with the details of the payments problem.

Despite the unhappy experience at the last meeting of the Working Group, my relations with all members of the group were very cordial. Some of them indicated to me privately that they had serious doubts about many aspects of the final report and tended to agree with my objections. However, I believe that for political reasons they were unwilling to go against Prebisch.

At the Panama City conference of the ECLA in May 1959, the U.S. representative, Harold M. Randall, expressed the position of the U.S. government in some detail with respect to the Mexico City Working Group report. Randall's statement, which was not published by the ECLA, may be summarized as follows:

1. The report fails to provide a definite schedule and timetable for creating a free trade area. It merely provides for an undetermined level of duty preferences at the end of ten years.

2. The system of duty reductions is based on lowering the overall average of duties rather than a step-by-step reduction of individual duties. Systems could be employed to maintain a high degree of protection for a number of commodities while simultaneously lowering the average by removing duties on other commodities.

Randall's findings were consistent with my own expressed at the Working Group meeting in Mexico.

The Montevideo Treaty

The Montevideo Treaty of February 18, 1960, established LAFTA with only six signatories—Argentina, Brazil, Chile, Paraguay, Peru, and Uruguay— later joined by Bolivia, Colombia, Ecuador, and Mexico. In some ways the treaty departed even further from a true FTA than the guidelines provided by the Working Group report. According to the treaty, the gradual elimination of duties and other barriers to intraregional trade would take place over twelve years. However, the reductions in duties were to be negotiated annually in accordance with the principle that each member is to obtain equivalent concessions or reciprocity in the form of reductions in trade barriers by the other members. Since equivalence in trade concessions was based on trade flows, each member would expect to increase its exports by an amount equivalent to the increase in its imports from reducing its restrictions. When this did not occur, the trade concessions would be renegotiated.

It is not surprising that little progress was made by the Latin American countries toward the goal of a free trade area under LAFTA. The insistence on "reciprocity" in lowering duties resulted in few cases of tariff and quota reductions. Only a few complementarity agreements were negotiated—which, incidentally, Prebisch believed to be an important means of combining increased trade with national economic controls.

In 1980 another agreement, the Latin American Integration Association (LAIA) treaty was negotiated by the same countries that were members of LAFTA. Much less ambitious, LAIA's purpose was simply described as the promotion and regulation of reciprocal trade, economic complementarity, and the promotion of economic cooperation, to contribute to market expansion. It was essentially a plan for creating an area for economic preferences composed of regional tariff preferences and bilateral trade agreements. Significant progress toward a regional free trade area was not made until the establishment of the "common market of the south" (MERCOSUR) involving Argentina, Brazil, Paraguay, and Uruguay in 1991.

In Retrospect

My experience working with Latin American groups emphasized that economic logic has little power to change policies that have strong political backing. Again, advice is accepted only after those who receive it come to believe that it was their own idea. This was certainly true in the case of Latin American trade policies, which in considerable measure were adopted in the 1990s along the lines that had been recommended in the 1960s.

Despite the controversies, the Latin American experience with trade issues was enjoyable and contributed to my teaching, writing, and future consulting. It afforded an opportunity to speak at Latin American universities and enabled me to serve my own university by attracting Latin American students and providing opportunities for University of Oregon faculty members to do research abroad. As to how much difference I made in Latin American economic history, I can only hope that some of my statements were remembered when those in power found it politically convenient to follow them.

Sources

The sources used in this chapter are mainly Mikesell (1962a) and publications of the U.S. Council of Economic Advisors (1962).

Raymond F. Mikesell

CHAPTER 9: THE ALLIANCE FOR PROGRESS

The Alliance for Progress became the symbol for U.S. and Latin American cooperation beginning in March 1961, following President John Kennedy's address to Congress on Latin American aid. In his address, Kennedy referred to the "Act of Bogota" (October 1960) as a "massive cooperative effort to strengthen democratic institutions through a program of economic development and social progress." The Act of Bogota was adopted by an OAS committee representing twenty-one Latin American countries as an agenda for improving living standards and social conditions. Topics covered included (1) agricultural productivity and rural improvement; (2) housing; (3) tax reform; (4) sources of external assistance; (5) promotion of trade within the Western Hemisphere; and (6) mobilization of internal, external, and private capital. No one could object to the broad recommendations, but as is often the case with political statements, specific measures for achieving them were lacking. The Bogota statement also recommended the creation of a special fund for social development to be administered by the Inter-American Development Bank (IADB), for which $500 million had been authorized but not appropriated by the U.S. Congress. In his March 1961 address, Kennedy called for an "Alliance for Progress" to achieve the objectives set forth in the Act of Bogota, and he asked the Congress to appropriate $500 million as a first step in U.S. cooperation.

Prior to the Kennedy address, I was working with a State Department Task Force on Latin America, which was engaged in preparing proposals for a program of hemispheric cooperation for realizing the economic and social objectives of the Act of Bogota. One of the questions I was asked to research was how much financial assistance would be available for Latin America from the resources normally provided by the World Bank, the U.S. Export-Import Bank, and the lending operations of the IADB over the next five years. I was also assigned to find out what additional financial resources would be required

from the U.S. government for financing all the Latin American development projects that were soundly conceived but unlikely to be funded by the World Bank or other sources. I came up with a total external financing requirement of $4 billion over the next five years, of which I estimated that $3.5 billion might come from other sources. My estimate of $500 million needed from the U.S. government was relayed to Richard J. Goodland, Kennedy's special economic assistant, and this amount was used in
Kennedy's address.

Prior to Kennedy's Alliance for Progress speech, I was invited to join a large intergovernmental meeting in the White House, where Kennedy and his aides outlined the principal elements of his speech. Although it was difficult to get the floor, I managed to say a few words about the inadequate Latin American Free Trade Association (LAFTA) plan for increasing intra-Latin American trade and suggested that a workable trading agreement be made a condition for our supporting the Alliance for Progress program. However, my suggestion did not make it into Kennedy's speech.

In my opinion, the Alliance for Progress lacked elements essential for success. It omitted both measurable goals and specific commitments by the Latin American countries. Its commitments were to broad principles rather than to specific actions. It emphasized sources of funds rather than governmental actions. Without specific actions, the goals could not be realized. It has required three decades for some of these countries to make significant progress in realizing the goals. Rapid progress required a substantial inflow of private capital along with public external capital, but the private capital inflow depended upon specific changes in laws and regulations on foreign investment conditions that were largely ignored in the Alliance for Progress program. For example, many Latin American countries barred foreign investment in mineral resources and in certain industries that would compete with domestic firms. Since it was generally agreed that expanding intra-Latin American trade was essential for regional economic growth, a free trade area agreement that went beyond the loose obligations of LAFTA should have been made a specific commitment by the Latin American countries.

Neither the Act of Bogota nor the Alliance for Progress program provided an organizational structure to coordinate the external sources of financial and technical assistance. The sources of assistance included the IADB, the World Bank, U.S. development aid, U.S. food aid under Public Law 480, and official European country aid. Unlike the Marshall Plan model, which included the Organization for Economic Cooperation and Development, no organization was responsible for monitoring or coordinating the various elements of the Alliance for Progress.

Those of us who worked in the OAS Secretariat were well aware of these deficiencies. We prepared memoranda calling for more effective programs, including the establishment of a multinational organization for reviewing country plans and programs, monitoring national policies, and coordinating the various sources of bilateral and multilateral assistance. But the representatives of the nations involved expressed little interest in creating a Latin American administrative structure which would undertake these responsibilities.

Work with Senator Wayne Morse

Senator Wayne Morse, former dean of the University of Oregon School of Law, chaired the Subcommittee on American Republics Affairs for the Senate Committee on Foreign Relations during much of the 1960s. I saw Morse frequently, both in Washington and in Eugene, and he and his wife were sometimes dinner guests in our home. I found Morse delightful as a person, but some of his political positions were derived more from prejudice and emotion than from facts and careful reasoning. In 1959 Morse asked me to serve as a consultant to his subcommittee.

With a deep interest in Latin American economic and political affairs, Morse attended a number of Latin American conferences, including the Bogota conference of 1960. I happened to be lecturing in Bogota at the time of the conference and attended as an unofficial observer. In his address to the Bogota conference, and in his report on the conference to the Senate Committee on Foreign Relations, Morse urged legal reform in Latin America, including the elimination of arbitrary expropriation of foreign or domestic investments.

Prior to the Bogota conference, I contributed to the preparation of several studies on Latin American economic problems for Morse's subcommittee. One, entitled *Problems of Latin American Economic Development*, was prepared under contract with the University of Oregon Institute of International Studies and Overseas Administration. As director of this institute, I wrote much of the study, with the participation of University of Oregon faculty members and graduate students. In the study we reviewed the weaknesses of the Latin American economies, including both low domestic investment and foreign direct investment, high rates of population growth, the failure to educate a substantial portion of the youth, the low level of intra-Latin American trade, high levels of inflation, and large balance-of-payments deficits. We pointed out the failure of financial policies in Latin American countries to achieve price stability, encourage savings, and channel governmental credit and foreign aid into the most productive sectors of the economy. We criticized Latin American trade and foreign exchange policies and the failure to promote domestic agriculture. We pointed out, too, that there were substantial sources of foreign public loans for Latin American nations from such institutions as the Export-Import Bank and the World Bank, but that the principal limit on lending was the lack of suitable loan projects and the low capacity of many Latin American countries to service additional foreign debt. Government controls impeded the direct foreign investment necessary to develop Latin America's rich natural resources, which could have provided the foreign exchange to service development loans.

The study suggested that entrepreneurship and technical and managerial skills were more critical and more scarce than financial capital in Latin America, and that efforts should be made to attract foreign investments by improving the legal and administrative climate for them. We criticized the international lending agencies for not providing more capital to the private sector, particularly to private agriculture and to small- and medium-sized industrial firms. The World Bank and other agencies made loans to the national development banks organized to provide loans to domestic firms, but these banks passed on a substantial portion of the loans to state-owned enterprises, which are notoriously inefficient.

Our basic recommendation on foreign aid was that "the United States, in cooperation with other industrial countries and with international agencies, should undertake to make available all the financial assistance that an individual Latin American country can productively employ in accordance with

Raymond F. Mikesell

reasonable standards of economic performance, until the country has achieved a satisfactory rate of growth on a self-sustaining basis. The application of this principle would, in effect, put much of the responsibility for determining the amount of external assistance to be provided on the country itself."

Such a recommendation did not correspond to the desires of the Latin American participants in the Bogota conference. Rather, they wanted more external assistance without conditions and argued that economic progress was a function of the amount of external assistance rather than the carrying out of governmental policies for promoting economic stability and freeing economies from governmental controls. With few exceptions, the adoption of the policy was delayed for more than three decades.

1962 Report for Wayne Morse

In addition to preparing studies published by the Subcommittee on American Republics Affairs, I frequently made confidential reports to Wayne Morse that were based on material acquired on my frequent visits to Latin America. These confidential reports contained information from U.S. Embassy and Agency for International Development (AID) officials, government officials of Latin American countries, Latin American businessmen, and university professors. A number of these people were personal friends, so I was able to obtain information and candid views not ordinarily available to those on short visits. During early 1962, I visited Argentina, Brazil, Chile, Ecuador, and Mexico, after which I gave a lengthy confidential report to Morse on economic conditions and the operations of U.S. aid missions in these countries. Portions of my study were later published under my name by the Senate Committee on Foreign Relations.

In my 1962 report for Morse, I pointed out that the past year had been marked by a slow rate of growth or virtual stagnation in the Latin American nations I visited. In addition, the region suffered from substantial inflation, a low rate of investment in the private sector, and a general lack of confidence that led to an alarming capital flight. For some countries, private capital flight well exceeded new private capital imports. I also pointed out that most of the countries had national economic plans, but they were little more than long-range targets for various sectors of the economy and little was being done to implement them. Political opposition forestalled legislation needed for carrying out economic and legal reforms. Since the plans' goals usually required changes in tax laws or land reform, politically powerful economic interests were usually able to defeat the required legislation.

I stated in my report to Morse that the U.S. foreign aid offices in our embassies were not equipped to carry out a development assistance program or to help the governments to create or improve their administrative machinery. Several AID mission directors told me they were simply not staffed to provide the technical and administrative personnel for appraising and monitoring projects that AID was requested to finance. AID funds were being employed largely to cover balance-of-payments deficits or for general budgetary support rather than for financing projects selected with a view to the investment priorities. I questioned whether we should continue to make balance-of-payments loans while permitting a continuation of the unsound economic and financial policies responsible for low exports, a high volume of imports of consumption goods, and large capital flight. I also criticized the IMF balance-of-payments loans for the same reasons. Despite being tied to agreements for eliminating fiscal deficits, the establishment of realistic exchange rates, and limitations on inflationary bank credit, the loan conditions were not being met.

The report concluded that U.S. aid programs generally did not give sufficient emphasis to directly supporting education and training. Latin America had a critical shortage of trained economists and public administrators. One area where I thought financial and technical assistance would make a difference was in promoting university contacts between Latin American universities and those of the U.S. and other Western countries. I found that Latin American universities were eager for such arrangements; in this way we could have an important influence on both Latin American governments and educators. I recommended that assistance to universities also take the form of programs for training Latin American university faculty members in the United States.

I reported that the U.S. AID mission in Chile had considerable difficulty in finding projects suitable for financing with funds appropriated by Congress in 1961 for reconstruction of the economy after an earthquake. Of the $100 million appropriated, only about a third had been turned over to the Chilean government. In the words of one AID official at the Chilean mission, "Funds are being turned over on the basis of just picking up projects here and there, which do not constitute new investment, e.g., paving streets and roads, and do not represent high priority projects in many cases, e.g, new airports." Knowledgeable officials in the U.S. mission stated that "much of our so-called project financing is little more than disguised balance of payments and budget support."

Several people in the AID missions had told me of their frustrations with the frequent diplomatic end-runs, in which high officials of the foreign governments had gone to Washington and obtained assistance or promises of assistance for their pet projects, at times without even consulting the AID mission chiefs. They said they could not administer U.S.-based development programs on the basis of short missions by high-ranking U.S. officials to Latin American countries.

I reported on the failure of LAFTA to achieve a reduction in barriers to intra-Latin American trade. I believed it was impossible to achieve development goals of individual countries in the absence of broad regional markets. Governments had been unwilling to adopt trade policies they believed would adversely affect special interests of particular industries that did not want foreign competition.

Finally, I observed that Latin American nations could not, over the long run, improve their structural balance-of-payments positions unless the rate of growth of exports kept up with the growth of import requirements and the increasing service payments on foreign loans. Export growth required a change in macroeconomic policies, such as monetary and credit restrictions, balanced budgets, increased foreign investment, and, in most cases, exchange rate depreciation.

Argentina is a case study of what bad government and political instability can do to a nation no matter how richly endowed it may be. An AID director in Argentina told me it was remarkable that a nation so rich in land and other resources, with a relatively well-trained and educated European-descended population, had made so little progress in recent years. He said that Argentina should have had a real per capita income approaching that of Western Europe by now. He had formulated concrete proposals for increasing Argentina's output of exports to Europe by at least 50 percent, but there was little he could do without the cooperation of the government. Meanwhile, the U.S. government had been providing enormous balance-of-payments assistance to cover capital flight, which had been reported at the annual level of $400 million.

The aid picture was similar in Colombia. Economic aid to Brazil had taken the form of balance-of-payments assistance, but the balance-of-payments outlook was more discouraging than ever. Few projects were sufficiently well formulated for the mission to act upon. A great deal of Brazilian capital had been wasted or misdirected to low-priority projects, such as urban construction and highways. Hundreds of millions of dollars were spent on highways in the vicinity of Brasilia to areas where there was little development.

In Ecuador I met with the head of the economics faculty at the University of Quito, and with the U.S. AID mission chief. The economics professor had prepared the government's development plan but complained that the country lacked experts to formulate specific projects. He asked the AID chief about the possibility of contracts with consulting firms or with American universities to supply the necessary personnel. I was impressed with the AID official's grasp of the development problems Ecuador was facing. As in the case of other mission chiefs, he was frustrated at being asked to do a capital financing job without trained, capable personnel in the mission. He expressed concern regarding the lack of guidance from Washington, D.C. When he invited me to give a talk at his staff meeting, I outlined the problems faced in the missions of other Latin American countries that were, in general, similar to his. The last time I visited Ecuador, in 1995, political problems still prevented adoption and implementation of policies that would promote sustained growth.

During a stopover in Mexico, I was given an excellent briefing by an old friend, Gary Smith, who was the economic counselor to the embassy. In contrast to most other major countries in Latin America, Mexico presented a picture of relative economic and political stability. Yet there was virtually no per capita growth in 1961, and the private sector in particular was lagging. Capital flight, at least $150 million in 1961, was covered in part by a $45 million general-purpose loan from the Export-Import Bank, by drawing on the IMF, and by private credits. I believed that the exchange rate was overvalued and the widespread belief that the peso would be devalued encouraged the capital flight. This sounds like a forerunner of the 1994 Mexican crisis—also brought on by capital flight.

Wayne Morse's Disillusionment with Foreign Aid

In my report to Morse, I outlined the basic economic problems of Latin America as I saw them: inflation, capital flight, regressive and inefficient tax administration, education programs that failed to reach the bulk of the population, and deplorable poverty. Despite these findings, I did not want to give the impression that the alliance was a failure, and I pointed to hopeful signs. I suggested that Latin America's progress would not depend upon the number of dollars supplied but upon institutional change and structural reforms that could only take place through democratic processes when people demanded them. In particular, I stressed the desirability of promoting education. I stated that the fundamental problem in Latin America was the mobilization of human, material, and financial resources for economic and social progress. U.S. money alone could not ensure development and political stability in Latin America or anywhere else in the developing world. This meant giving greater attention to the staffing of our missions, to coordinating various sources of external assistance, and to mobilizing nongovernmental sources of personnel, including people from foreign universities, labor unions, and private business. The more I study economic development, the more I am convinced that it is basically a process of changing the hearts, minds, and capacities of the people. This job cannot be done simply by writing checks.

Although my oral and written reports to Morse were positive regarding what external aid might be able to accomplish if properly managed, I believe he was more impressed with the failure of Latin American governments to adopt correct policies and with my criticisms of the aid missions. These criticisms, plus Morse's distaste for the use of aid as a tool for fighting the Cold War and his strong objection to U.S. involvement in Vietnam, led him to become a critic of *all* U.S. foreign aid. He came to the conclusion that U.S. aid programs largely supported political objectives rather than economic development. In my talks with Morse in the late 1960s and early 1970s, I tried to dissuade him from what I saw as an overgeneralized negativity toward all development assistance. His position distressed me very much, and thereafter he ceased to call on me as a consultant.

The Organization of American States

In the early 1970s, the Organization of American States (OAS) made an effort to induce the Latin American governments to adopt policies and programs in support of the objectives of the Alliance for Progress. It appointed a group of leading Latin American economists, including Rolf Luders, Jorge Marshall, Raul Saez, and Roberto Campos (the group known as the "Nine Wisemen"), to make recommendations on a number of economic policy issues. Some of these people, including Campos (Brazil), and Saez and Luders (Chile), later became heads of ministries in their countries. As a consultant to the OAS, I was assigned to work with this group, mainly on the development of Latin American capital markets.

Capital markets are very important for developing countries because saving and productive investment are major conditions for growth, and high rates of growth can only be achieved by high rates of saving and productive investment. Capital markets should channel savings into the kinds of investments that promote growth. The capital market includes not only markets for stocks and bonds but all the avenues by which saving is channeled into investment, including savers who invest directly in their own businesses. The amount of saving and the opportunities for profitable investment are closely related, and there is a need to increase savings in all developing countries.

Under a 1969 contract with OAS, I prepared a study of savings in Latin America, with the assistance of Professor James E. Zinser of Oberlin College. Our major policy conclusions concerned the role of government policy in encouraging or discouraging savings. Inflation in Latin America has tended to reduce real savings since most saving is done in banks and savings institutions that pay rates of interest that often do not rise with inflation; thus the savers receive zero or negative rates of interest. This rules out for such savers the important role of allowing compound interest to add to their savings. Savings by urban firms and wealthy landowners are promoted by a desire to make new investments in business, and government controls that dampen the incentive to invest reduce their incentive to save. The absence of institutions in which savers can invest in the stocks of domestic companies or buy privately issued bonds at rates of interest higher than rates paid on government bonds or on savings deposits also reduces both savings and investments. The absence of domestic savings outlets paying reasonable real rates of return leads higher income residents to channel their savings abroad. Another major cause of low savings is fiscal deficits, which constitute net dissaving by the government and thereby offset private savings.

Assessment

Latin America is rich in natural resources, including arable land. Although some countries have large populations of indigenous people, in countries such as Argentina and Costa Rica, descendants of European immigrants constitute the vast majority. Per capita gross domestic product (GDP) in Latin America averages less than one-fourth that of the United States, and in some countries it is less than 15 percent of U.S. per capita GDP. Social conditions are even more backward, and there is great inequality of income and lack of opportunity for the poor. Yet Latin America has made considerable progress since the early 1980s. There has been substantial trade liberalization, and some of the regional trading arrangements appear to be working. Foreign exchange and capital markets have been liberalized substantially, and the movement toward privatization of industries, including utilities and natural resource industries, has gained momentum. Latin American countries still have economic problems, but a number of them now appear to be on the road to sustained economic development. Chile, which stagnated for decades despite its rich natural resource heritage, has become a model for economic and social development for all developing countries. The Chilean universities whose faculties have studied abroad are no longer champions of governmental planning, ownership, and control; their students have been exposed to the economic advantages of competition, private ownership, and free markets. Businessmen who come in contact with foreign investors and who have participated in conferences in Latin America and abroad have learned that economic freedom enhances their wealth more than dependence on government to protect them from competition.

I am among hundreds of economists who have carried this message in various ways during the postwar period. We have helped lay the foundation for changing the views of governmental, business, and educational leaders. What Latin American countries need most now is social reform, which should include more equitable income distribution, rural development, and universal opportunities for education and training. Progress has been slow in this area and will depend heavily on the democratization of the political process. It will also depend upon priorities of international institutions, such as the IMF and the World Bank, and upon foreign aid administrators for providing assistance that emphasizes social reform, governmental responsibility, and the concept that development is not measured simply by the rate of growth in GNP but by the degree to which all members of society share in its benefit.

Sources

Information for this chapter was taken from Mikesell (1962a).

Raymond F. Mikesell

CHAPTER 10: AT THE WHITE HOUSE

In the early 1950s, I was an economic adviser to three presidential committees: the Gordon Gray Committee of 1950; the President's Materials Policy Commission (Paley Commission), appointed in 1951; and the Randall Commission on Foreign Economic Policy, appointed in 1953. I was able to work with these committees while teaching at the University of Virginia by spending two days a week in Washington, D.C., during the school year and full time during summers and school vacations. My office and most of the meetings of the committees were in the Executive Office of the President. Occasionally there was a meeting at the White House when cabinet members and the vice president attended. My committee work was followed by an appointment in 1955 as a senior economist on the President's Council of Economic Advisors, chaired by Arthur Burns.

The presidential commissions with which I worked played a significant role in the formulation of U.S. postwar foreign economic policies. Although we tend to take most of these policies for granted today, they were quite controversial in the 1950s. The reports of the Gray Committee and the Randall Commission have been largely forgotten, but the report of the Paley Commission is frequently cited.

The Gordon Gray Committee
Immediately following World War II, several U.S. programs were designed to aid the reconstruction of individual European nations. Experts soon realized that a unified economic assistance program, closely integrated with an organization to coordinate individual national programs and promote intra-European trade, was needed. This was the major theme of then Secretary of State George Marshall's famous Harvard speech of June 1947, the principles of which were embodied in the Economic Cooperation Act of 1948, called the Marshall Plan. A convention in April 1948 established the Organization

for Economic Cooperation and Development (OECD), whose immediate tasks were to prepare a joint recovery program for Europe and to develop an intra-European trade system. The Soviet Union was invited to participate in the Marshall Plan and the OECD but declined, and none of the East European satellites controlled by Russia joined. Although European production rose rapidly after the war and the European Payments Union (EPU) facilitated the expansion of intra-European trade, European countries were slow to restore their markets where payments were made in dollars in order to meet their demand for imports requiring dollars. This came to be called the "dollar shortage," which suggested that world recovery depended upon an increase in U.S. dollar payments to the rest of the world through both aid and trade.

Although the Marshall Plan had barely started, both the Truman administration and Congress were dissatisfied with the progress of European economic recovery. Their concern was not simply with the welfare of the people of Western Europe. The onset of the Cold War with the Soviet Union gave urgency to the promotion of a European economy that would enable our allies to build their military strength for resisting invasion and create economic conditions that would eliminate or weaken internal Communist forces. In April 1950 President Truman appointed Gordon Gray, former secretary of the army, to undertake a study of U.S. foreign economic policies with special reference to European recovery. Gray appointed Edward S. Mason, professor of economics at Harvard University, as his deputy and a small group of economists—including Kermit Gordon, Griffith Johnson, Walter Salant, Philip Trezise, and me—as his staff. I had not known Gray previously; Ed Mason, whom I had known for several years, was responsible for my appointment to the staff. Although Gray was not an economist, he knew a great deal about military aid—an important issue since the European recovery plan was integrated with the creation of the North Atlantic Treaty Organization (NATO). I spent the summer of 1950 and part time in the fall working on the Gray report, which was submitted to the president on November 10, 1950.

In 1949 the United States had a surplus on current account with every major area in the world and an overall surplus of $6.2 billion, an amount approximately equal to U.S. government loans and grants plus disbursements by the IMF and the World Bank. Of major concern was what would happen

Raymond F. Mikesell

to the world economy if this large supply of loan and grant dollars were sharply cut. Both the U.S. Congress and the Truman administration wanted foreign countries to become less dependent on U.S. aid, and this could only be achieved by expanded foreign production. Rejecting the idea that the world's major problem was a shortage of dollars, the staff approached economic recovery in terms of how the European nations could meet their import requirements by producing more. There was no shortage of world demand or surplus of world producing capacities. We believed that if countries maintained open markets and the correct macroeconomic policies, they could produce and export enough to meet their domestic requirements for economic growth. We also believed that the exchange rates of most developing countries were overvalued and should be adjusted so that producers would have an incentive to produce and export in accordance with their comparative advantage.

When information on the U.S. balance of payments became available after the Gray Committee was organized, it was found that the U.S. surplus on current account had declined from $6.2 billion in 1949 to an annual rate of only $2.9 billion in the first six months of 1950, and that foreign countries had accumulated over a billion dollars in gold and dollar assets. By the third quarter of 1950, the U.S. current account surplus had almost disappeared. During a meeting in the fall of 1950, we reviewed the current trade and balance-of-payments statistics and decided that the world's supply of dollars had dramatically increased. Some of us asked whether any special study and report was necessary, since the principal problem that led to the appointment of the Gray Committee seemed to have disappeared. No radical change in current U.S. foreign economic policy appeared to be needed to achieve our economic objectives for Europe.

The Gray report stressed the importance of freeing markets and trade, including the operation of the EPU, which had just been inaugurated. We believed, however, that U.S. economic aid to Europe should continue for another three or four years, and that the NATO countries should receive substantial military assistance for defense against any possible Soviet attack. We also recommended a centralized economic and military assistance program in close cooperation with the OECD.

There really was not much new in our recommendations. Reports by the International Development Advisory Board and by the Brookings Institution that came out about the same time as the Gray report reached more or less the same conclusions. European recovery proceeded more rapidly than most of us expected. The German economy rose to be the dominant European economy, but it was well integrated with the rest of Western Europe. Fears expressed by Treasury officials, White, and Morgenthau that Germany would be preparing for World War III soon faded with the emergence of a democratic West Germany.

The Paley Commission

Prior to World War II, the U.S. was nearly self-sufficient in energy and in a number of minerals such as copper, but our dependence on foreign supplies was increasing rapidly. During the war there was relatively little exploration and investment for expanding supplies of natural resources. Immediately following World War II, world demand for natural resources, especially energy and nonfuel minerals, increased enormously. There was concern that world supplies would not expand in line with world demand, and that supplies of some vital resources such as petroleum might, for political reasons, be denied to the U.S. This insecurity was enhanced by the Cold War success of the Soviet Union in promoting Communism in a number of developing countries that exported minerals needed by the U.S. and Western Europe. Projections were made of the demand for raw materials by the year 1980 based on the rates of growth in their consumption between 1900 and 1950. These projections showed that U.S. demand for petroleum and certain minerals, such as aluminum, would increase more than 100 percent between 1950 and 1980, Free World demand for petroleum would increase by 275 percent, and demand for aluminum (based on bauxite) would balloon by 415 percent. Projected demand for minerals by 1980 far outstripped supply. As it turned out, these projections proved to be wide of the mark because they did not take into account the effects of technological developments that increase potential supplies by making it possible to mine lower ore grades or obtain larger amounts of petroleum from oil fields, and by the substitution of more abundant resources for those that are less abundant.

In response to the growing national concern over the availability of natural resource products, in January 1951 President Harry Truman established the Materials Policy Commission to prepare a report on U.S. and world natural resources and make recommendations for U.S. government resource policies. Truman asked William S. Paley (chair of Columbia Broadcasting) to chair the commission. He was joined by four other members: George R. Brown, Arthur H. Bunker, Eric Hodgkins, and Edward S. Mason—the only economist on the commission. None of the commissioners had an outstanding reputation in the field of natural resources. Although not a resource economist, Mason knew a good deal about the subject and was well acquainted with leading specialists in natural resources. He provided a link between the commission and the first-rate economists who were appointed to the staff. The director of the executive staff, Philip H. Coombs, did an excellent job of mobilizing a number of full- and part-time specialists, including outstanding natural resource people such as Harold Barnett, Orris C. Herfindahl, Eugene E. Oakes, Sam Schurr, Sidney S. Alexander, Raymond W. Lusher, and Arnold C. Harberger. Altogether there were nearly 100 professionals on the staff, which I think was far too many people to prepare a report in a few month's time.

Due mainly to my friend, Ed Mason, with whom I had served on other governmental assignments, I was appointed director of foreign resources and given a professional staff of about ten people. My team was responsible for projecting foreign supplies of mineral and energy resources and for recommending U.S. policies that would promote world supplies. I was glad for the opportunity but had never before been asked to direct a staff of this kind. All I could think of was how to do the job myself rather than assigning portions to several people and waiting for their reports before putting all the pieces together. Moreover, most of my professional staff members were only part time, and I feared that I would not have a full report by the deadline. Not everyone on my staff was a specialist in natural resources. For example, Kingman Brewster was a law professor who later became president of Yale University, and Herbert Feis was a political specialist in the State Department.

At the first staff meeting, I passed out an agenda for our work. Instead of assigning specific tasks to each member, I told them to select the topics they wanted to work on and send me a note on what they planned to do. I was consumed by the responsibility of completing a report by the deadline three months hence, and I felt that unless I prepared the report myself it would not be ready. I said to my staff, "I'll make a bargain with you. If you don't bother me for the next month or so, I won't interfere with anything you are doing." In two months I had ready the basic report, which was later enriched by the material produced by my staff.

Because I was teaching in Virginia, I could only devote myself full time to the commission in the summer of 1951. When school began in October 1951, I turned the responsibility for directing the resources work over to Isaiah Frank, whom I had known for several years. Frank was also an academic but was free to work full time in the fall of 1951 and spring of 1952. We collaborated on most of our reports to the commission.

The duties of the commission as outlined in Truman's letter of January 22, 1951, were quite broad. An important objective was to determine U.S. needs for military security, civilian welfare, and continued economic growth. However, the commission wanted to consider the outlook for world demand and supplies over the long run—at least through the twentieth century—not simply for the next decade or so. Although we did undertake some long-run projections, we were not equipped nor did we have time to do so. We mainly summarized and evaluated projections made by others. I had little confidence in long-range projections because we simply could not forecast changes in technology, often induced by increases in prices for minerals, which would affect future long-run demand and supply. I regarded my group's contribution as the formulation of governmental policies to promote, if not actually ensure, the availability of world supplies for meeting world requirements. This meant reviewing existing government policies and recommending changes we regarded as important for realizing the objectives.

The range of natural resources considered by the commission and staff was not confined to energy and hard minerals. It included timber and agricultural resources, water, and power. We took into account the raw material requirements for our defense industries and those of our NATO allies, and we allowed for the possibility that the Soviet Union would gain control of natural resources in some developing countries.

U.S. foreign resource issues included foreign aid for promoting resource development; policies that affect private investment in resources, such as taxation and the negotiation of investment treaties; and international trade policies that would be conducive to expanding world trade and investment in resources. For example, to what extent should the United States seek to be self-sufficient in petroleum or certain other minerals, in contrast to increasing its dependence on foreign resources by reducing its trade barriers? Many in Congress favored policies designed to make the United States self-sufficient in petroleum, copper, lead, zinc, and other minerals by restricting imports. In most cases, such policies reflected the desire by individual congressmen to promote mineral production in their own states. Such policies, of course, are costly for American consumers and taxpayers, and American self-sufficiency could not be maintained in the long run. We examined the desirability and feasibility of accumulating stockpiles of commodities that might be in short supply in the future. By and large, our studies and recommendations favored free world trade and the uninhibited flow of investment as providing the best insurance that the growth of supplies would keep up with world demand.

The final report of the President's Materials Policy Commission, *Resources for Freedom*, was published in June 1952. It constituted the most comprehensive analysis of U.S. and world natural resources that had ever been published. Its approach was dynamic in the sense that it recognized the role of technological advances in both world demand and supply, and it avoided conclusions based on projections that assumed a static world economy. The report contrasted sharply with the narrow national industry-oriented policies that many congressmen advocated in the interest of their constituents, and it was consistent with the free trade and open-economics policies represented by the Bretton Woods Agreements and the GATT. For example, the report rejected a policy of U.S. self-sufficiency in petroleum. The reason was that even if the government could stimulate a substantial increase in output, it would hasten the time when the U.S. would become much more dependent on foreign petroleum sources as reserves were depleted. Security was improved by keeping more of our petroleum in the ground rather than subsidizing high-cost production in the short run.

The high quality of the report reflected the quality and objectives of the staff. A report by the same group of commissioners, supported by a typical congressional committee made up of people with close ties to special interests, would have been quite different. The report stimulated research on natural resources by private organizations and by international agencies such as the OECD. Some of the economists associated with the preparation of the report subsequently joined together to obtain a grant from the Ford Foundation for the establishment of Resources for the Future (RFF), which has become the world's leading research institution on natural resources and the environment. My own research activities were substantially influenced by RFF, which partially financed and published four of my books on minerals. These studies established my reputation as a mineral economist and created a demand for my consulting services.

The Randall Commission

While serving on the faculty of the National War College in October 1953, I received a call from Alfred I. Neal, director of research for the President's Commission on Foreign Economic Policy, asking if I would be interested in working part time with the commission staff. Since my academic duties were almost entirely confined to the mornings (in the afternoons I was expected to sit through boring lectures, primarily by U.S. government officials, including several cabinet members), I said I would like to work with the staff in the afternoons, provided the commandant of the National War College gave his permission. Neal asked a presidential assistant to call the commandant, and I was free the following day to work as a consultant to the White House staff. As it turned out, I not only worked in the afternoons but frequently at night as well. One commission member, John Hay "Jock" Whitney, frequently invited two or three of us for dinner in his hotel suite, where we worked until 10 p.m. or 11 p.m. I was acquainted with about half

Raymond F. Mikesell

of the commission staff members, and several had national or international reputations as economists. They included Raymond Vernon, a Harvard professor of economics and a leading analyst on trade policy; the Brookings Institution's W. Adams Brown, who wrote a monumental history on U.S. foreign economic policy; and Arthur I. Bloomfield of the Federal Reserve Board. I was also well acquainted with Emilio D. "Pete" Collado. He had left the World Bank to become treasurer of Exxon Corporation but devoted some of his time to the commission.

Eisenhower appointed the commission in the spring of 1953. Clarence B. Randall, head of Inland Steel Company, was chair, and Lemar Fleming of Houston, Texas, was vice chair. Other presidential appointees included David J. MacDonald, a labor leader; Cola G. Parker; Jesse W. Tapp; Jock Whitney; and John H. Williams, an economics professor at Harvard and adviser to the Federal Reserve Bank of New York. A leading opponent of the Bretton Woods Agreements, Williams was one of the most conservative economists in the country. Despite the fact that he was the only economist on the commission, he rarely attended meetings and had relatively little influence. Jock Whitney was one of the most active members and worked more closely with the staff than any other commissioner. Whitney was a New York financier who was famous for falling off horses and had an undeserved reputation as an idle playboy. He later became U.S. ambassador to Britain. Also listed as members of the commission were several senators and congressmen, but I do not recall their being present at the working sessions.

Why did President Eisenhower appoint yet another commission on foreign economic policy? The Republican administration inherited from the Roosevelt and Truman administrations a large and complex set of national and international institutions, programs, and policies that had not existed at the time of the last Republican administration under Herbert Hoover. Many of these programs were subjected to substantial criticisms by Republicans, who maintained that foreign aid was a waste of money and involvement in international organizations compromised U.S. sovereignty. Eisenhower himself supported the Marshall Plan and international economic cooperation, and he had substantial experience with foreign policy—more than any member of his commission. Eisenhower wanted a Republican-dominated group to review U.S. foreign economic policy, with the expectation that their report would not depart substantially from existing policy. Thanks in considerable measure to the staff, Eisenhower got what he wanted!

The staff consisted mainly of internationally minded economists, some of whom had considerable experience in foreign affairs. The staff did a first-rate job of reviewing the major issues in U.S. foreign economic policy: foreign aid; foreign investment; international trade; international commodity agreements; and U.S. obligations as a member of the IMF, the World Bank, the GATT, the OECD, and a variety of United Nations agencies. Memoranda prepared by the staff reviewed criticisms of U.S. policies and outlined issues on which the commission should make recommendations. Papers prepared for the commissioners did not put forth direct recommendations on the issues, but our analysis provided strong arguments for continuing the major policies and institutions inherited from the Roosevelt and Truman administrations. We also drafted the commission's report and defended the positions we had taken. Although the commission listened to criticisms of current U.S. government policies by Congress and spokesmen for a variety of private interests, the recommendations made in its report published in February 1954 were generally in line with existing policies, programs, and institutions.

The first section of the commission's report dealt with the postwar dollar problem. The staff seemed more willing to accept the existence of a dollar problem than was the Gordon Committee in 1950. In essence, the report defined the dollar problem as an inadequate world supply of dollars for meeting the transaction and reserve requirements of a world payments system in which all major currencies were convertible into dollars. Some of us doubted the theoretical basis for this position, but it was useful in convincing noneconomists to support liberal U.S. trade policies and continuation of foreign aid. The final report recommended the steps—consistent with U.S. political, economic, and security interests—the country should take toward solving the world's dollar problem.

It suggested that a drastic reduction in U.S. foreign assistance in the short run would exacerbate the dollar problem and impair Western European recovery and defense programs, and it recommended a continuation of existing U.S. grant and loan programs. Regarding foreign private investment, the commission favored government action to encourage private investment abroad; negotiating investment treaties to establish fair treatment of foreign investment; reducing the corporate tax rate by at least 14 percentage points on income from investment abroad; and removing certain restrictive tax provisions affecting foreign investment. It favored establishment of a program of government guarantees against expropriation or inconvertibility. U.S. foreign investment was a controversial subject in the United States, both then and now. Labor wanted to discourage foreign investment that might reduce American jobs, while most international economists believed that foreign investment was likely to create more jobs in the U.S. than it would displace. Much of my work with the commission, in collaboration with Pete Collado, had to do with supporting the case for encouraging foreign investment.

The commission opposed the use of international buffer stocks to stabilize world prices of raw materials and foodstuffs. It believed that prices should be determined in free competitive world markets. The report opposed U.S. import restrictions to promote national self-sufficiency in raw materials on security grounds. The report favored military stockpiles, the cost of which should be borne by the defense budget. It favored negotiations through the GATT for reducing tariffs and other trade restrictions. Although it rejected labor's arguments for import restrictions to save American jobs, it did adopt MacDonald's amendment that "no tariff concessions should be granted on products made by workers receiving wages which are substandard in the exporting country."

The commission's report was what might be expected from conservative businessmen who favored free international trade and capital movements and international economic cooperation. It tended to justify a number of economic policies from a business standpoint rather than from the point of view of American consumers and wage earners, and it failed to show the relationship between U.S. economic policy and American foreign policy. Gardner Patterson, director of the International Finance Section at Princeton University, organized a conference attended by about twenty leading economists to review the Randall Commission report. The conference was critical of the commission's report, more because of what it did not say than what it did.

Some commission members expressed reservations on a number of the recommendations in the majority report. As might be expected, MacDonald had reservations on the tax and other measures to stimulate private foreign investment; in a lengthy statement, he advocated assisting industries whose workers were adversely affected by increased imports resulting from tariff reductions. Others objected to the commission's recommendation on U.S. agricultural trade policy favoring the removal of restrictions on world trade in agricultural products. The staff pointed out that existing agricultural price support programs, which held domestic prices above world prices by means of import controls, restricted U.S. foreign markets and were ultimately harmful to American agriculture.

Some of the congressmen associated with the commission seriously criticized the report. The most comprehensive criticism was made by Senator Eugene D. Millikin, a Republican from Iowa, who objected to U.S. government promotion of foreign investment and to the recommendation giving the president authority to reduce tariff rates by 50 percent *ad valorem.* Congressmen Daniel L. Reed and Richard M. Simpson issued a minority report separate from the commission's. However, the minority report mostly agreed with the recommendations of the majority.

I enjoyed my experience with the Randall Commission and benefitted from the contacts made, perhaps more than from what I actually learned. It was a welcome escape from the National War College, which presented nothing more challenging than an occasional lecture and service as chair of the seminar on foreign economic policy. However, I was impressed with the knowledge and enthusiasm of the military officers, who were much less conservative than I had imagined. A favorite topic was U.S. relations with China, with which we did not have diplomatic contact or formal diplomatic relations until Nixon's famous trip. My seminar group took a vote on whether the United States should recognize the Communist government of China and establish diplomatic and economic relations with the country. To my surprise, the group voted heavily in favor of such actions; the Republican administration and most congressmen were solidly in favor of isolating China as much as possible.

An Incident Involving Vice President Nixon

As a historical footnote, I will relate an incident that occurred when I was serving with the Randall Commission. One evening Jock Whitney asked me why Nixon did not like me and considered me a threat to the administration. I told Whitney that I had never met Nixon personally, but that I had long been critical of him because of the things he did in the senatorial election against Helen Gahagan Douglas, whom I had met several times in Oregon and abroad. Whitney explained that Randall had received a call from one of the vice president's assistants asking that I be removed from the White House staff as soon as possible. The only reason given was that I was *persona non grata* to the vice president of the United States. Randall took the matter to Eisenhower, who told Randall to ignore it. Actually, there were many occasions when Nixon had sought to interfere with activities in the president's office and was rebuffed by Eisenhower. I asked Whitney if he could find out what Nixon had against me. I told him about the action taken earlier by Harold Stassen and suggested that perhaps Nixon had seen the list of alleged Communists prepared by Stassen. Whitney met Nixon at a White House party a few days later and reported to me that he asked Nixon point blank, "What do you have against Ray Mikesell?" Nixon looked him straight in the eye and responded without a sign of reflection, "I never heard of Ray Mikesell." Nixon indicated he did not want to discuss the matter. I was treated extremely well by the members of the commission and by the White House staff, all of whom were aware of Nixon's attitude.

The Council of Economic Advisors

In the spring of 1954, Arthur Burns asked me to become a senior economist with the President's Council of Economic Advisors (CEA) with primary responsibility for international economic activities and policies. I was able to obtain a leave of absence from Virginia during the fall quarter of 1954, but I told Burns I would have to be part time the following year until summer, when I could again work full time. I worked with the CEA until August 1957, when I left to teach at the University of Oregon. Other members of the CEA were Joseph S. Davis and Raymond J. Saulnier; the latter became chair in December 1956 when Burns resigned to chair the Federal Reserve Board.

My relations with all three council members were excellent, and I was very impressed with the staff, some of whom were later appointed to the council. For most of the year, the council was a pleasant and relaxing place to work because ordinarily we were not subject to short-term deadlines. I kept the council informed on developments in foreign trade, the balance of payments, and foreign investment—largely based on statistics generated by the Department of Commerce and other agencies—and prepared analyses of the activities of the U.S. and international agencies having to do with international economics. Burns met periodically with the president; he was also on a cabinet-level economic committee, whose meetings were attended by the vice president as well as the Treasury, State, and Commerce secretaries. Occasionally, I was invited to accompany one of the CEA members to the cabinet-level meetings in the White House. I worked more with Davis, who had a special interest in foreign economic activities, than with other council members. The weekly meetings of the entire council and professional staff were very informal, and everyone was free to bring up any matter he wished. I recall that the most junior member of the professional staff, Charles L. Schultze (who became chair of the CEA in January, 1977), frequently took issue with Burns on some question; Burns was sufficiently flexible to occasionally agree with Charlie.

Burns, who had come from the National Bureau of Economic Research to the CEA in March 1953, was a good person to work under. He precisely outlined the duties of the staff and was a good listener who always pressed you for details. He insisted on having all the factual information relating to a subject before reaching a conclusion. He kept up-to-date on all statistics being prepared on the U.S. economy. Charlie Schultze usually came to Burns's office late Friday afternoon carrying a stack of new statistical material, which Burns would review at home over the weekend. Eisenhower had full confidence in Burns, and I cannot remember any instance in which the president did not accept Burns's advice.

When I joined the CEA staff, several staff members were outstanding scholars with whom I was very proud to be associated. These included Alfred E. Kahn (later U.S. Wage and Price Commission director), and George P. Shultz (later secretary of state). Several of the people with the council attended my wedding in Washington, D.C., in February 1956, and I still cherish their gifts; a small letter holder given to us by George Shultz and his wife still sits on my desk.

No outstanding controversial issues on foreign economic policy arose during my tenure with the CEA. The Eisenhower administration maintained a liberal trade policy and supported the foreign assistance programs that had been established by the Roosevelt and Truman administrations. The council favored extending the Trade Agreements Act and increasing the authority of the president to reduce tariffs.

Personal Matters

My new wife, Irene, and I became acquainted at the Atlantic City conference in 1944. At the time we met, she worked on trade policy in the State Department. In 1946 she attended the Paris Peace Conference and in 1948 participated in the London conference that established the GATT. Just before our wedding, she was an executive assistant to the director of the Office of Economics in the Federal Trade Commission. After moving to Eugene, she was so busy looking after my twin sons from a former marriage, George and Norman, and editing my writings that she had neither time for nor interest in a job outside the home. We had a wonderful life and she accompanied me on nearly all my long foreign trips. She died at our home in Eugene in 1996. I married my present wife, Grace, a year later.

My work on the presidential commissions and with the CEA during the 1950s gave me intimate knowledge of U.S. international economic policies. It also prepared me for the foreign missions and international conferences in which I participated in the negotiation of foreign policy issues during the next thirty years. Knowledge of the formulation of policies contributed significantly to the process of implementing them. Working one or two days a week in Washington, D.C., plus most of my summers and vacation periods, took time from teaching, but I do not believe I neglected my graduate students. The Economics Department at Virginia was very liberal in allowing me to be away and take occasional leaves; in fact, it encouraged my consulting work. The president of the university, Colgate Darden, sometimes chided me for being away so much, but since he used my external activities in his annual report to show that his faculty was active in national and world affairs, I did not concern myself with his casual criticisms. In my eleven years in Charlottesville, 1946–57, I published several books and a number of journal articles as well as giving papers at academic conferences. Thus I was able to utilize the information from my consulting to promote my professional reputation. I shared my external activities with my Ph.D. students by providing them with research topics and jointly authored with them several publications based on their dissertations. Because of my governmental contacts, I was able to help many of them obtain jobs when they graduated.

Sources

The primary sources for this chapter are my own memoranda and reports of the commissions (*President's Materials Policy Commission.*, 1952; Commission on Foreign Economic Policy, 1954).

CHAPTER 11: ADVENTURES IN FOREIGN MINING

My work with mining companies not only provided knowledge of the industry and experience in negotiating mining contracts but took me to fascinating areas of the world. I visited mines in the Amazon jungle, took helicopter rides through narrow canyons in the Andes, visited native communities in Papua New Guinea, snorkeled in the Coral Sea off the coast of Bougainville, trekked through wildlife parks in Africa, and—more exciting than I wanted—experienced the chaos in Iran shortly before U.S. embassy personnel in Tehran were taken hostage.

My consulting work with mining companies started in 1959 through a friendship with Myron (Bernie) Bernstein, a geologist living in Eugene, Oregon, who worked for St. Joe Minerals Corporation. Shortly after we met, he became the company's international exploration manager. I accompanied him on trips to prospective mineral areas in foreign countries and later he sent me on missions to mining areas in four continents.

Latin American Mining Company Missions

In the summer of 1975, a geologist working with Bernstein found what he believed to be an exciting copper-gold prospect in Chile. Bernstein asked me to go with him to Santiago to help appraise the project and begin negotiation on a contract with the Chilean government. When we arrived in Santiago, I studied the latest data from the field and estimated that the gold content of the ore alone would produce a highly profitable mine, provided the reserves were large enough. The deposit had been found by a geologist, Dave Thompson, during a visit to an assay office in a small coastal town where he learned that a man living in a remote area of the Andes had been bringing down very rich ore on donkeys. Thompson contacted the family that was extracting the ore to get an idea of the size of the area where the ore was located, but he did not do any prospecting. Minimal prospecting of the area, which was called El Indio, revealed the likelihood of substantial reserves.

While in Santiago on this trip, I did some preliminary work on the El Indio mining contract, which by law had to be negotiated with the government before a foreign company could engage in exploration and mine development. The Pinochet government, which had recently come to power, had not negotiated any mining contracts; the Allende government that preceded it had a policy against foreign investment in the resource industries. I knew my way around Santiago since I had been there several times previously, including three occasions during the Social Democratic regime and one when Allende was in power. Pinochet had put some of the university professors with degrees from U.S. universities in his ministries. I knew some of them and learned a good deal about the government's foreign investment policies. However, it took another year and two additional trips to Santiago before we negotiated an agreement for the El Indio mine. El Indio proved to be one of the most profitable mines St. Joe Minerals had ever discovered and it is still operating.

Over the next twelve years, Bernstein sent me on several trips for St. Joe Minerals to West Germany, Norway, South Africa, Egypt, and Iran. In addition, I visited several other Latin American countries for St. Joe: Argentina, Peru, Uruguay, and Brazil. Most of these visits were to research the mining laws and interview government officials in the geologic and mining departments to determine the nature of the contracts that could be negotiated.

Cairo and Tehran

During the spring and summer of 1980, St. Joe geologists found interesting mineral prospects in Egypt, but they needed to know the conditions under which exploration and mining contracts could be negotiated there since no foreign mining investment had been made recently. The Egyptian government was moving toward more liberal economic policies, but there were disputes within the government over foreign investment policy. Since I had been in Egypt during World War II and several times after that, I was asked to spend a week or ten days in Cairo on behalf of St. Joe. I thought the assignment would be interesting, despite the fact that I always felt depressed in Cairo because of the poverty, dirt, and occasional threatening mobs in the streets.

Although I had the names of several government officials, I learned that the person in charge of all exploration was the head of the government's geologic department. I spent many hours in his office, which was hot and generally uncomfortable. The employees at an American petroleum office in Cairo that was associated with St. Joe made life pleasant for me. I stayed at the best hotel in the city and revisited the famous Egyptian geologic museum, the pyramids, and other historic places I had first seen in 1943–44.

After hearing what I needed to know, the geologic official told me he was in the process of writing up the conditions for foreign mineral investments but needed to check a few details with the minister of finance and other ministries. He advised me to return the following morning. On my return he said he had not been able to get the approvals he sought but would certainly have them by the following day. I returned again and the process was repeated for several days. Meanwhile, I received a telegram that I was to proceed to Tehran for several days after finishing my business in Cairo. This possibility had been discussed before I left New York and I had agreed to go. My Cairo contact continued to say he still had not received all the approvals needed but that he would send me a draft contract. The contract never came, no investment was made, and I felt I had wasted a week in Cairo. I have since become used to such experiences in developing countries.

Leaving Cairo for Tehran, I stopped for a pleasant day in Beirut, where I enjoyed a swim in the Mediterranean and a visit with some faculty members at the American University of Beirut. In Tehran I was to discuss with government officials and mining companies the possibility of negotiating exploration and mining contracts in areas known to St. Joe geologists. I found Tehran in an uproar, with mobs in the streets shouting epithets at the Shah. Since I had no governmental contacts, I went to the American Embassy to see the commercial and economic counselors about arranging appointments. I had always found American Embassy personnel cordial and helpful, sometimes even to the point of giving me an office and making available a car and driver. But here I was neither helped nor treated cordially. They probably wondered what company in its right mind would want to make an investment in Iran at that time. After a few days I saw some people in the geologic office and a few executives in the state mining company, but I had already decided my report would be a highly negative one—not only because of civil unrest but also because Iran's laws and regulations were not conducive to a profitable investment.

A couple of days before my plane was to depart, I left the hotel to buy a book on doing business in Iran. The area I visited was very crowded and there was no place to park, so I asked the driver of my hired car to wait while I went into a bookstore. When I returned I found him having a terrific argument with a policeman. After I got in the car, the driver hit the policeman, who then arrested the driver. He ordered both of us to the police station although I had nothing to do with the dispute. I thought it best to get out of the car, so I rushed across the street and entered a British bank. I explained to a bank official that I needed to get back to my hotel and asked if the bank could call someone to take me. He said they had no way to get me back to the hotel, so I walked down the street until I found a garage where they spoke a little English and bargained with a driver to get me to my hotel.

At the hotel I found it no longer accepted credit cards; I was expected to pay a large bill in cash, which I did not have. Also, I learned that my original driver was given a big fine by the police and demanded that I pay it. If I did not pay, he would make sure I did not leave Tehran. I immediately contacted my wife in Eugene and asked her to call St. Joe Minerals in New York, requesting that they send me $3,000 immediately to pay my hotel bill and, if necessary, bribe someone to protect me from the driver. I got a call the next morning from a British bank that had received the money. When I went to pick it up, they tried to pay it all to me in Iranian riyals, but I wanted it mostly in dollars to pay my hotel bill. No doubt the bank was anxious to get rid of the riyals, but I managed to get most of the money in dollars. It was very important for me to catch my plane out of Tehran, since so many people were anxious to escape Iran that all airlines in any direction were booked for six months.

I managed to leave just in time. A week or so later the Shah formally resigned, the revolutionary government took over, and American Embassy

Raymond L. Mikesell

personnel were taken hostage. When I made my report to St. Joe in New York, the vice president who had been most anxious for me to go to Iran had to endure a lot of kidding. I had lunch with St. Joe's president, Jack Duncan, to whom I related my experience in Tehran. He expressed appreciation for my frustrating trip.

Chile, Peru, and Bolivia

Shortly after my Iranian experience, St. Joe Minerals was taken over by another company, which Bernstein did not want to work for. Bernstein formed his own exploration company with headquarters in Santiago, Chile, but did exploration work in other Latin American countries as well. On several occasions he invited me to visit Santiago or Lima, Peru, where he also operated, to do studies of economic or political conditions, tax situations, and other matters important to prospective investors. He combined my findings with a geological analysis and survey of exploration and sold the package to multinational mining companies that were interested in investing in either Chile or Peru.

Bernstein had a Bolivian mineral prospect whose profitability he wanted me to appraise. I had always wanted to visit Bolivia and indulge my fondness for skiing by spending a few days visiting a ski area at an altitude of 16,000 feet. It took me two days to become acclimatized sufficiently in La Paz (which is at 12,000 feet) to do much work. I had great difficulty getting the data I needed from the company holding the property that Bernstein was interested in acquiring. I had made a reservation to leave Bolivia in advance and needed to get back to Eugene in time for fall classes. I was unable to visit the ski area since it took me a week to get the information I needed to make my report, which Bernstein greatly appreciated.

Once Bernstein took me to an area high in the Andes north of Santiago. Flying into a narrow canyon, our helicopter rose several thousand feet and emerged at a small meadow where a prospecting camp was located. That afternoon, two geologists accompanied us as the helicopter flew very close to a canyon wall and Bernstein indicated where he wanted the geologists to take samples of the rock. We flew so close to the wall that I felt I could almost touch it from the helicopter. Later we landed at a spot where we could walk on a narrow rocky trail; samples were taken and analyzed on the spot. Based on the data obtained, I made some quick calculations about the value of the minerals in the ore samples.

In February 1980 Bernstein asked me to go to Peru to assist a Peruvian mining firm, San Ignacio de Morococha, which was planning a foreign bond issue to finance an expansion of the mine. The mine manager was Eduardo Rubio, a close friend of Bernstein who later moved to Santiago to work with him. Rubio asked me to write the section of the prospectus for the bond issue dealing with economic and political conditions in Peru and an appraisal of the financial condition of the mine. Located in eastern Peru on a tributary of the Amazon, the mine produced lead and zinc. I told Rubio that I would like to see it before writing my report, so he drove me from Lima across the Andes to eastern Peru, where I spent several days at the mine. The manager was a notoriously fast driver who tended to take the middle of the road on blind curves. At the summit of the Andes we were at about 16,000 feet with ten feet of snow on either side of the road, but traveling through narrow canyons of ice did not inspire caution by the driver. I asked Bernstein about him nearly two decades later, and found to my surprise that he was still alive and uninjured!

The mine was carved out of the rain forest close by the river—host to beautiful birds and large numbers of monkeys. As I was escorted through a number of mine shafts, I was impressed with the operations, which were more labor intensive than those of other mines I had visited. I was able to make a favorable report, and the company got the money it needed for expanding the mine. My only regret was that the mine expansion would desecrate some of the forest.

On our return to Lima from the mine, I was asked to discuss a proposed tax on mineral exports with a group of mining officials. With the expectation that I might help dissuade the government from imposing the tax, they invited me to accompany them to a meeting with Peruvian government officials the following day. I said I did not want to represent them in lobbying the government but would be glad to give an economic analysis of the proposed tax. At the meeting, I pointed out that an export tax on minerals would increase the production costs of Peruvian mines that were exporting copper, zinc, and other minerals in highly competitive markets. I said the proposed

Raymond L. Mikesell

tax would likely reduce Peruvian mining output and discourage both foreign and domestic investment in mining. The government did not impose the tax, but I am not sure whether my economic arguments influenced this outcome.

Missions for Mining Companies in Papua New Guinea

A considerable portion of my consulting work for mining companies was contracted by a small Washington, D.C.–based consulting firm. It was owned and operated by Al Blackburn, Robert Kilmarx, and me, but we hired people to undertake overseas missions from time to time. We did work for several multinational mining companies—much of it research on the economic, political, and legal environment for mining investments in developing countries. We also provided information on the outlook for mineral prices and served as the eyes and ears in the United States for a large Australian company, Conzinc Riotinto Australia (CRA). CRA did not maintain an office in this country, even though it borrowed millions of dollars from, and had partners in, the U.S. Our contract with CRA provided a fixed annual payment of $100,000, which paid our office rent for several years. I made two trips to Australia and Papua New Guinea (PNG) for CRA and later visited PNG again to do research on the Ok Tedi mine (majority owned by CRA).

Bougainville

My first mission for CRA was in 1974 to the island of Bougainville, which at the time was a part of PNG. Formerly both PNG and Bougainville were under a UN trusteeship held by Australia. When PNG gained its independence in 1972, Bougainville became a part of the new nation. The island is 500 miles east of PNG, but the two economies are not integrated.

The CRA mine, which produced copper and gold, proved to be quite profitable both to the corporation and to the PNG government, which received tax revenue on net income and on income as a minority shareholder. Operations began in April 1972. I was asked to prepare an objective analysis of the economic impact of the mine on PNG and the island of Bougainville. An important goal of my study was to determine the net contribution of the mine to Bougainville. Because all of the tax revenue went to the PNG government and the operating company did not pay taxes to the local government, Bougainville gained little from the mine. Payments were made to local landowners, but they represented less than 1 percent of the projected annual retained value (value of gross revenue from the mine less mine imports and salaries of expatriates transferred abroad). The PNG government made some expenditures on the island not related to the mine, but they were small. The principal benefit to the island was in wages paid to local inhabitants and in expenditures by the mine for domestic products, mainly agricultural. The vast bulk of retained value went to the PNG government, the foreign shareholders, and payments on foreign loans owed by Bougainville Copper Ltd. (BCL). The payments to local workers and purchases of domestic products increased the income of the population and promoted the island's agriculture and small industrial sector. However, many local inhabitants of this tribal society believed that the social costs of altering the nature of the island's economy and social structure exceeded the economic benefits. Also, most inhabitants believed that a portion of the PNG tax revenue should have gone directly to the local government.

After reading all I could find about Bougainville, which geographically is a part of the Solomon Islands, I spent about two weeks on the island during the summer of 1974. Although I was not asked to pass judgment on the revenue distribution, which had been determined by agreements and laws passed by the PNG government, I felt that not enough attention had been paid to the interests of the Bougainville inhabitants. I interviewed local business people, who were cautious about saying anything critical of BCL. Unfortunately, I had little opportunity to interview the tribal leaders, since I did not speak their language and had to depend on company translators to whom they were reluctant to express their feelings about the company. It became clear to me that tribal leaders regarded BCL as an intrusion on their culture; they did not consider the wages paid to the workers who came from the tribal society as a social contribution. Undoubtedly, most of the workers themselves thought otherwise, since their wages liberated them from living in a tribal community with little monetary income.

Although I was asked not to include recommendations in my formal report, which the company later published, in private I told BCL officials that more revenue should go to the local government and that greater efforts should be made to provide education for workers and community services.

Since I knew that most inhabitants would eventually want development to provide income to buy products of the modern world, I believed the mine could be instrumental in transforming the local economy by providing income for education, health, and other social services. This transition was never permitted to take place. In the late 1980s, local leaders led a revolution on Bougainville; the inhabitants declared independence from PNG and shut down the mine. Since it appears unlikely that the mine will reopen, the PNG government and the foreign investors have lost several hundred million dollars. I believe this might have been prevented if Bougainville Copper Ltd. and the government had followed different policies.

I enjoyed my recreational experiences on Bougainville—both hiking on the island and visiting the coral reefs in the Coral Sea on a cruiser. The snorkeling was more exciting than any I had done before. It was like swimming in a marine museum filled with beautiful tropical fish. I also saw some sharks and had a close encounter with a giant manta ray some twenty feet across, but they are not carnivores. Incidentally, despite the name "Bougainville" there is no native bougainvillea plant on the island, and I do not know the history of how the island was named.

Mission to Botswana

My most interesting experience as a mining company consultant was a visit to Botswana for the American mining company American Metals Climax (AMAX). In 1982 I was asked to prepare a report on the Selebi-Phikwe nickel-copper mine, in which AMAX had a substantial investment. I was delighted to go. Botswana is the most democratic and stable country in Africa today, has been successful in promoting development, and is a fascinating place to view wildlife. My association with AMAX arose from work done with the Fund for Multinational Management Education (FMME), a foundation devoted to research on international investment projects and arranging conferences attended by officials of multinational mining companies, governments, and others interested in the field. I became acquainted with F. Taylor Ostrander, head of the AMAX Foundation. He told me that AMAX wanted someone outside the company to study the operations of Bamangwato Concessions Ltd. (BCL), which operated the Selebi-Phikwe mine. The major shareholders of BCL were AMAX and the Anglo-American Corporation

(AAC) of South Africa, with equal shares and the Government of Botswana, with 15 percent of the shares. AMAX and AAC jointly guaranteed Botswana's debt to the World Bank, which financed the infrastructure needed for the mine. Ostrander had negotiated with FMME to sponsor the study with some financial contribution from the AMAX Foundation, and he asked me if I would be interested in doing the study.

AMAX wanted an independent analysis of its investment in BCL for several reasons. The mine had suffered some large cost overruns during the previous decade, and the company wanted to know whether to reduce or eliminate its investment and guarantee obligations by selling its interest. Second, AMAX wanted to investigate any opportunities for investment in other Botswana minerals, including gold and diamonds. The company therefore needed information about the political climate of Botswana and the nature of any investment agreement the company might make with the Botswana government. Finally, AMAX's managers wanted to submit to its board an investment history—prepared by an independent source—including an analysis of the several negotiations with the government. Apparently there had been some criticism of the management by members of the board.

I spent more than two months, including three weeks in Botswana, on the project. On my own initiative I added a section dealing with the contribution of BCL to the Botswana economy—a topic not specifically mentioned in the outline provided by AMAX. After spending several days at AMAX headquarters in Greenwich, Connecticut, collecting documents and interviewing officials who had experience with the Botswana project, I traveled to London specifically to interview Sir Ronald Prain. He was a leading official in the development of mining in Northern Rhodesia (now Zambia) as well as in other areas in Africa. Prain chaired Rhodesian Selection Trust, which had gained a concession in 1959 to explore for minerals in Botswana. This interview, and a number of documents Prain gave me, provided an excellent historical background for my case study of BCL. From London, I flew to Johannesburg on South African Airlines and from there to Gaberones, the capital of Botswana, on a small local airline flying DC3s.

The Botswana government intrigued me. It had evolved out of the tribal government, which, except for its foreign relations, had been largely independent of Britain. The first president, Seretse Khama, was British educated in law, was married to a British white woman, and participated in the tribal government for many years. Knighted by the British government, he was officially Sir Seretse Khama, B.E., LL.D. He had also been associated with various agreements with BCL.

Unlike some of the other English colonial possessions that became independent after years of conflict, the Botswana government had good relations with Britain and other Western powers, and foreigners experienced virtually no discrimination. Botswana was also fortunate in not having large foreign-owned landholdings, as was true in Zimbabwe. The leading political party was dominated by middle-class cattle herders and urban businessmen. The government sought to maximize its returns from foreign investments in the country and had negotiated investment agreements which contributed to its economic and social development. For many years Botswana's principal foreign policy concern was maintaining its independence from the Union of South Africa. To this day Botswana is heavily dependent on South Africa for trade and foreign capital.

While in Gaberones, I conducted interviews with government officials and domestic and foreign business people who had anything to do with minerals policy or the investment climate in general. I spent several days at the Selebi-Phikwe mine, located in a mountainous area in east-central Botswana. I traveled by a car arranged for by BCL and stayed at a modern hotel. At the mine, officials described mine operations, including costs and technical problems, which would affect future profitability. I also gathered information about the impact of the mine on the local community. The mine is near the city of Francistown, which has benefitted from the power and other facilities associated with the mine. Most of its workers live in a nearby community which appeared to provide adequate living conditions.

The financial problems of AMAX as a partner in Bamangwato Concessions Ltd. did not stem from a failure of the Botswana government to honor its agreements. They were the result of technical problems arising from the nature of the copper-nickel ore and the failure of the initial plant to properly process the ore. Similar but less serious technical problems cropped up at the Soroako nickel project in Indonesia, and at other nickel mines I had investigated. World prices of both copper and nickel declined sharply after the mine began operations, and the company considerably underestimated costs other than those associated with technical problems. In the dozen or more case studies of foreign mining ventures that I prepared in the 1970s and 1980s, I found that disappointing financial returns were due more to technical problems and other nonpolitical factors, such as unexpectedly low mineral prices and a sharp rise in fuel costs, than to adverse governmental actions.

Botswana's investment climate for future undertakings in mining compared quite favorably with that in other developing countries. I stated in my report that it was difficult to think of a country with a lower degree of political risk. On the other hand, the conditions demanded by the government before obtaining a mineral lease—such as providing free equity participation to the government—were less favorable in Botswana than in a number of other developing countries. Another disadvantage was a marginal tax of 75 percent on personal income in excess of $50,000. This tax made it difficult to obtain professional and managerial personnel, most of whom came from outside the country.

In my final report to AMAX, I did not deal directly with the issue of whether AMAX should withdraw from the project immediately. I did discuss this question with AMAX officials on my return to the United States. Since my outlook for both nickel and copper prices was not optimistic, I concluded that it would be desirable for AMAX to sell its investment in BCL and eliminate its guarantee obligations. I believed that BCL would never be very profitable and that AMAX could earn higher returns on an alternative investment. To my knowledge, the company made no effort to sell its investment in BCL. My case study on Bamangwato Concessions Ltd. was published by FMME in 1983, in the same volume with a dozen other case studies of mineral projects I had prepared (Mikesell, 1983).

While I was in Botswana, its president died and I was unable to make appointments to see any government officials for several days. I took advantage of this opportunity to visit the Okavanga Wildlife Refuge in the northern part of the country. Since no tourist camps were available, I stayed at a hunting camp, where I was able to both see and eat wild game. The hunters were mostly Americans from Texas who brought their game to the camp.

Choice pieces of impala, gazelle, wildebeest, and warthog were spread over a huge grill every evening. The people who ran the camp were very cordial and knowledgeable about wildlife. A well-informed woman who was related to the camp manager took me out in a boat every day to view birds and animals, which were more abundant than in other African countries I have visited. Since my 1982 visit I have returned to the area twice—the last time in the fall of 1997 with my wife, Grace, on our honeymoon. Botswana has an excellent wildlife management system. The natives work in tourist camps, and their communities receive a portion of the income from tourism. Happily, the animals are threatened more by overpopulation than by extinction by poachers.

Visits to Zambia and Zaire

During the 1970s and 1980s, I visited Zambia on three occasions—twice for research on mining agreements and the climate for foreign investment in minerals, and once as a member of a UN Technical Assistance Group. Zambia is one of the best examples of a nation that is heavily dependent on mineral exports but has neglected to develop its agriculture and manufacturing. For much of the twentieth century, Zambia's principal export has been copper, which at times has constituted 90 percent of the country's foreign exchange earnings. The copper industry was developed by British, American, and South African capital when the country was under British rule as Northern Rhodesia. After the country became independent in 1970, President Kenneth Kaunda nationalized much of the copper industry by acquiring 51 percent of the equity of the country's two major copper mines, Roan Consolidated Mines and Nchanga Consolidated Mines. The mines continued to be operated for a time under management contracts with the former owners. In 1974, however, the Zambian government canceled the management and sales contracts with the foreign mining companies, and the minority foreign investors were left with virtually no voice in management and a very small return on their investment. Zambia's foreign exchange earnings from copper exports declined sharply during the 1970s, in part because of a fall in copper prices, and in part because of inefficient mine operations and a reduced flow of foreign capital into the industry. Much of Zambia's foreign exchange income has been spent on large urban office buildings, roads between urban centers, and other infrastructure of benefit mainly to the urban upper class.

On my visit to Lusaka in 1976, the U.S. ambassador took me to hear Kaunda's annual address to Parliament, and by chance we met the president as he was leaving the hall. In the course of a fifteen-minute conversation, I mentioned that the fully lighted four-lane highway from the airport to Lusaka was as good as any I had seen in any country, but that I was stricken by the large number of peasants and workers walking in the mud on both sides of the highway. This group of pedestrians was fully fifty times the number of people in the modern cars using the highway. Getting my point, he said he had thought about putting some gravel on the side of the road where the pedestrians walk but had been unable to finance the project. I feared I had embarrassed our ambassador, but she told me later that she was glad I had spoken up. On my next visit, I found that no graveling or other improvements had been made.

When I returned to Zambia in 1978, the new U.S. ambassador was Oliver L. Troxel, an old friend with whom I had worked in the State Department. He provided an office in the American embassy and transportation in embassy cars while I talked to people in the mining industry. I also planned to visit Lumbumbashi, Zaire, the principal city in the Zairian copper mining region, where I wanted to interview the Belgian manager of the nationalized Zairian mining company. I had wanted to travel across the border by car, but my ambassador friend told me that the border between Zambia and Zaire was too dangerous for me to cross. Thus he arranged for me to fly on Air Zaire. I had made a plane reservation several days before the trip, and before I was taken to the airport, the embassy reconfirmed my reservation. When I arrived at the ticket desk I found a number of travelers complaining that all reservations had been canceled. Those of us with reservations were herded into a room with the possibility that we might be able to board. We soon discovered that the Zairian soccer team, which had played the Zambian team the night before, decided they wanted to take that plane from Lusaka into Kinshasa instead of an earlier one. Only after the team members were stowed aboard the plane, were a few of us called to board. After further delay, the packed plane started to taxi to the runway. Just then another member of the team began running across the airfield toward the plane. Those on board knew that one of us would be taken off. The plane stopped and soon an official came back and ordered a man out who looked very much like a cleric. He sadly collected his baggage and left while the soccer player took his place. For reasons of national prestige, developing countries in Africa and elsewhere have devoted large amounts of capital to establish national airlines, nearly all of which lose millions of dollars a year.

I had a good meeting with the Belgian managing director of the Zairian copper mine. He was quite candid in his review of conditions since the nationalization of the mine. Efficiency was low, he said, and it was difficult to attract foreign investors because of lack of trust in agreements made by the Zairian government. A couple of days later, I flew on to the Zairian capital of Kinshasa, where my visit was disappointing and unpleasant. Since the hotels in the city were poor and the area unsafe, I stayed in a foreign-operated motel about fifteen miles from the city. Although I had made appointments to meet some government officials in charge of mining, most of these were not kept. I learned very little except the usual derogatory things about state mining enterprises. Zaire did allow new foreign investment in mining, but the economic and political climates were poor, a condition that continues today.

Experience with United Nations Workshops

During the period 1975–79, I participated in several workshops organized by the United Nations Centre on Transnational Corporations under the direction of Walter A. Chudson, with whom I had worked in the government. The purpose of the workshops was to train officials of developing countries in the negotiation of agreements with transnational corporations, and I was to direct the workshops on government negotiations with foreign mineral companies. I participated in UN workshops in Buenos Aires, Argentina (November 1973), New Delhi, India (March 1975), Lusaka, Zambia (January 1976), Georgetown, Guyana (September 1977), and Khartoum, Sudan (December 1977). In May 1979 I participated in a similar workshop sponsored by the Georgetown University Law School. Held in Bridgetown, Barbados, it was attended by representatives from several Caribbean nations.

I began these workshops with lectures on the various types of arrangements found in mining agreements and their impacts on government revenue and other government interests. Topics included conditions for exploration and mineral development, government equity participation, taxation, foreign exchange and trade transactions, relations with workers, environmental regulations, and the establishment of mining communities. Mining legislation usually provides a legal framework for mining agreements, but in most cases the provisions relating to taxation, government equity participation, and other conditions affecting the distribution of rents are negotiable. I outlined how various arrangements affect the net returns to both the government and the foreign investor, and how they would affect income stability and risk for both parties. I showed how the choice of different tax arrangements constituted a trade-off between prospective revenue and the risk of no return or even loss. For example, taxes on output usually yield less revenue than income taxes for a profitable mine. However, revenues from income taxes are more volatile than revenue from royalties or output taxes, because mines often operate without earning profits.

The interest of the government is not simply in maximizing government revenue from the exploitation of natural resources; it includes the control of mining operations having a special effect on the national economy, the welfare of the workers, and the protection of the environment. At times these interests conflict. The primary interests of the foreign investor are maximization of profits and the ability to transfer those profits to the investor's home country. Profit maximization requires bringing in expatriate personnel, importing equipment and raw materials, and operating mines and processing plants—all without undue government interference. Governments frequently have an interest in interfering with these activities, but the nature of such interference is often an important issue in the negotiations.

During the last three days of my workshop sessions, I would divide the participants into two groups, one representing government and the other representing the foreign investor. I would then ask the groups to negotiate a mining agreement on the basis of assumptions regarding revenue, production costs, and other conditions I stipulated. Most mining agreements deal with three broad issues: (1) ownership and control; (2) division of the net income produced by the mining enterprise; and (3) administrative procedures, such as dispute settlement and contract revision. In the negotiating exercise, we

Raymond L. Mikesell

concentrated on the division of mineral rents, which constitute the revenues from the sale of the products less all operating costs and the payments on borrowed capital. Because most mines are built with borrowed capital, interest and repayments on borrowings are not a part of net mine revenue. The return on the capital invested must be sufficient to attract the investor after taking account of political and economic risk.

In setting up the negotiating problem, I would outline for the group the assumptions regarding revenues and costs, but the *minimum* return acceptable to the investor was usually held confidential by the investor. The government might also adhere to a minimum share of the rent it was willing to accept. While the members of my group were negotiating, I would stand ready to calculate for them the rates of return that would result from a particular set of tax and other provisions in the contract.

The minimum rate of expected return required by a prospective investor is a function of risk, and different types of contracts provide for a different sharing of the risk between the foreign company and the government. The greater the investor's share of the risk, the larger the return he demands. For example, if the foreign investor were to bear all the risk, say, by paying a certain sum for the right to mine, he might be unwilling to pay any taxes or share his net revenues in any other way. On the other hand, if the government were to put up half the capital for developing the mine, the company would expect to pay taxes on its share of the net revenue since the risks were shared equally with the government. Most agreements involve payments to the government in several forms: royalties, which depend solely on output; profits taxes, which depend on the financial success of the mining venture; and income from a share of the equity, say, 10 to 25 percent to the government, either without cost or a minimum payment. Usually the company bears the risk of the initial exploration to determine whether a mine is feasible, following which the government may be given the right to buy shares in the company. Both risk and expected returns need to be evaluated by the negotiators.

During the role-playing sessions, the bargainers entered into the spirit of the game and worked very hard to win the best bargain without losing the investment by not being able to reach an agreement. This taught them not only the rules of the bargaining game but also an appreciation of the problems faced by foreign companies and how companies make investment decisions. I do not think this role-playing approach had ever been used in a training program involving the negotiation of mining agreements.

Most of the participants in my workshops on mine negotiation were fairly sophisticated, but some insisted on introducing ideological issues relating to foreign investment in natural resources. I firmly discouraged such discussion, because I wanted to teach the techniques of negotiating without dealing with the question of whether such negotiations were in the national interest. It was important for them to understand the incentives and the objectives of transnational companies. Why, for example, should companies require an expected rate of return of 20 to 25 percent on their equity investment when they should have been satisfied with a more modest return, such as that on relatively risk-free bonds? The answer is that an expected rate of return must be adjusted by the probability that the return will be realized. An expected return of 20 percent with a probability of realization of .5 provides a probability-adjusted return of only 10 percent. The idea that the terms of a contract determine the way in which risk is shared between the foreign investor and the government was the most difficult to get across. Measuring risk and calculating probability-adjusted rates of return involve concepts that are unfamiliar to most people.

As UN officials, we were treated cordially and often entertained by the government officials of the host country and by members of U.S. embassies. We visited areas not ordinarily seen by tourists. In the Sudan, we took a memorable trip up the Blue Nile from Khartoum and sat by the river, where tall peasant women came from villages many miles away to get water. They carried the water on their heads in five gallon cans and sang beautifully while walking. In Barbados, we enjoyed the beaches and attended native dances and musicals. In Guyana, some of us were taken in native boats on narrow rivers in the rain forest to see an abundance of birds and other animal life.

Although I am usually depressed by the poverty and squalor of large Indian cities, I rather enjoyed the UN mission to New Delhi. One day we were taken to Agra, where we visited the Taj Mahal, which I had not seen before. We did tire of the highly spiced vegetarian Indian food. One evening we were taken to a restaurant in a very old building in Old Delhi, where they

Raymond L. Mikesell

specialized in steak and other red meat. Thereafter most of us headed for Old Delhi for the evening meal. One event that we witnessed several times was the almost military entrance of some two dozen Russians from their embassy, seated at a large table near us.

Alaska

In 1980 I was asked to consult for the Bering Straits Native Corporation (BSNC), one of the Alaska Native corporations established under the Alaska Native Claims Settlement Act of December 1971. Agreements between the regional corporations and mining companies are similar to those between multinational mineral companies and foreign governments, so my acquaintance with foreign investment agreements was relevant.

My Washington, D.C.–based consulting firm was first contacted by an Anchorage lawyer representing BSNC for assistance in preparing exploration and lease agreements with mineral companies. We were also asked to draft an agreement among the twelve regional corporations for sharing a substantial portion of all revenues received from timber and subsurface resources. Initially, I did my work on these assignments in Eugene. Later, officials of the Aleut Corporation invited me to Anchorage to participate in two days of negotiations with a mining company. I found the officials of the Native corporations and their legal advisers to be quite knowledgeable and very hard bargainers. During these meetings I limited my intervention to explanations and examples rather than appearing as a principal in the bargaining. I also met with Aleut Corporation officials in advance of the negotiations to suggest strategies.

In addition to revenue, the Alaska Native corporations were interested in having the mining companies provide job training and infrastructure that served both the mineral industry and the general economy. They also wanted a substantial portion of the equity, but I pointed out to them that they could be paying too high a price in terms of additional risk for the income that they might gain from having a share of the equity. In my view, control over such matters as labor relations and the environment can best be achieved through an agreement for setting up joint supervisory boards in which the company does not have majority vote. For example, an environmental board made up of governmental, tribal, and company representatives could decide on issues relating to the environmental impact of the mining projects. Such issues might include air pollution caused by the smelter or a demand by labor for better safety in the mine.

I have spent dozens of summers hiking the Brooks Range, rafting rivers to the Arctic Sea, and kayaking in Glacier Bay, but the idea of living in Alaska full time through the long, dark winter days terrified me. My experience with the Native corporations gave an opportunity to see how Alaskans live other than in the summer. In Anchorage I learned that many professional people took as much as two months off between late November and the end of January to live in Hawaii or some southwestern state. Most of them owned a boat or small plane, which took them to exotic spots in Alaska. This is not a bad life. I think if I were sixty years younger, I might have chosen Alaska as the preferred place to spend my life.

South Africa

In 1976 I spent two weeks in Johannesburg, South Africa, on a mission for St. Joe Minerals. St. Joe had sent geologists to South Africa to look into exploration opportunities, and two top officials of St. Joe planned to visit the nation following my visit. However, before committing themselves, they asked me to meet with a number of government and mining company officials to discuss specific mining projects. They also asked me to undertake an economic and political evaluation of South Africa—both because of security concerns generated by apartheid and conflicts between the black majority and the government, and because of the threat of a United Nations–sponsored investment boycott.

South Africa is best known for its gold and diamond production, but it possesses a large portion of the world's known reserves of several industrial minerals: chrome (74 percent), platinum (70 percent), manganese (60 percent), and uranium (30 percent). At the time of my visit, U.S. corporate investment in South Africa was about $1.5 billion, nearly half of which was in mining. It included investments by such major companies as Phelps Dodge, U.S. Steel, Newmont, Union Carbide, and Allied Chemical.

I obtained details on a number of mining opportunities, including the interest of South African companies in joint ventures with St. Joc Minerals. My most challenging task was evaluating the economic and political conditions. I obtained a good deal of information from members of the business administration faculty at the University of South Africa in Pretoria. One of these professors, a black man, favored a strong federal government to guarantee the constitutional rights of minorities, and he was highly critical of the government's "homelands" approach creating strictly black states. Instead, he favored genuine integration of the country because he came from a minority tribe that was afraid of being dominated by the Zulus, a majority black tribe. The minority tribe felt it needed the protection of a federal government.

I had a long visit with Dr. W. J. Breytenbach, director of the African Institute and a leading scholar on South African political and social movements. Breytenbach believed that the greatest threat to political stability was urban unrest, but he was optimistic that security could be maintained if the government moved ahead with sufficient speed to eliminate economic discrimination and improve the economic position of non-whites. The non-whites include not simply blacks but also the large population of immigrants from India and other countries who constitute a substantial portion of the middle class. His concern about urban unrest as a major threat to South Africa has been borne out since the establishment of the Mandela government. Urban unrest and the failure of urban blacks to cooperate with the present integrated federal government continue to be sources of disturbance, which has limited South Africa's industrial and social progress. This became quite evident when my wife and I made a short visit to South Africa in the fall of 1997. I learned that several black mafia groups in Johannesburg prevented the government from taking the necessary steps to improve the economic and social conditions of the black masses. The city has no public transportation system because the taxicab mafia has destroyed the existing buses. There is 50 percent unemployment among blacks in Johannesburg, and most of the unemployed are living in slums.

On one trip to South Africa, I accepted an invitation to speak at Rand Afrikaans University in Johannesburg. My talk dealt with the importance of getting rid of apartheid in the interest of promoting the country's industrial and agricultural development. I was a guest at the home of Theodore Beukes, a member of the economics faculty whom I had known for several years. He and I planned a study of the mining industry in South Africa, but we were unable to secure funding from a South African source we had counted on. My friend and his family had a beautiful home with a swimming pool, tennis court, and several servants. I could not help contrasting it mentally with the black slum visible nearby.

I made a moderately optimistic report on South Africa's economic and political future to St. Joe Minerals in 1976, but I would not do so if I were asked to evaluate conditions today.

Conferences and Associations on Natural Resource Investment

Perhaps more than any other foreign activity, my work with mining companies and the United Nations provided material for books and articles, which in turn led to invitations to give papers at a number of conferences and workshops around the world. My lectures usually dealt with some aspect of investment in minerals or the outlook on the demand and supply of minerals. In the Netherlands I gave a series of five lectures at the Institute for Social Studies at The Hague (Mikesell, 1980) and a lecture at the International Chamber of Commerce conference in Amsterdam. On the latter occasion I attended a dinner given by Prince Bernhart, husband of Queen Juliana. I wanted to talk with the prince about the duties of a house-prince to a queen but had no opportunity to do more than formally greet him. In the United States, I addressed the American Mining Congress on a couple of occasions, and since U.S. commercial banks are heavily involved in lending to mining ventures throughout the world, I twice gave papers at the annual American Banking Conference.

The U.S. Department of State has a special interest in promoting U.S. private investment in developing countries as a complement to, or substitute for, U.S. foreign aid. I gave several talks on foreign investment at the State Department that were sponsored by the department's Bureau of Intelligence and Research. The bureau published and circulated these talks. One of them

Raymond L. Mikesell

described the workshops on mining contract negotiations I gave at the UN missions in several countries.

My work on foreign investment in the resource industries led to my appointment to the Advisory Council of the Overseas Private Investment Corporation (OPIC), a U.S. government agency responsible for guaranteeing foreign investments against political risk. I attended a number of meetings of the Advisory Council in Washington, D.C., and gave talks at OPIC meetings in Houston, Texas, and other cities. My interest in world petroleum led to a consultantship with the U.S. Department of Energy, where I prepared papers on how the U.S. government could promote greater exploration and investment in foreign petroleum production. This work enabled me to renew my friendship with Jim Schlesinger, at the time secretary of energy, who was a colleague in the economics department at the University of Virginia in the 1950s.

The British–North American Committee

My association with the British–North American Committee (BNAC), whose members were leading British, Canadian, and U.S. business executives plus a few academics and research institute directors, provided an opportunity to get acquainted with several leading mining executives. The BNAC undertook a study in 1978–79 of world investment in minerals in relation to growing world requirements. I was asked to prepare a paper on the relationship between conditions essential to foreign mineral investors and those being demanded by host governments, together with approaches to reconciliation of foreign investor–host country positions. I was able to participate in several meetings of the group, both in the United States and abroad. Most of our meetings were held in Washington, D.C., but in March 1978 we met at Christ Church, Oxford University, where I renewed acquaintance with Oxford professors whose classes I had lectured in some years before. Another meeting took place in Palm Beach, Florida, where we were housed, wined, and dined in the luxury of one member's magnificent home. I gave a short talk at a press conference and, according to my notes, said the following: "We are not going to run out of any minerals that will impair our economic growth during the present century, and when I am ninety years old in 2004, I don't believe I or anyone else will be worrying about running out of minerals.

This will disappoint the apostles of zero growth, but I do not believe we will need to renounce our civilization anytime in the next century and perhaps beyond, if we are lucky enough not to collide with a large meteorite."

My optimism was endorsed by the Workshop on Mineral Supplies, which I attended at the mineral economics department of Pennsylvania State University in May 1978. The workshop was organized by William A. Vogely, a professor of mineral economics and one of the world's leading specialists on a number of minerals. Vogely is one of the most remarkable people I have ever met. Despite great physical handicaps his accomplishments are outstanding. Vogely has stumps for limbs and only one hand is functional. He transports himself on a small platform with four small wheels and pulls himself onto chairs without assistance. He does not even allow people to carry his tray in the cafeteria. He travels all over the world to meetings. On one occasion a group of us attending an East-West conference in Honolulu were all going to lunch in Waikiki. On the way out of the building, he asked me if I would like to ride with him to the restaurant. I said, of course, and supposed he had someone to drive the car. It turned out that he drove a type of car first used by Franklin Roosevelt following his bout with polio. Vogely was far more crippled than Roosevelt but handled the car beautifully. Vogely and I both served as members of the National Materials Advisory Board (NMAB) in 1981–83, and it was he who recommended my appointment. The NMAB is appointed by the National Research Council, which is under the National Academy of Sciences.

Frankfurt Institute

Another institute concerned with mineral resources with which I have been associated is the Institut für Ausländisches Internationales Wirtschaftrecht of Frankfurt, Germany. I visited this institute several times and gave lectures to audiences at the University of Frankfurt. On one occasion in 1976 I was coming from New Delhi, India, on an all-night flight and arriving in Frankfurt in the morning. I was met by people from the institute who handed me an agenda that included a morning talk, a lunch talk, a mid-afternoon talk, and an evening lecture. Since they knew I had spent the night on the plane, I do not know why they believed a sixty-five-year-old man could fulfill such a schedule. I did reduce my talks to two, but they were not among my better performances.

In 1978 the institute sponsored a conference of leading mineral economists from various countries of the world, and I was invited to give a paper. The conference was an opportunity to renew my acquaintance with a number of people working in the same field—most of them were academics. One afternoon all the members of the conference were loaded into two buses for a tour of the Rhine near Frankfurt. We visited several wineries and an eleventh-century church that contained a statue of the purported mother-in-law of Jesus. After our visit to the church, whose fourteenth-century organ was played for us, we went to a monastery that produced a substantial amount of wine for commercial sale. When the monks had seated us comfortably, they began passing out small glasses of their wines—fifteen glasses in all. After a lecture on each wine, and after serving us fifteen more glasses of the same wines from bottles with no labels, we were asked to name each of the wines we had consumed. We were all glad that the bus drivers were not participating in this exercise.

On another visit to the Frankfurt Institute, I spent a day being driven along the Rhine from one winery to another. This day was memorable because we drove onto a Rhine ferryboat and went several miles down the river before we disembarked on the other side. With its magnificent fairy-tale castles, this is one of the most picturesque areas of the Rhine. It was memorable for me because I had passed this same area when I was seventeen years old on an all-day cruise down the Rhine to Cologne.

Sources

The sources for this chapter are mainly my own memoranda and several of my publications on mining.

CHAPTER 12: WORK ON ENVIRONMENTAL ISSUES

My work on environmental issues over the past twenty-five years has taken a number of forms, including chairing the Sierra Club's National Economics Committee, serving as a consultant to the World Bank's Environment Department, participating in a study group sponsored by the Council on Foreign Relations, and teaching courses on environmental economics at the University of Oregon. I was also active in the Environmental Defense Fund and the Wilderness Society. I am currently working with the University of Oregon's Center for Environmental and Resource Economics, which I founded and financed in 1998.

Today most economists are conscious of environmental values, but environmentalists frequently regard the application of economic values and methodology to analyze environmental issues as improper. Economists believe that the application of basic economic principles, such as social benefit-cost analysis, is essential to any rational discussion of environmental issues. Social costs and benefits, as contrasted with private costs and benefits, are borne or enjoined by society as a whole. Many environmentalists oppose any amount of air or water pollution, while economists believe account should be taken of how much additional social costs of pollution abatement should be incurred to remove additional units of pollution. This means that economists view resources for abolishing pollution as scarce, and they consider whether the additional social benefits provided by reducing an additional unit of pollution are greater than the additional social costs. Suppose that 98 percent of a pollution source can be eliminated from a region for $100 million in cost to the producers, but to achieve a 99 percent elimination would cost about $1 billion dollars, which is inevitably passed on to consumers in the form of higher prices. Economists would not favor achieving 99 percent elimination, because the additional expenditures could be used in other ways that might more significantly improve the environment. Economists believe other social costs should be taken into account in public decisions on environmental matters. For example, we might be able to improve the environment by monitoring how households handle their waste, but such government intrusion could be so invasive of personal privacy that it would harm overall social welfare. On the other hand, some government outlays for projects, such as dams, are designed to increase output but have adverse impacts on the environment. In such cases, the social cost of the environmental deterioration must be weighed against the social benefits of increased output.

As a professional economist, I sometimes have difficulty working with lay groups organized to promote social causes. Such groups often adopt general principles to be applied without qualification to a range of social activities. Principles such as "thou shalt not pollute" or "thou shalt never impair the services of natural resources" become an ideological framework for judging all social activity. Economists tend to think instead in terms of maximizing *net* social benefits. Such judgments, of course, require measuring social benefits and costs. For example, how do we measure the social cost of one human life or a certain amount of local discomfort from pollution when comparing that cost with a loss of $10 billion worth of output? To many environmentalists, the value of one human life is infinite, but in my opinion there is a limit to what society should sacrifice for one life. Economists also measure risk in terms of the probability that a particular harm will occur; thus the social cost of potential harm is adjusted for the probability of the event, say, one in 10,000 or one in a million people will be harmed. Economists argue that society cannot afford the cost of eliminating all risk. The social cost of an event with a probability of occurrence of one in ten million may be minuscule in comparison with the social cost of lost output from avoiding the risk.

The conflict between national output and the environment is reflected in the attitude of many environmentalists toward international trade. Because there are cases in which trade restrictions, say, on imports of food that has been subject to harmful chemicals, may provide environmental protection, some environmentalists regard free or unrestricted trade as antithetical to environmentalism. This translates into a general support of trade restriction, and the rejection of international agreements for reducing trade barriers such as the World Trade Organization (WTO) and the North American Free Trade

Area (NAFTA). Economists, on the other hand, contend that reducing trade barriers provides far larger worldwide social benefits from increased output and employment than any resulting environmental costs. My support of free trade has frequently put me in conflict with members of environmental organizations with which I have worked.

Work with the Sierra Club

My love of the wilderness areas of the Pacific Northwest—the old-growth forests, the magnificent coast with rocks towering above tidal pools, and the scenic lakes and rivers—led me to believe that these aesthetic values should be preserved for all time. Therefore, I joined the Sierra Club shortly after my arrival in Oregon because it was the most important institution fighting for environmental preservation. I became active in club work in 1975 when Richard A. Tybout, chair of the Economics Committee (EC), asked me to become a committee member. I was invited to be cochair with Tybout in 1983, and the following year I became chair following Tybout's resignation. The idea of establishing an EC to advise the club was initially Tybout's, but he was frequently at odds with members of the Sierra Club's Executive Board. One reason was that Tybout would occasionally introduce resolutions that dealt with subjects under the jurisdiction of other committees, such as the Air Pollution Committee or the International Committee. For example, he tried to get through a resolution that the Sierra Club would always take into account balancing social benefits with social costs in making decisions on environmental policies. Although I supported Tybout in this effort and made a short statement before the board in its favor, the board was uncomfortable with a resolution requiring the application of quantitative economic principles in reaching decisions about environmental problems, and Tybout's resolution was defeated. I came to the conclusion that the EC would be more effective in applying economic logic by working with other committees in supporting their resolutions with which the EC agreed, and that it should operate as a service organ by giving advice on economic aspects of environmental policy questions. This was the course I tried to follow during my tenure as chair.

Of the various types of environmental regulations, the EC nearly always favored economic incentives rather than direct governmental controls. The EC often demonstrated how the social cost of achieving a particular environmental goal, such as a specific percent reduction in pollution, is nearly always lessened with economic incentives. For example, where firms are required to pay a fee when they exceed a certain amount of pollution—as opposed to being required to reduce pollution by a specified amount—companies with high-cost pollution abatement pay the tax, while companies with much lower costs meet the abatement requirement without paying the tax. Thus, for a specific amount of industrial pollution abatement, the overall cost incurred by firms will be less under the fee system than under a specific abatement control system. Minimizing costs for achieving a specific pollution reduction goal is desirable because the amount of environmental protection the public is willing to accept depends heavily on the costs it may be required to pay in higher prices and unemployment.

Most committees accept this reasoning, but some who have ideological objections to any consideration of economic costs prefer direct governmental control. For example, there were objections to using marketable permits for specific amounts of pollution emission on the grounds that firms should not be able to purchase the right to pollute. Costs of reducing emissions vary dramatically among industries and among firms within industries. Marketable permits have been shown to achieve substantial cost saving for a given overall reduction in pollution.

A contentious issue within the club concerned taking account of risk, as measured by the probability of a harmful event occuring, in setting environmental standards. As a member of the Sierra Club's Risk Task Force, I was at odds with the chair, who rejected consideration of the probability of environmental harm but instead favored the elimination of all risk, regardless of the probability of harm. Thus, avoiding a 100-million-to-one risk of harm to human health was regarded as having the same benefit as avoiding a ten-to-one probability of harm. The report to the Sierra Club by the Risk Task Force was split on this issue, and so far as I know, the board never really faced the question.

As a member of the International Committee of the Sierra Club, I dealt with issues such as proposed international agreements on greenhouse emissions for protecting the global environment, on assistance to developing countries, and on government controls on international trade and foreign investment. I had no problem considering international agreements on activities affecting the global environment. But I disagreed with some International Committee members who wanted the U.S. government to apply trade sanctions against foreign countries that maintained environmental or labor policies different from our own. For example, should the U.S. government stop importing from countries that do not have the same standards on labor, safety, and health that exist in the United States, or should the U.S. government restrict U.S. investments in such countries? The attempt to dictate foreign environmental policies by means of such sanctions would result in retaliation against U.S. exports or investments by these countries. I argued that as long as the imports do not impose health or safety risks on American consumers, such import restriction constituted interference with the sovereignty of the foreign countries. In my view, changing the environmental practices of foreign countries requires persuasion and the negotiation of agreements rather than unilateral sanctions. This issue was at the heart of some environmentalists' objections to U.S. membership in international trade organizations.

The environmental community has for many years been critical of the World Bank and of the regional banks, such as the Inter-American Development Bank and the Asian Development Bank, for financing projects that are environmentally harmful. For example, the World Bank has financed the construction of multipurpose dams that generate power for urban centers but at the same time cause the evacuation of thousands of peasants from their land and reduce the availability of water for irrigation in certain areas. International banks have also been criticized for making loans to finance roads and mining projects in rain forests—resulting in deforestation that contributes to global warming.

Because I was interested in the operation of international banks, I decided to write a book on their environmental policies and, if possible, have it published by the Sierra Club. I invited Larry Williams, the club's senior

Raymond L. Mikesell

international representative, to be my coauthor because of his special interest in the subject, although I wrote most of the book. The Sierra Club published it in 1992 under the title *International Banks and the Environment: From Growth to Sustainability, An Unfinished Agenda.* It traced the evolution of environmental policy by the multinational banks and provided case studies of bank loans with environmental consequences. We found that the international banks' environmental policies had improved considerably in recent years. We recommended certain additional improvements having to do largely with monitoring projects the banks finance and making loans conditional upon the improvement of environmental laws and regulations of the borrowing countries. An environmental assessment study must now be undertaken before the World Bank will finance a project or program, and the results of the study must be embodied in the project proposal.

The book was well received, particularly by my friends in the World Bank's Environment Department, for which I served as a consultant from time to time. Both Williams and I were disappointed with the sales of the book due to what I believe was a poor distribution system. I regretted that we did not have it published by a commercial publisher.

NAFTA and the WTO

When NAFTA was being negotiated with Canada and Mexico during the Bush administration, environmentalists were concerned with how its trade rules would affect the ability of the United States to use trade restrictions on imports that violated U.S. health and safety regulations, or on imports produced under conditions that violated U.S. environmental regulations on production. However, little attention was paid to environmental issues in the negotiation of NAFTA. When the Clinton administration presented the treaty to Congress for ratification, there was an effort by U.S. environmental organizations to make the treaty more environment-friendly. Many environmentalists opposed any trade agreements that would limit U.S. governmental control over imports. Several memoranda from the Sierra Club's Economics Committee pointed out how NAFTA might deal with possible conflicts between trade rules and the environment and also promote regional environmental objectives, including regional rules governing production of products entering into trade. We argued that all governmental actions taken in accordance with existing and future multinational agreements on environmental issues, such as the Montreal Protocol on Substances that Deplete the Ozone Layer, should be permitted under the rules of NAFTA. We also suggested that in administering trade rules, global environmental protection should be regarded as a legitimate argument in disputes between the exporter of a product and a nation imposing import controls in the interest of the global environment. For example, Mexico charged the United States with violating GATT rules because the U.S. restricted imports of tuna that were caught under conditions that did not protect dolphins. U.S. fishermen were prohibited by U.S. law from catching tuna using certain methods that killed dolphins. We believed the government should have been able to argue that the destruction of dolphins impaired the U.S. environment because of its impact on the global environment.

Some of our memoranda were used by the Sierra Club to lobby for changes in the NAFTA treaty before it was ratified by the U.S. Congress, and the Clinton administration obtained agreements with Canada and Mexico on some of the proposed changes. About the same time, the administration asked Congress to ratify the WTO agreement. Changes in this treaty were proposed by environmental organizations, but the treaty was not renegotiated.

I was not wholly satisfied with the provisions of either NAFTA or WTO as they related to the promotion of U.S. environmental objectives. However, I believed that the benefits from our membership in these organizations far exceeded the possible harm. The strength of the U.S. in negotiating disputes over environmental questions was such that our positions would be sustained. If they were systematically defeated, we could always threaten to withdraw from the organization. The environmental risks were small in relation to the gains in the national product that could be achieved through freer regional and multinational trade. Both NAFTA and WTO do provide for the harmonization of practices affecting the environment, and they could be used for improving the global environment.

However, the Sierra Club leaders opposed congressional ratification of both agreements, and some of their objections to NAFTA and the WTO actually had little to do with either agreement. NAFTA was faulted because it did not do more to improve environmental conditions on the U.S.-Mexico border, but these conditions would not have been better—and perhaps would have been worse—if NAFTA did not exist. It was argued that lower environmental standards in Mexico would induce U.S. firms to invest there. However, NAFTA provides for the enforcement of Mexican environmental regulations, which are nearly equivalent to our own. Little in NAFTA would induce more U.S. investment in Mexico, since lower Mexican import duties favor U.S. exports to Mexico over production of the goods in Mexico. Also, all the empirical studies I have found indicate that environmental standards do not constitute a significant factor in the decisions by U.S. firms to invest abroad. The members of the EC believed that the social benefits of U.S. membership in these two trade organizations far outweighed the risk-adjusted environmental costs. Moreover, U.S. membership in the organizations would provide opportunities for the U.S. to promote special agreements that would have a favorable effect on the environment, especially on production methods that impaired the global environment.

Break with the Sierra Club

While preparing memoranda on NAFTA, I met occasionally with club leaders, including Michael McCloskey, the chair, and Larry Williams, and members of the International Committee to discuss club policy on trade and the environment. I agreed fully with the club's environmental objectives and with most of what the club leaders sought in the final texts of both NAFTA and the WTO. But we differed sharply on one principal point: my unwillingness to agree that, as a condition for participation, the U.S. government should have the right to restrict trade with other members (either exporting or importing) because the country employed production practices that differed in some way from U.S. practices. I felt certain that such a position would be unacceptable both to other nations and to the U.S. government. The U.S. certainly would be unwilling in general to allow foreign nations to use trade restrictions as a means of inducing us to adopt their domestic production practices. (Such cases do, however, occur. Canada has refused to accept certain U.S. agricultural products because of our production practices, and the European Economic Community has refused to import U.S. livestock because of the industry's use of growth hormones.)

This difference of opinion led to my resignation from the EC. In the spring of 1994, while NAFTA was being considered by Congress, the EC was facing a dilemma. Our report to the club encouraged support of NAFTA. The Sierra Club leaders opposed it. Most EC members felt that the club's unwavering official opposition to NAFTA, as well as to WTO membership, conflicted with our principles to the extent that we could no longer work for the club. Therefore, the entire EC, save one, resigned. This was a difficult decision for me, because I enjoyed my work with the other members of the club and knew I would miss the association. However, as strong believers in free trade, as are the vast majority of economists, we were embarrassed that the club would take a position against NAFTA and the WTO, both of which we believed were very important for U.S. economic welfare. Our split became public when one EC member sent a copy of our committee report to the U.S. Foreign Trade Representative, and it was released as a White House document. This should not have occurred since it was an internal document. Our committee was accused by Sierra Club leaders of sabotage. Since that time I have made several efforts to get the club to appoint another economics committee, which would serve as a purely advisory body without taking committee positions. The club leadership has expressed no interest in having an economics committee of any kind.

Looking back on this unfortunate episode, I believe that some club leaders were greatly influenced by their relationship with labor leaders against all trade agreements because they feared that American workers would be displaced by low-cost imports from lower-wage nations. I believe this vision is short-sighted from the standpoint of maximizing our social benefits. While imports may replace some low-skilled workers, the exports they help to finance increase the demand for goods produced by U.S. higher-income workers.

It is unfortunate that an organization as large and broadly based in terms of public interests as the Sierra Club condemns a long-time volunteer as a heretic because he disputes one of the club's positions. These autocratic and ecclesiastical practices discourage objective scholars from becoming closely involved with the club leadership, and it may explain why there are no longer any economists in the club leadership. Environmentalism is not a creed to which one must be faithful; it is an appreciation of the legacy of the natural world and devotion to its preservation by whatever means are appropriate and rational.

One of the most painful experiences following the breakup of the EC was severing my relations with the club's international representative, Larry Williams, with whom I had worked very closely for many years. I had always been available to produce memoranda, run to Washington, D.C., for a special meeting, or obtain some information he urgently needed. We had been close personal friends, spent time in each other's homes, and were joint authors of a book published by the Sierra Club of which we were both quite proud. My rejection of the Sierra Club's position on NAFTA led him to regard me as a traitor to the club, and he expressed no interest in seeing me again or using my advisory services.

Work with the World Bank's Environment Department

Beginning in 1990, I served as a consultant to the World Bank's Environment Department. I participated in several conferences and wrote memoranda on environmental assessment of proposed projects, two of which were published.

Along with other environmental economists, such as Salah el Serafy, I regard natural resources as capital assets. Their depletion should be treated as a social cost analogous to the depreciation of a building or other man-made asset. I developed a model for calculating resource depletion based on el Serafy's work. Depletion of any natural resource should be regarded as a production cost—with the amount of the cost saved and invested in the economy to avoid reducing resource capital. The principle of treating natural resource depletion as a reduction in social capital is an important element in "resource accounting."

If natural resource–producing countries were to adopt resource accounting practices, it would reduce their GDP to reflect depletion of the resource assets. This is true because traditional national accounting practice, including U.S. accounting, does not deduct depletion of nonrenewable natural resources from the GDP but does deduct the depletion of man-made capital. If countries properly accounted for the degradation of natural assets, such as soil, their GDP would be lower because their depletion of capital assets would lower their future output. The annual depreciation of these capital assets should be saved and accumulated so that the nation will not be consuming capital on which future generations depend for income. One way of accomplishing this would be for the government to tax natural resource depletion and invest the receipts from the tax in new capital assets. I wrote memoranda on resource accounting for the World Bank and published several articles on the subject.

Some of my associates in the Environment Department of the World Bank were ecologists who believed that unless output in industrial countries ceased to grow, the world's environmental and natural resource assets would be so depleted that modern civilization could no longer be sustained. I took the position that technological progress could both avoid and partially offset this depletion if proper resource policies were followed by governments and the output of goods and services could continue to grow.

Mining

It may seem paradoxical that someone who has spent a considerable amount of time advising multinational mining companies could also be dedicated to environmental protection, especially since mining is one of the most environmentally destructive industries. As a consultant to mining companies, I was not asked to prepare a program for restoring mines and petroleum fields to their natural state after operations were closed down, or to limit the output of sulfur dioxide created by their smelters. Until recently, most countries were not especially interested in including environmental regulations in their mining agreements. But some have passed strict environmental laws after the mines went into operation. I therefore advised my clients to adopt the most advanced environmental technology with the expectation that, sooner or later, environmental regulations would be applied to them. Since it is not always possible to anticipate all environmental problems in advance, I recommended that mining contracts provide for committees—on which there would be representatives from government, the company, labor, and the community—that would deal with environmental complaints and agree on solutions. While mining is destructive, I do not

Raymond L. Mikesell

believe we should stop using minerals because of its environmental impact.
With proper economic incentives and sensible regulations, production for
satisfying human wants and enhancing per capita income need not be antithetical to maintaining humankind's environmental heritage.

Council on Foreign Relations

In 1992 I participated in a Council on Foreign Relations Study Group on
trade policy and the environment. The council considered this an important
subject because it concerns whether the U.S. will continue to be a leader in
reducing barriers to international trade. A major source of controversy has
been the Clinton administration's effort to obtain congressional approval of
"fast track legislation" in negotiating international trade agreements. This
legislation, which was in force during several previous administrations but
expired in 1990, provided that Congress would not attempt to change the
provisions of any trade agreement reached by the administration as a condition for approving the agreement. In the absence of such legislation, Congress
is likely to approve the agreement with certain changes, which would then
require the administration to renegotiate the agreement and return it to
Congress for approval. Meanwhile, the other parties to the agreement might
accept the changes our Congress wanted only on the condition that other
changes be made in the agreement, which Congress might in turn find
unacceptable. Negotiation of trade agreements is virtually impossible under
these conditions.

Many environmental groups, including the Sierra Club, oppose fast
track legislation because they would be unable to pressure Congress to make
changes in a trade agreement. In addition, some environmentalists believe
that trade agreements will reduce the authority of the United States to dictate
environmental conditions in the foreign production of goods we import.
Labor has opposed fast track legislation because the agreements may result in
increased imports of goods that compete with domestic products and thereby
cause unemployment. Some leaders in the president's own political party have
opposed fast track legislation in response to the objections of their environment and labor constituents, while Republicans have generally supported it.
The division in government between a Republican-controlled Congress and

a Democratic administration has made it impossible, as of the time of this writing, to obtain a majority in both the House and the Senate to pass the legislation.

Members of the study group, about 150 in all, included specialists in environmental organizations, such as the Sierra Club and the Environmental Defense Fund, U.S. government officials representing the EPA, the Office of the Trade Representative, and the State Department, World Bank representatives, and a dozen university professors. The one-day meetings offered little time for serious debate because nearly everyone in attendance expected to be able to speak. A number of papers were prepared, including one of my own that emphasized two ideas: (1) the social welfare advantages of expanded trade are very great and can be realized only by increases in both bilateral and multilateral agreements for reducing trade barriers, and (2) there should be international agreements on environmental practices affecting all nations; this would meet the concerns of environmentalists in the U.S. who fear that the country would be flooded with goods produced by countries with low environmental standards, particularly processes that impair the global environment.

It was impossible for such a large and diverse group to issue a single recommendation—especially since the vast majority of the economists present favored free trade, while many environmental group representatives were strong believers in trade restrictions in support of environmental objectives. Instead, Ford Runge of the University of Minneapolis was asked to write a book drawing heavily on the discussions at the regional meetings, but the book was to be "on his own responsibility" and not viewed as a consensus document for the study group. Runge's book, *Free Trade in a Protected Environment: Balancing Trade Liberalization and Environmental Interests*, was published by the Council on Foreign Relations. It provided an excellent overview of how U.S. commitment to free trade and to membership in GATT, the WTO, and NAFTA can be entirely compatible with national and world environmental values. Runge believes strongly in both free trade and environmental principles. He had also been a member of the Sierra Club's Economics Committee.

Personal Evaluation

Environmental problems are enormously complex, especially since the social values in protecting the environment conflict with other social values. Implementation of environmental objectives in a way that minimizes social costs and thereby elicits greater public support requires intensive empirical study and analysis. Environmental organizations are vital for educating the public and lobbying legislatures, government regulators, and business and labor groups. However, environmental organizations need the support and advice of social scientists who can justify environmental objectives in terms of net social welfare and advise them on how objectives can be implemented at a minimal cost to society. I believe that social scientists should be doing more research on environmental and resource issues, and they should cooperate closely with private, governmental, and environmental organizations.

CHAPTER 13: RESEARCH ON ECONOMIC POLICY

As every economist knows, there is much more to foreign development aid than handing money to a needy government. The basic problem is how to transfer external assistance and direct the aid toward uses that will promote an increase in both per capita output and general welfare. This means more than selecting the channels through which external aid is used in the economy. A more difficult task is influencing the governmental and nongovernmental organizations whose policies and practices will ultimately determine whether the objectives of the aid will be realized. As a student of foreign aid and witness to its effects, I reached a number of conclusions that were critical of U.S. and international agency aid policies during the early postwar period.

Foreign Aid for Development

Foreign aid for development has advanced substantially since the 1950s when it was used largely to finance specific projects such as dams, roads, and steel mills. To be successful, in my view, development aid must promote a change in the economic structure by freeing markets and substituting economic incentives for government control. But equally important are investment in education and health, and increased opportunities for the bulk of the population. Recently, the Western developed world has been seeking to establish a global economy in which all countries participate, so that doing business in Uruguay or Nigeria will differ little from doing business in Portland, Oregon. To a considerable extent, globalization has succeeded in achieving rapid economic growth in a number of nations, but a substantial portion of the world has still made no economic or social progress. In fact, in many of these nations, social welfare has declined. Development aid programs in these countries have failed, and we have much to learn about how to change their governmental policies and social structures. This may be more of a political than an economic problem.

U.S. aid policies have undergone significant changes in the postwar period. Except for humanitarian aid and shipments in response to disasters, foreign aid did not exist before World War II. In the period 1950–70, foreign aid models used by the U.S. government were based on the approach—popular with many economists and with international organizations—that made capital imports a major determinant of economic growth. According to these models, to achieve a positive rate of growth in per capita output, a country required a critical amount of external capital until domestic saving could finance a sufficient level of investment to maintain growth without foreign aid. Foreign aid had to, therefore, supply any shortfall in required capital.

I became dissatisfied with the models used by the U.S. government to determine its foreign aid policies, for several reasons. First, I believed these models put too much emphasis on external capital for determining the rate of economic growth. My research in developing nations convinced me that establishing competitive domestic markets and free international trade could contribute more to economic growth than foreign grants and loans made to governments. Such loans were often invested in inefficient state-owned enterprises or in infrastructure that made little or no contribution to output or technical progress.

Second, I believe the best form of capital imports is private foreign direct investment in both resources and manufacturing, and that such investments are especially effective in the form of joint ventures with domestic firms. What is needed most is a political environment that encourages private investment in agriculture and manufacturing. In many developing countries, ample domestic saving is available for such investment but incentives and technical knowledge are lacking.

Third, I believe that poor economic performance, with or without foreign aid, is largely caused by improper fiscal and monetary policies that lead to restrictions on foreign trade and controls on domestic commerce—both of which are immensely harmful to economic progress.

Fourth, I believe too much emphasis has been given to the rate of economic growth in terms of GDP and not enough to broader contributions to development, such as education and health. Inequality of education denies most people the opportunity to increase their productivity and to become entrepreneurs; it also keeps the economy at a low stage of development.

Finally, I believe that foreign aid can speed development, but it should be accompanied by conditions on its use and on the recipients' economic policies. One criticism of the U.S. foreign aid program—which I share with most international economists—is that during most of the postwar period, U.S. government decisions have been made more in support of political objectives than by what is required to promote economic development. U.S. assistance has been provided to keep friendly governments in power or to prevent countries from maintaining close economic and political relations with the Soviet Union. This policy led us to support dictatorial governments that not only denied human rights to their citizens but failed to promote satisfactory growth and broad social development.

Although a number of economists were making much the same criticisms of our foreign aid models and policies, I was eager to write a book that would critically review the theoretical underpinnings of our foreign aid policies. In 1966 I received an invitation to write such a book from Harry G. Johnson (who held professorships at both the University of Chicago and the London School of Economics). He asked me to contribute to the Aldine Treatises in Modern Economics series, which he edited. The books in the series were written by leading economists in the U.S. and Britain, including Alan O. Waters, Martin Bronfenbrenner, Carl Shoup, and Herbert Stein. My book, *The Economics of Foreign Aid*, has been used since 1968 as a supplementary text in a number of economics departments in the U.S. and abroad.

My interest in broadening the concept of development beyond simply increasing the rate of growth of GDP led to an invitation to spend the summer of 1972 working for the World Bank. My chief function was to prepare an index for measuring development progress, including social progress in such fields as education, health, and broadening economic opportunities for all classes of society. This study was circulated within the World Bank and the U.S. government. Later, my development index was greatly expanded by including statistical measures of social progress for all the members of the World Bank. Using many indices for each country, today the Bank publishes annual statistics on overall development progress.

Raymond L. Mikesell

The UN Conference on Trade and Development

While on a sabbatical leave from the University of Oregon in 1963, I was invited to serve as a visiting professor at the Graduate Institute of International Studies in Geneva, Switzerland, during the spring semester of 1964. It was a delightful experience since my teaching duties were light and both seminars were on Friday; this left the rest of the week for my wife and me to travel. Shortly before leaving for Geneva, I was asked to serve as an adviser to the U.S. delegation at a UN conference in Geneva to prepare a charter for what became the UN Conference on Trade and Development (UNCTAD). Since my duties to the U.S. delegation were very light, I gladly accepted the invitation. In addition to my advisory and teaching duties in Geneva, a good part of my time was devoted to giving lectures at various European universities under a State Department lecture program. All this provided a very busy semester, but I enjoyed the contacts made at the conference and at the various universities. I gave lectures at Oxford in the classes of Sir Roy Harrod and Sir John Hicks, both of whom were distinguished economists. I also lectured at the Universities of Paris, Munich, and Berlin. While in Berlin, my wife and I visited Soviet-controlled East Berlin under the guidance of a former Oregon student who had lived in the area.

Unlike most international conferences, which have been organized by developed country governments, this one was called at the request of the UN General Assembly. World development and trade policies were regarded by most developing countries as being dominated by leading industrial countries. In the early 1960s, there was a strong movement within the UN to establish an organization to promote the positions of Third World countries, which were often in conflict with those of the IMF, the World Bank, and especially the GATT. Raul Prebisch, my former colleague at the Mexico meeting of the Working Group, had considerable influence in the UN General Assembly and played a major role in both organizing and directing the conference.

The UN conference was dominated by developing country leaders who introduced resolutions on trade and economic policies that were generally opposed by the developed countries, particularly the United States. For example, these countries wanted exceptions for low-income countries to GATT trade rules while at the same time demanding discriminatory reductions in import duties imposed by the developed countries. Developing country delegates also opposed conditions for foreign assistance imposed by the IMF and the World Bank. They wanted a UN-sponsored program of international commodity agreements designed to support world prices of agricultural and mineral commodities of importance to developing countries in world trade.

While the developing countries achieved some of their objectives at the conference, UNCTAD has never been very effective in influencing policies favored by the Third World. The GATT rules applied to developing countries have not significantly changed, the international aid organizations have attached even more conditions to their largess, and the few international commodity agreements negotiated were not successful in raising commodity prices. Although many developing countries still criticize the economic domination of the industrial countries, the more successful ones have adopted the economic policies of the developed world.

Foreign Aid Study for the Treasury Department

During much of the postwar period, I served as a consultant to the Treasury Department and belonged to a panel of nongovernmental economists who, from time to time, met with the secretary or undersecretary of the Treasury Department. This panel, whose membership largely comprised university professors, was often used by the secretary to "test" some of his ideas. We often strongly opposed them. I recall one occasion, shortly before the U.S. abandoned the gold exchange standard in 1971, when the secretary proposed a new method of maintaining fixed exchange rates among the major countries. The panel rejected the idea of fixed exchange rates, much to the secretary's disappointment. While economists generally favored fixed exchange rates at the time of Bretton Woods, most favored freely fluctuating rates by the late 1960s.

After the inauguration of the Reagan administration in 1981, I was called to Washington, D.C., by Beryl W. Sprinkel, undersecretary of the Treasury Department, for consultation, but was not told in advance what I was to do. Republican leaders had been critical of the Democratic administration's foreign aid policies, including the amount of foreign aid as well as its allocation. Because foreign aid was a controversial issue among Republicans and the new administration wanted to be cautious about major changes in foreign policy, officials in the State and the Treasury Departments wanted a report on the subject prepared by an independent source.

I saw the invitation to prepare the study as an opportunity to circulate some of my own views on foreign aid. Although much U.S. aid was motivated by political objectives, I did not deal with the relationship between foreign aid and U.S. political interests. Rather, I confined my report to how the U.S. might help countries achieve self-sustaining development. This means maintaining a reasonable rate of growth in per capita GDP while making progress in realizing basic social goals. I stated that, to the maximum extent possible, foreign aid should go to stimulate the private sector of the economy, particularly private agriculture and small manufacturing, rather than to loans to state-operated enterprises or balance-of-payments loans to governments. The type of foreign aid I was recommending required considerable administration by the donor. A substantial portion of aid should go to social programs, such as education and health; such aid should be administered as much as possible by local governments and community organizations, rather than by national governments.

All development aid should be contingent on the adoption of appropriate fiscal and monetary policies by the national government. This means avoiding inflation and instituting a progressive tax program that will raise sufficient income for the government's operations. Foreign aid should be contingent on performance in accordance with agreements reached with governments regarding the ways in which aid was to be used. Aid conditioning is often resented by foreign governments, and some Americans thought the U.S. government should not involve itself in the internal activities of foreign governments. I did not agree, because unless our aid makes a difference in how governments and social institutions operate, it is unlikely to realize its objectives.

My report was completed by December 1981; with a few changes suggested by State and Treasury Department officials, it was published in February 1982. On the day the report came out, Undersecretary Sprinkel was meeting with President Mubarak of Egypt, which was having some balance-of-payments problems and seeking additional aid from the U.S. The undersecretary gave him a copy of my report and suggested he would find it very useful. I have no idea whether he read it. His country's economic performance in the following years suggests that even if Mubarak read it, the Egyptian government did not take it seriously.

My report was well received in the government by those who favored continuation of the U.S. foreign aid program, but it was probably a disappointment to conservative congressmen who had criticized the program as a waste of resources. I cannot claim that there was much new in my report. Most of what I wrote was in line with the thinking of other economists who specialized in economic development and foreign aid. Although the report was widely circulated in the government, it did not receive broad circulation in the media. Unlike earlier similar reports, it was not subject to hearings by any congressional committees. The reason was that the report was not signed by a high government official or endorsed as government policy. Given permission to publish the report myself, I arranged for publication by Westview Press of Boulder, Colorado.

Research on Foreign Exchange

My continuing work with the Treasury Department introduced me to a number of foreign exchange problems, including an analysis of the sources of supply and demand for foreign exchange and the effects of changes in foreign exchange rates on a country's balance of payments. In the immediate post–World War II period, foreign exchange was highly complex, with only a few countries maintaining free exchange markets. Most nations controlled their exchange rates and transactions in their exchange markets and used several exchange rates. For example, one rate might apply to essential imports, another to imports of luxury goods, and still another to government transactions. Usually a free market rate applied to transactions not controlled by the government, such as private capital transactions. I wrote articles analyzing the effects of these systems on trade and the balance of payments of the countries using them, but there was a need for a comprehensive study of the foreign exchange systems that had emerged after the war.

In 1951 a Twentieth Century Fund (TCF) official, who had been studying current foreign exchange systems, asked if I would be interested in writing a book on foreign exchange for TCF—both to explain the highly complex systems that currently were in operation and to analyze their effects on world trade. I was delighted with this opportunity, since it fit well into both my research and teaching at the University of Virginia. I spent most of one summer researching at the IMF headquarters in Washington, D.C., which had the best information on the subject. The result, published in 1954, was one of my most popular books, *Foreign Exchange in the Post-War World.* It was widely used in graduate economics courses throughout the world, and sections of it were translated into other languages.

In addition to providing a detailed description by country and regional grouping of the foreign exchange systems in the early 1950s, and an analysis of why countries adopted the controls on foreign exchange rates that they did, the book showed how the systems impaired world trade. I discussed how the International Monetary Fund might operate to gradually eliminate these distortions. However, I took the position that the European Payments Union (EPU) should be maintained for a time since it tended to free trade within the region, even though the system involved discrimination against non-European currencies such as the dollar. The IMF had initially opposed the EPU, as did the U.S. government.

One of the conclusions reached in this book was that there was a need for an expansion of international reserves, which then consisted mainly of gold and dollars. I pointed out that in 1938, the world's gold and dollar holdings outside the United States represented about 70 percent of total world trade, but by 1952 the corresponding percentage was only about 25. I stated that the establishment and maintenance of full currency convertibility by most countries was unlikely without a substantial increase in world reserves. Since that time, world reserves have expanded substantially as a consequence of U.S. balance-of-payments deficits that increased dollars in the hands of foreigners, the increase in IMF quotas, and the allocation of billions of dollars of Special Drawing Rights.

Eurodollar Study

I continued to write papers on exchange problems, including several monographs published by the Princeton University International Finance Section, but my most ambitious undertaking was a study of the Eurodollar market. In 1971 J. Herbert Furth, then senior economist with the Federal Reserve Board, asked if I would be interested in writing a book on the Eurodollar market. A Eurodollar is a time deposit in a non-U.S. bank denominated in dollars. Although most of the Eurodollar deposits are held in European banks, a bank anywhere in the world outside the U.S. can accept deposits denominated in dollars, and they are also called Eurodollars. There were a number of questions on the effects of Eurodollars (which grew to many billions of dollars) on U.S. and world trade and payments, and there were conflicting views on the subject. For example, do Eurodollars expand the world's supply of reserves? How do Eurodollars affect the U.S. balance of payments? I agreed to do a study with Furth, and we applied for a grant from the National Bureau of Economic Research (NBER), one of the world's most prestigious nongovernmental economic think-tanks. Furth did much of the theoretical work for our project while I concentrated on gathering and analyzing the data.

The best source of data on Eurodollars is the Bank for International Settlements (BIS) in Switzerland, the bank that the Bretton Woods conference recommended be abolished because of its alleged dealings in Nazi gold and other assets. I spent a month in the course of two visits to Basel doing research on the Eurodollar market, and economists there gave me their fullest cooperation and cordiality. The result of our research was a jointly authored book entitled *Foreign Dollar Balances and the International Role of the Dollar*, published by NBER in 1974.

During the postwar period Eurodollars rose rapidly, from almost none in the 1950s, to $9 billion in December 1964, to $54 billion in December 1971. A sizable amount of Eurodollars are held by central banks as a part of their reserves, a substantial portion by commercial banks, and the remainder by individuals and corporations. U.S. citizens also hold Eurodollars. Why were Eurodollars introduced as a substitute for holding dollar deposits in the United States? The principal reason is that interest rates paid on Eurodollar deposits are often higher than on dollar deposits in the United States. Generally, interest rates in the U.S. have been lower than in Europe. Also, European bank customers who wanted to hold deposits in dollars found it easier to do it there than open a deposit account in a U.S. bank. Finally, nations with foreign exchange controls sometimes prevented their residents from acquiring dollars held in the United States, while permitting them to own Eurodollar deposits in their own nations.

We found no direct evidence that the Eurodollar market had an effect on the U.S. balance of payments. However, Eurodollars can be substituted for dollar reserves held in the United States. Because many central banks held Eurodollars as reserves in place of deposits in the U.S., the amount of foreign central bank reserves held in the United States was reduced. We found no correlation between the increase in central bank Eurodollar holdings and their dollar reserves in U.S. banks.

Another question is the extent to which Eurodollars increased the total amount of international liquidity. Although Eurodollars are not used in making payments for current international transactions, they do augment international liquid reserves. World reserves were being increased by a number of sources during this period. We concluded that the Eurodollar market did not have a major impact on the world's payment system. It is worth noting that the Eurocurrency market has continued to grow since the 1970s. I believe our main contribution in the NBER study, which was the first in-depth analysis of the role of Eurocurrencies in the world's payment system, was to reply to those who believed that somehow the Eurocurrency market was having a major impact on the U.S. balance of payments and the world's payment system generally. These instruments were simply a part of the trend of expanding international liquidity and the exchangeability of assets held in different currencies.

The opportunity to undertake the NBER study and be appointed a Fellow of the NBER enhanced my professional standing and led to other opportunities. This and other publications were in part responsible for my receiving academic offers from more prestigious universities. However, I was completely wedded to Eugene, Oregon, a small university city where high mountains and ski lifts are only an hour-and-a-half away and a rocky and sandy seacoast is about the same distance.

My continued interest in foreign exchange was stimulated by a University of Oregon colleague, Henry Goldstein, with whom I collaborated on a monograph on floating exchange rates that was published in 1975 by the Princeton International Finance Section. It was also stimulated by supervising several Ph.D. dissertations in the foreign exchange field, in particular that of Michael Hutchison, currently professor of economics at the University of California, Santa Cruz. His dissertation dealt with the ability of central banks to control foreign exchange rates through exchange market intervention. In 1986, Hutchison and I published a monograph in the Princeton International Finance Section series.

Work with Washington, D.C., Research Institutes

During the late 1960s and early 1970s, I became associated with two Washington, D.C.–based research institutes, the Center for Strategic and International Studies (CSIS), which is a branch of Georgetown University, and the American Enterprise Institute (AEI); both sponsored and published my research. CSIS published several of my studies on U.S. trade issues. These studies, which are listed in the bibliography of this book, largely reflected my research for the Gray Committee and the Randall Commission. In 1977 I was made cochair, with Walter Lacquer, of the center's Research Council. The council had several well-known economists as members, such as Fred Singer, John Wallace, Karl Brunner, and Murray Weidenbaum. I think my position as cochair was more honorary than anything else, since the decisions on the studies sponsored by the center were made by the full-time officials of CSIS, usually without discussion or input from the council. CSIS held conferences from time to time, both in Washington, D.C., and abroad, and I usually gave talks on these occasions.

One of my monographs published by the AEI was *The Rate of Discount for Evaluating Public Projects* (1978), which dealt with the controversial issue of how public projects should be valued for purposes of determining the priority of the project and whether the social benefits justified the costs. The benefits of a project are usually determined by calculating the present value of the expected future benefits. A major issue is what the rate of discount should be for determining present value. Should it be the rate on government bonds or the rate of return required by private investors on similar projects? This is an important issue: if the discount rate is too low, the present value of the benefits is overstated, and the costs may actually be greater than the benefits when they are properly determined. This issue was raised by President Jimmy Carter, who deleted a number of water resource projects from the administration's 1978 budget on the grounds that the rate of discount used for valuing these projects (in accordance with the rate provided by law at the time the projects were authorized) was much too low. If a higher rate of discount were used, the projected costs of the projects often exceeded the present value of their expected benefits. For example, a project that yielded $1 million a year for fifty years would have a present value of $26 million when calculated at a rate of 3 percent, but only $10 million when calculated at a more realistic discount rate of 10 percent. I argued that government projects should be valued by using a rate of interest equal to that required by private firms when evaluating similar projects in which they might consider investing. This rate will be considerably higher than the rate on riskless government bonds. Whether a project is built by government or private investors, there is substantial risk of cost overruns and of disappointing benefits from the project. Therefore, government projects such as dams and utilities should be valued by using a rate of discount corresponding to that used in the private sector on similar projects. Although my monograph did not have wide circulation, it continues to be referred to in studies on evaluating public projects.

My 1986 AEI monograph, *Stockpiling Strategic Minerals: An Evaluation of the National Program,* deals with economic and strategic issues that should determine decisions for the U.S. government's stockpiling program. In this study I presented some guidelines for the optimum size of a stockpile, based on the annual requirements for producing commodities essential to military needs and for the operation of the economy. I have no idea what impact this study had on the stockpiling program. In the past, political rather than economic considerations have determined the content of the stockpile. In this and other studies involving social risk, I have argued that the cost of the insurance against risk (in this case the cost of stockpiling) should be limited to the present value of the benefits as determined by the risk-adjusted value of the loss incurred if the materials were in short supply.

Research on IMF Policies

During the years following my retirement from teaching in 1993, much of my research has been in international finance with special interest in the financial crises of the East Asian and Latin American countries during the 1990s. This research is closely related to my longtime interest in the IMF. In addition to publishing a monograph in 1994 on the Bretton Woods debates and participating in the fiftieth anniversary conferences mentioned in Chapter 4, I have presented papers at several international financial conferences. In March 1998 I participated in a panel on the IMF at a conference held by the Milken Economics Institute in Santa Monica, California. (Milken is well known as the popularizer of "junk" bonds.) I was very impressed with both the Milken Institute and its founder, Michael Milken, who played an active role in the conference by chairing some of the seminars. Despite his difficulties with the Securities and Exchange Commission, Milken is an intelligent and charming man who has devoted his life since leaving prison not only to his economics institute but to raising money for cancer research and educational problems. The conference was attended by a number of well-known economists, including four Nobel laureates.

My papers at the above conferences dealt with aspects of the international financial crises in East Asian and Latin American countries and with the way I believe such crises can be avoided. The countries in crisis have received financial assistance and advice from several sources including the U.S. government, but the principal source has been the IMF, which committed larger credits to individual countries than at any other time in its history. The recent financial crises in countries that have liberalized their foreign exchange and capital markets by opening them to the world financial community were different from the traditional balance-of-payments problems of members requesting financial assistance from the Fund. The crises were caused mainly by the withdrawal of foreign capital and a loss of confidence in the foreign exchange value of the currency. These events were caused by economic disturbances within the countries themselves, such as bank failures and the inability of firms that had borrowed abroad to meet their debt service obligations. The IMF aid for dealing with the recent crises has been accompanied by conditions requiring monetary and fiscal restrictions, which have caused sharp increases in interest rates, a reduction in credit availability for business, and reduced domestic investment. This has resulted in reduced output and employment that plunged the countries into recessions. Since there was little inflation or fiscal deficits, these policies were inappropriate and the reduction in output has been especially hard on the poor.

Jeffrey D. Sachs, director of the Harvard Institute for International Development, has served as an adviser to a number of developing governments. He criticized the IMF for applying the "wrong medicine" in helping developing countries through their financial crises. My own position is in accord with Sachs's. In my papers I have addressed the need for the Fund to help countries maintain production and investment rather than to assist them in maintaining the foreign exchange value of their currency or in meeting their foreign debt obligations. I argued strongly in favor of market-based controls that would reduce the vulnerability of countries to financial crises. These include special taxes and other incentives for reducing short-term capital imports, especially those used to finance investments in real estate. I also argued that once a financial crisis occurs or is threatened, the country should prevent capital exports from reducing the exchange value of the currency used for financing imports of goods and services. This could be achieved by the creation of a free capital market, which would be separate from the foreign exchange market used to finance imports and exports of goods and services.

Although most economists, myself included, do not like government controls over markets, I believe that the costs of financial crises are so great that countries need to take action to prevent large capital exports from creating conditions that lead to reduced output investment and employment. I have been somewhat surprised by the absence of criticism I received following my lectures. However, I have noticed increasing acceptance of controls designed to insulate the economies of developing countries from financial crises. I strongly believe that globalization provides important contributions to development through increased imports of capital and technology. Still, it is important for governments to protect their economies against recession, which tends to reduce social and economic progress and is especially hard on the poor, who are the first to suffer and the last to recover.

Sources

The sources for this chapter are mainly my personal memoranda and publications.

CHAPTER 14: CONCLUSIONS

Every book is supposed to end with a conclusion but I have difficulty drafting a conclusion for a memoir of my professional life. I can say that my life has been rewarding and a personal success. But an objective evaluation of my contributions to society will be left to others. In place of a conclusion, I will make a few statements about my social philosophy and how it has affected my career. Many if not most readers may regard these statements as gratuitous, but I think they will be appreciated and understood by my friends.

During much of my life, I could not distinguish the pleasure of work from that of play. My career choices have been based more on what I believed I would enjoy doing than on a desire for money, influence, or enlarging social welfare. I am convinced that the right career choice is the key to lifelong happiness, and that the more extensive one's academic education and cultural experience, the greater are the opportunities for career choices. My opportunities have been due in large measure to good fortune and the support of others.

My views on economic and social issues have changed substantially over my career, usually as a consequence of my professional experiences. When I took my first college course in economics in 1931, I was secretary of the Socialist Party chapter of Lima, Ohio, and proud of my acquaintance with Norman Thomas and other national Socialist leaders. Gradually, I became convinced of the superiority of private enterprise and free markets. I learned how inefficiency, vulnerability to corruption, and suppression of human rights can arise from government ownership and control. My support for universal opportunities for education at any level, a floor on real income for everyone, and a comprehensive social program financed (but not directly managed) by government has never waned. It is this philosophy that explains my approach to economics and to the development policies in the many nations I have visited and studied. Textbooks define economics as the study of how humankind makes a living. I also regard economics as a social science guided by the objective of maximizing social welfare. Social welfare, however, is difficult to define and apply in decisions on public policy. It is measured by the degree of equality in opportunities for education, by the equality of medical benefits, by the distribution of income, and by the support given to preserve natural resources for the enjoyment of future generations. Although social welfare is much more than maximizing per capita GDP, increasing GDP is essential for promoting social welfare.

Is social welfare an objective that ends at the national border, or does it encompass the human race? I have given priority to my nation's welfare, partly on the grounds that our welfare can greatly influence world welfare. I believe that, in the long run, preservation of our civilization depends upon the achievement of fundamental world welfare objectives.

In my view, social welfare has many attributes. It must include a minimum level of living for all humans, including adequate nutrition, housing, and medical care. It does not mean universal equality of income, although social welfare could be greatly improved by reducing the vast inequality of income within nations and between nations. I do not believe that multimillion-dollar corporate salaries contribute anything to the GDP, and we would be just as productive if professional incomes were not ten times those of the lowest-paid workers. Much more important than greater equality of income is *equality of opportunity*, including universal availability of education and training, freedom of choice in occupation, and the absence of discrimination by race, sex, and social class. In the case of developing nations, the fact that education is available for only a small portion of the population constitutes a major reason for their low per capita income.

I do not see how equality of opportunity can be realized in an economic system other than one that fosters private enterprise and competition. Communism never provided as much equality of opportunity as we have in the United States and in other Western nations. On the other hand, equality of opportunity requires a large role for government as a supplier of funds for public services. It also requires a progressive tax regime that will provide sufficient funds for the public services that promote social welfare. However, expenditures for public services should be guided by benefit-cost principles that require not only that social benefits exceed social costs but that social expenditures be allocated among uses so that marginal social cost is equal to marginal social benefit. This approach requires more intensive application of social benefit-cost analysis than we are presently practicing, and it requires more research by social scientists.

One of my greatest satisfactions comes from feeling that I have made a difference in terms of promoting social welfare. This goes beyond the contributions I have made to the lives of my family and close friends, from whom I receive more immediate satisfaction. As a teacher, I regard my most important contribution to be my influence on the careers of my students. This is impossible to gauge for each of the thousands of students who have attended my classes. But because much of my academic work has been with doctoral students, I have some evidence based on the careers of some sixty Ph.D.'s whose dissertations I have supervised. In my fortieth year of teaching at the University of Oregon, my department, together with other faculty members and the president of the university, honored me by inviting all Ph.D. recipients whose committees I chaired to the university for seminars and receptions—in the course of which they reviewed their careers and expressed what university training had contributed to their lives. Each of the twenty-five Ph.D.'s who attended the program—they came from all over the United States and two from abroad—paid a special tribute, indicating how their work with me had made a difference in their careers. As recognition of my service to the University of Oregon, I was presented with the university's Distinguished Service Award in March 1999.

The particular effects of service with government, international agencies, and private organizations are difficult to weigh. Because many individuals influence the outcome of negotiations and conferences that in turn influence policies, it is impossible to determine the degree to which the participation of one adviser has made a difference. It is also difficult to determine whether the outcome itself has advanced social welfare. Even the failure of achieving a desired outcome may affect future outcomes by influencing the thinking of others. All I can say is this: I believe that in most of these activities my advice pointed in the right direction.

Finally, in considering the influence of my twenty-six books, two dozen monographs, and hundreds of articles, I haven't a clue whether I have contributed significantly to social welfare. This goes beyond whether the reviews are favorable or how many references are made to my books and articles, or even the number of my publications that have been sold. I doubt if my views on any of the topics I have addressed have resulted in a critical change in thinking. Many voices make up a chorus of influence on particular questions, and rarely can such influence be attributed to one individual. I do know that the economic theory and policy positions I have espoused have been consistent with my concept of social welfare maximization.

As I write at age eighty-seven, I have some advice about retirement. Don't retire! Productive activity contributes to psychological and physical health. Everyone should plan to work until the day he or she dies. Retirement should be no more than a change of productive activities. I have been blessed with good physical and mental health, and with the opportunity to continue most of the activities that have brought me so much satisfaction over the sixty years of my professional career. They now include giving lectures at universities and papers at academic conferences, writing books and articles, and participating in the work of the University of Oregon's Center for Environmental and Resource Economics.

One final observation. The evaluation of one's career is usually based on objectives achieved and lifetime goals realized. In thinking about my own career, I believe the achievement of goals is not the most important measure of success. It is not the goals, it is the journey that is truly rewarding.

BIBLIOGRAPHY

Acheson, Dean. 1969. *Present at the Creation: My Years in the State Department*, New York: Norton.

Altman, Oscar L. 1956. "Quotas in the International Monetary Fund," *International Monetary Fund Staff Papers* 5 (August): 136–41.

Bank for International Settlements. 1998. *Sixty-Eighth Annual Report.* Basel, Switzerland (June).

Black, Stanley W. 1991. *A Levite Among the Priests: Edward M. Bernstein and the Origins of the Bretton Woods System.* Boulder, Colo.: Westview Press.

Blum, John M. 1967. *From the Morgenthau Diaries: Years of War 1941-1945.* Boston: Houghton Mifflin.

Bretton Woods Commission. 1994. *Bretton Woods: Looking to the Future.* Washington, D.C.: Bretton Woods Committee.

Daly, Herman E., and John B. Cobb, Jr. 1989. *For the Common Good: Redirecting the Economy toward Community, Environment, and a Sustainable Future.* Boston: Beacon Press.

ECLA Secretariat. 1959. *Report of the Second Session of the Working Group.* Mexico City, p. 50. Unpublished.

Eddy, George and Raymond F. Mikesell. 1948. "A Program to Improve the Monetary System of Saudi Arabia." (November). Jidda. Unpublished.

Ganin, Zvi. 1979. *Truman, American Jewry, and Israel, 1945–1948.* New York: Holmes and Meier Publishers.

Gardner, Richard N. 1969. *Sterling-Dollar Diplomacy.* New York: McGraw-Hill.

Great Britain Palestine Royal Commission. 1937. Report of the Palestine Royal Commission. Parliament Papers by Command, No. 5479. Geneva: League of Nations.

———. 1947. *British Proposals for the Future of Palestine, July 1946–February 1947*. British Command Paper, No. 7044. London: His Majesty's Stationery Office.

Halevi, Nadav and Ruth Klinov-Malul. 1968. *The Economic Development of Israel*. New York: Praeger. Appendix Tables 9 and 10: pp. 294–97.

Harrod, Sir Roy Forbes. 1951. *The Life of John Maynard Keynes*. London: Macmillan.

———. 1965. *Reforming the World's Money*. New York: St. Martin's Press.

Haynes, Stephen, Michael Hutchison, and Raymond F. Mikesell. 1986. *Japanese Financial Policies and the U.S. Trade Deficit*. Essays in International Finance, No. 162. Princeton, NJ: International Finance Section, Department of Economics, Princeton University.

Hurewitz, J. C. 1950. *The Struggle for Palestine*. New York: Norton.

Institute for Latin American Integration. 1984. *The Latin American Integration Process in 1983*. Buenos Aires, Argentina: Institute for Latin American Integration.

Institute for Social Studies. 1980. *Mining for Development in the Third World*. New York: Pergamon Press. Published in cooperation with the Institute of Social Studies at The Hague. Contains three lectures by Mikesell given at the Institute.

International Monetary Fund. 1969. *The International Monetary Fund, 1945–1965: Twenty Years of International Monetary Cooperation*, ed. J. Keith Horsefield. Washington, D.C.: International Monetary Fund. Volumes 1, 2, and 3.

———. 1991. *Financial Organizations and Operations of the IMF*. Pamphlet Series, No. 4, second ed. Washington, D.C.: International Monetary Fund.

Kindleberger, Charles Poor. 1950. *The Dollar Shortage*. Cambridge, Mass.: M.I.T. Press.

Lash, Joseph P. 1982. *Love, Eleanor: Eleanor Roosevelt and Her Friends*. Garden City, N.Y.: Doubleday.

Lloyd, E. M. H. 1956. *Food and Inflation in the Middle East, 1940–45*. Stanford, Calif.: Stanford University Press.

Merrow, Chester E. 1962. *Report of the First Annual Review of the Alliance for Progress, by the Inter-American Economic and Social Council, Organization of American States.* October 1–28, 1962, Mexico City. Washington, D.C.: U.S.G.P.O.

Mikesell, Raymond F. 1947. "Monetary Problems of Saudi Arabia," *The Middle East Journal.* 1 (April).

———. 1951. "Negotiating at Bretton Woods, 1944." pp. 101–16. Raymond Dennett and Joseph E. Johnson, eds., *Negotiating with the Russians.* Boston: World Peace Foundation.

———. 1954a. *The Emerging Pattern of International Payments,* Essays in International Finance, No. 18. Princeton, N.J.: International Finance Section, Department of Economics and Social Institutions, Princeton University.

———. 1954b. *Foreign Exchange in the Post-War World.*

———. 1959. "Possible Alternatives for the Establishment of the Latin American Regional Market" (February). Mexico City. Unpublished.

———. 1960. *Problems of Latin American Economic Development.* Washington, D.C.: USGPO. p. 6.

———. 1962a. "Confidential Report on Economic Conditions in Certain Latin American Countries and the Operations of U.S. AID Missions in these Countries." Memorandum to Wayne Morse from Raymond F. Mikesell, April 27, 1962 [Mikesell files].

———. 1962b. *Some Observations on the Operation of the Alliance for Progress, The First Six Months: A Study.* (August 3). Washington, D.C.: USGPO.

———. 1968. *The Economics of Foreign Aid.* Chicago: Aldine Publishing.

———. 1975. *The Eurocurrency Market and the Recycling of Petrodollars.* National Bureau Report Supplement. New York: National Bureau of Economic Research.

———. 1978. *The Rate of Discount for Evaluating Public Projects.* Washington, D.C.: American Enterprise Institute for Public Policy Research.

———. 1978. "New Taxation Formulas in Mine Investments: Sharing the Risks and the Rents," *International Mining Investment.* Vol. 2 (Papers and Proceedings of the AIW Institute Conference). Frankfurt, Germany.

————. 1980. *Mining for Development in Third World Countries.* Netherlands: The Hague.

————. 1983. *Foreign Investment in Mining Projects: Case Studies of Recent Experiences.* Cambridge, Mass.: Oelgeschlager, Gunn & Hain for project sponsored and administered by the Fund for Multinational Management Education.

————. 1986. *Stockpiling Strategic Materials: An Evaluation of the National Program.* Washington, D.C.: American Enterprise Institute for Public Policy Research.

————. 1989. "Depletable Resources, Discounting, and Intergenerational Equity." *Resources Policy.* (December): 292–96.

————. 1992. "Project Evaluation and Sustainable Development." In *Population, Technology, and Lifestyle: The Transition to Sustainability.* ed. Robert Goodland. Washington, D.C.: Island Press.

————. 1992. "The Limits to Growth: A Reappraisal," *Resources Policy.* 21 (June): 127–32.

————. 1994. "Environmental Assessment and Sustainability at the Project and Program Levels." pp. 20–28. In *Environmental Assessment and Development.* ed. Robert Goodland and Valerie Edmundsen. Washington, D.C.: The World Bank.

————. 1994. *The Bretton Woods Debates: A Memoir.* Essays in International Finance, No. 192. Princeton, N.J.: International Finance Section, Department of Economics, Princeton University.

————. 1995. "Sustainable Development and Mineral Resources." *Resources Policy.* 20 (June).

————. 1995. *Proposals for Changing the Functions of the International Monetary Fund (IMF).* Working Paper No. 150. Annandale-on-Hudson, N.Y.: Jerome Levy Economics Institute, Bard College.

————. 1996. *Revisiting Bretton Woods: Proposals for Reforming the International Monetary Fund Institutions.* Public Policy Brief No. 24. Annandale-on-Hudson, N.Y.: Jerome Levy Economics Institute, Bard College.

————. 1998. "The International Monetary Fund." *Proceedings of the 1998 Milken Institute Global Conference.* March 11–13, 1998, Santa Monica, Calif. Los Angeles, Calif.: Milken Institute. pp. 89–92.

————. 1998. "The Future of the Bretton Woods Institutions." *Jobs and Capital.* 7 (Spring).

Mikesell, Raymond F. and Hollis Chenery. 1949. *Arabian Oil: America's Stake in the Middle East.* Chapel Hill, NC: University of North Carolina Press.

Mikesell, Raymond F. and Henry N. Goldstein. 1975. *Rules for a Floating Rate Regime.* Essays in International Finance, No. 109. Princeton, N.J.: International Finance Section, Department of Economics, Princeton University.

Mikesell, Raymond F. and Merlyn Nelson Trued. 1955. *Postwar Bilateral Payments Agreements.* Essays in International Finance, No. 4. Princeton, N.J.: International Finance Section, Department of Economics and Social Institutions, Princeton University.

Mikesell, Raymond F. and James E. Zinser. 1973. "The Nature of the Savings Function in Developing Countries: A Survey of the Theoretical and Empirical Literature," *Journal of Economic Literature.* Vol. 11, No. 1 (March): pp. 1-25.

Mikesell, Raymond F. and J. Herbert Furth. 1974. *Foreign Dollar Balances and the International Role of the Dollar.* New York: National Bureau of Economic Research.

Mikesell, Raymond F., Robert A. Kilmarx, and Arvin M. Kramish. 1982. *The Economics of Foreign Aid and Self-Sustaining Development.* Boulder, Colo.: Westview Press.

Mikesell, Raymond F. and Larry Williams. 1992. *International Banks and the Environment: From Growth to Sustainability, An Unfinished Agenda.* San Francisco: Sierra Club Books.

Nathan, Robert R., Oscar Gass, and Daniel B. Creamer. 1946. *Palestine: Problems and Promise.* Washington, D.C.: Public Affairs Press, American Council on Public Affairs.

Oliver, Robert W. 1975. *International Economic Co-operation and the World Bank*. London: Macmillan.

Passell, Peter. February 12, 1998. "The IMF Must Go, Critics Say, But Who Will Cope with Crises?" *New York Times*. p. C2.

Patinkin, Don. 1959. *The Israel Economy: The First Decade*. Jerusalem: Falk Project for Economic Research in Israel. pp. 52–53.

Rees, David. 1973. *Harry Dexter White: A Study in Paradox*. New York: Coward, McCann & Geoghegan.

Ritchie, Donald A. 1980. *James M. Landis, Dean of the Regulators*. Cambridge, Mass.: Harvard University Press.

Robbins, Lord Lionel. 1971. *Autobiography of an Economist*. London: Macmillan.

Roosevelt, Kermit. 1948. "The Partition of Palestine: A Lesson in Pressure Politics." *Middle East Journal* 2 (January).

Runge, C. Ford. 1994. *Freer Trade, Protected Environment*. New York: Council on Foreign Relations Press.

Sachs, Jeffrey. 1997. "The Wrong Medicine for Asia." *New York Times*, November 3, 1997: p. A19.

Sachs, Jeffrey D. and Steven Radelet. 1998. "Next Stop, Brazil." *New York Times*. October 14, 1998: p. A25.

el Serafy, Salah. 1989. "The Proper Calculation of Income from Depletable Natural Resources," in *Environmental Accounting for Sustainable Development*, ed. Yusuf H. Ahmad, Salah el Serafy, and Ernst Lutz. Washington, D.C.: The World Bank.

Shultz, George P. 1995. "Economics in Action: Ideas, Institutions, Policies." *American Economic Review*. 85:3 (May).

United Nations. 1959. "Report of the Second Session of the Working Group." *Latin American Common Markets*. New York: United Nations. pp. 38–50.

U.S. Commission on Foreign Economic Policy. 1954. *Report of the President and the Congress*. Washington, D.C.

U.S. Council of Economic Advisors. 1956, 1957, 1958. *Economic Report to the President*. Washington, D.C.

————. 1962. *United States–Latin American Relations.* A study prepared for the Subcommittee on American Republics Affairs, Senate Committee on Foreign Relations. August 3.

U.S. Department of State. 1945. *Anglo-American Financial and Commercial Agreements.* Washington, D.C.: U.S. Department of State.

————. 1946. *Foreign Relations of the United States, Diplomatic Papers.* Vol. 7: *The American Republics.* Washington, D.C.: U.S. Department of State.

————. 1948. *Proceedings and Documents of the United Nations Monetary and Fiscal Conference.* Bretton Woods, New Hampshire. July 1–23, 1944. Vol. 1. Washington, D.C.: U.S. Department of State.

————. 1948. *Foreign Relations of the United States, Diplomatic Papers.* Vol. 5, Part 2: pp. 248–50.

————. 1948. *Bulletin.* Washington, D.C.: U.S. Department of State.

————. 1965. *Foreign Relations of the United States, 1944.* Vol. 5: *The Near East–South Asia and Africa–The Far East.* Washington, D.C.: U.S. Department of State.

————. 1986. *Foreign Relations of the United States, 1952–1954,* Vol. 9. Washington, D.C.: USGPO.

U.S. President's Materials Policy Commission. 1952. *Resources for Freedom: A Report to the President.* Vol. 1: *Foundations for Growth and Security.* Vol. 2: *The Outlook for Key Commodities.* Vol. 5: *Selected Reports to the Commission.* Washington, D.C.: U.S.G.P.O.

U.S. Treasury Department. 1943. "Replies to Questions on the International Stabilization Fund Submitted by the Experts of Various Governments Participating in the Technical Discussions in Washington." Division of Monetary Research, Washington, D.C. (May). Unpublished.

Van Dormael, Armand. 1978. *Bretton Woods: Birth of a Monetary System.* New York: Holmes and Meier Publishing.

White, Harry D. 1944. "Memorandum for the Secretary." June 23 [Mikesell files].

Williams, John H. 1937. "The Adequacy of Existing Currency Mechanisms Under Varying Circumstances," *American Economic Review.* Supplement (March): pp.151–68.

Williamson, John, and Marcus H. Miller. 1987. *Targets and Indicators: A Blueprint for the International Coordination of Economic Policy*. Washington, D.C.: Institute for International Economics.

Williamson, John, and C. Randall Henning. 1994. "Managing the Monetary System," *Managing the World Economy: Fifty Years after Bretton Woods*, ed. Peter B. Kenen. Washington, D.C.: Institute for International Economics.

Wilson, Harold. 1981. *The Chariot of Israel: Britain, America, and the State of Israel*. New York: Norton.

Young, Arthur N. 1983. *Saudi Arabia: The Making of a Financial Giant*. Ithaca: New York University Press.

Young, John Parke. 1950. "Developing Plans for an International Monetary Fund and a World Bank." *Bulletin* 23. Washington, D.C.: U.S. Department of State. (November 13): pp. 778–90.

INDEX